Springer

Berlin
Heidelberg
New York
Barcelona
Hong Kong
London
Milan
Paris
Tokyo

Ingomar Kloss
Editor

More Advertising Worldwide

With Contributions by
I. Abdullah · A. Batraga · R. Boddy · D.R. Chang · U. Dimigen
C. Etayo · G. Frigkas · M. Lee · M.O. Lwin · T. Meenaghan
C. Mondada · J. Rothlauf · S.L.M. So · P. O'Sullivan · T.D. Szabó
B. Thompson · B. Tsakarestou · M. Vanetti

With 94 Figures
and 151 Tables

 Springer

659.1
M835

Professor Dr. Ingomar Kloss
University of Applied Sciences
Zur Schwedenschanze 15
18435 Stralsund
Germany
E-mail: ingomar.kloss@fh-stralsund.de

ISBN 3-540-42994-8 Springer-Verlag Berlin Heidelberg New York

Library of Congress Cataloging-in-Publication Data applied for
Die Deutsche Bibliothek – CIP-Einheitsaufnahme

More Advertising Worldwide / Ingomar Kloss (Ed.).
With Contributions by I. Abdullah .... – Berlin; Heidelberg; New York;
Barcelona; Hong Kong; London; Milan; Paris; Tokyo: Springer, 2002
   ISBN 3-540-42994-8

Springer-Verlag Berlin Heidelberg New York
a member of BertelsmannSpringer Science + Business Media GmbH

http://www.springer.de
© Springer-Verlag Berlin Heidelberg 2002
Printed in Germany

Cover design: Erich Kirchner, Heidelberg

SPIN 10860038   42/2202-5 4 3 2 1 0 – Printed on acid-free paper

Preface

The first volume of this reader was on the subject of advertising conditions in Australia, Belgium, Finland, France, Germany, India, Japan, Russia, South Africa, Taiwan and the USA. Not forgetting Marieke de Mooij's chapter on the impact of culture on advertising.

With this second volume the title "Advertising Worldwide" becomes a little bit more true. Again other important countries are investigated with respect to their specific advertising structures. The authors of the different countries had the same briefing as in the first volume:

- What are the social, cultural or religious features of advertising and advertising practices?
- Are there any taboos?
- Which legal restrictions apply?
- What kind of advertising infrastructure is there? Are there any institutions, federations or boards of advertising?
- Which media are readily available?
- How are media data collected? What are the methods of gaining advertising data?
- How can specific target groups be addressed?
- Are there any particular preferences concerning the use of media?

Assessing the choice of countries in the two volumes of "Advertising Wordwide" one has to conclude as a first resume that it is not primarily the more theoretical question of standardization or differentiation which dominates the advertising strategy (at least for consumer goods) but the very practical necessity of adapting to the respective specific advertising conditions of each country. A standardized global, even multinational advertising campaign has to be considered the exception, rather than the rule. Thus international advertising is more a question of *effectiveness* and not of *efficiency*. The more an advertising campaign matches local needs, local infrastructures, local regulations and local habits the more likely is its acceptance.

The paradigm of Marketing is differentiation. Competitive advantages for exchangeable products can only be obtained by giving the consumer an argument why to buy this product and not the competitor's one. If the competitor's product is more or less identical – the normal case in saturated markets – the argument has to be based on a factual or non-factual difference. If this is true on a national basis can it be false on an international basis?

Then what about the undeniable success of campaigns like Coca-Cola, Marlboro, Nike? How can one explain that people all over the world smoke the same cigarettes, eat the same burgers, drink the same soft-drinks and walk in the same sneakers? Looking at the different eating-habits in Asia and Europe this sounds rather unlikely.

Although considered as the exception from the rule an explanation is necessary. I offer a personal opinion. The success of global campaigns is based

- either on a uniqueness of the advertised product (Coca-Cola)
- or on a uniqueness of the communicational concept (the Marlboro Cowboy)
- or – and this is a necessary condition for the two points mentioned first – a supra-socio-cultural identification platform. Just to provoke: Would Coca-Cola, Marlboro and McDonald's be as successful if they came from France, Italy or Japan? Or is their success based on the fact that these products represent the "American Way of Life" which seems to be attractive for people in all continents?

Again in this introduction some highlights of the respective chapters:

- Until recently, in *Bulgaria* legislation limited the amount of advertising in certain TV-programs. There was not supposed to be advertising on national TV during prime-time hours – from 7 p.m. to 10 p.m. Now there are certain limitations, such as no commercials during children's programs and a maximum of 15 minutes of advertising per hour, of which not more than five minutes may be in a block.
- In the 90s, the advertising market in *China* was mainly driven by multinational advertisers and the emerging local advertisers. In recent years, the confidence and assertiveness shown by local enterprises are especially encouraging. As the local marketers have more experience in marketing, they have come out of the shadows of foreign brands. All top 10 advertising products are local brands. Together they account for 7 per cent of total advertising in China. As for foreign products, an international brand leader Coca-Cola ranked 20th among the most advertised products in 2000.
- During the economic recession 1995 in *Greece* the opacity of media buying negotiations gave rise to a big issue: the transparency of the tariffs. The debates under the self-regulation umbrella failed to result

in mutual understanding and agreement between the interested parties. As a consequence the Hellenic Ministry of Press and Mass Media enforced a law to regulate and control the advertising practices. Five years on one can trace the repercussions of the new law on advertising industry. In 1996 and 1997 the adspend as percentage of GDP falls to 1.43% and 1.00% respectively compared to 1.86% in 1995. Advertising agencies see a 15% cut to their gross income.

- The fact that a mixture of English and Chinese is still the dominant form of language used reflects *Hong Kong* consumers' language habits. Therefore, a mixture of languages is the unique character of Hong Kong advertising and it enhances the association of the Hong Kong local audiences with the content of the ads.

- *Hungary* has a quite well developed advertising industry with sophisticated media research information systems and expenditure monitoring systems. But there is no official information for the total advertising industry.

- The issue of 'overspill' media, principally from its nearest neighbor, the United Kingdom has also had a profound effect on the *Irish* media market. It is increasingly common for advertisers and agencies to plan advertising campaigns on an All-Ireland basis which includes both the Republic of Ireland and Northern Ireland.

- Almost a uniquely *Korean* characteristic is the presence of The Korean Advertising Broadcasting Company (KOBACO) that was founded in 1981 by the Korean government. Its perhaps most controversial role is that it acts as an exclusive agent for the sale and placement of broadcast advertising space. For this role it receives a commission that varies depending on the type of agency (in-house versus independent agency) that buys media placement from KOBACO.

- In the Republic of *Latvia* approximately 70% of the whole advertising investments consist of resources of foreign companies for advertising goods and services. It is very hard for the local producers to compete with the foreign companies. The foreign companies are more technologically advanced and the prime cost of goods and services is lower than for producers of goods and services in Latvia. Wherewith foreign enterprises can afford to waste considerably more money for advancement of their goods and services in the market, while the local companies cannot.

- In *Malaysia*, scenes of an amorous, intimate or suggestive nature are forbidden on television. Also not permitted are commercials for pork and pork products, liquor and alcoholic beverages since they are forbidden in Islam. In addition, provocative scenes that show naked or scantily clad models are also not allowed to be shown. Recent changes in the code of advertising include forbidding certain advertisements such as those that highlight western values and project and promote inspirational lifestyles as well as advertisements on feminine napkins.

- One of the particularities of advertising in *Spain* is the fact that non-classical media is as important as classical media.
- The existence of three main races in *Singapore*, Chinese, Malay and Indian makes it a challenge for advertising to have national appeal.
- A major consideration for everyone who is going to advertise in *Switzerland* is that there are not only four written languages (German, French, Italian and Rhaeto-Romanic), but in addition many dialects of the Swiss German, which may be considered a fifth language. This means that although the other elements of the marketing mix may remain the same, at least the advertising mix has to be changed if a large share of people in Switzerland is not to be ignored.
- In the UK the amount of advertising air time permitted on the Independent Television Authority ITV, Channel 4, and Channel 5 is strictly regulated at seven minutes per clock hour during the day and seven point five minutes per hour peak time. Air time is sold in a pre-emptive auction system which tends to maximize the yield for the station. The permissible EU average of nine minutes is allowed to satellite and cable services and there is an active debate as to whether terrestrial stations should be allowed this level of advertising. It might in fact lead to a weakening of price achieved and an increase in clutter.

Again my thanks to the authors for their cooperation.

Ingomar Kloss

Contents

Multicultural Management Insights

Prof. Dr. Jürgen Rothlauf
University of Applied Sciences, Stralsund

Success and survival are the key goals in the fierce competition of today's global marketplace. Companies are in constant competition for customers, who in turn are increasingly demanding and discriminating. Losing customers means more than simply losing revenues; it means losing market share to competitors in a global fight to be a major player. The toughest question a manager in the complex global playing field is facing is how to secure a competitive advantage.

First of all, management today is increasingly multicultural. This has come to pass in the last quarter to the 20th century, as national populations have become more informed, heterogeneous, and less isolated. With continued movement toward a global marketplace, growing transborder exchanges are leading to trade agreements and economic unions. Thanks to stunning technological advances in communications and transportations, the world's cultures are increasingly starting to interact with one another.

Because of the significant social and political changes that are currently under way, there is a real opportunity for world traders and entrepreneurs, free of ideologies, to engage in peaceful commerce for the benefit of humankind. The globalization of the mass media has shown many people the possibilities available within modern society, and has made them desire improvements in their quality of life. Such market needs can only be met on a global scale when a new class of managers and professionals come prepared with multicultural skills. Such cultural competencies are critical as we transition into 21st century.

1   Diversity in the Multicultural Workforce

For business people the challenge remains one of simultaneously managing diversity and change. The wordwide competition will continue to foster partnerships and joint ventures, mergers and acquisitions within its national territory and across its borders.

A business firm's decision to internationalize its operations does not simply mean expanding into new geographical areas. It involves moving into and operating in different economic, political, legal, sociocultural and financial environments. The ability of the firm to identify these environmental differences, understand their implications for its business and adapt its operations and products accordingly, will be important in determining the success or failure of its international expansion.

One of the key issues for managers in international organizations is the problem of integrating employees from several cultures. At one level the problem is familiar one of overcoming value and behavioural differences that arise when employees from different cultures must work together. For example, an organization with its headquarter in a country which gives considerable deference to leaders may encounter difficulties in promulgating its policies in a country in which consultation among supervisors and subordinates is the norm.

One conclusion out of this scenario is that the domestic work environment in most countries is becoming more complex. Most national workforces are experiencing a population growth among traditional minorities, who also seek to move beyond entry-level jobs. Improved access to education and training for people in such microcultures fuels their vocational ambitions. Gender barriers are also slowly being eliminated, and many women are now in supervisory, management, and other executive positions.

Everywhere, people are moving beyond their homelands in the search for a better life, creating worker pools that call for cross-culturally sensitive managers. In this post-industrial information age, a new work culture is emerging. One of its norms is competence, regardless of one's race, colour, creed, or place of origin. High-technology industrial parks around the world are being staffed by technical types of many nationalities, hired because of their scientific ability, as the current green card discussion in Germany underlines, and regardless of the cultural background. Operating high-tech plants requires the best of multicultural management, whether it will take place in the „Silicon Valley" of California or the „Biocon Valley" of Mecklenburg-Westpomerania. Those companies that are not cross-culturally prepared will definitely fail.

2 Mergers and Acquisitions

As companies expand into the global marketplace mergers and acquisitions become more and more important. A critical multicultural management challenge often ignored occurs when two or more systems are reorganized into one enterprise. Whenever a merger, acquisition, or joint venture is formed by two or more existing companies, distinct organizational cultures must be combined. It is ineffective when one entity simply tries to impose its culture upon another. It is more productive to seek a cultural synergy between and among the systems involved. But the latter calls for finesse, the practice of sophisticated multicultural management. Nowhere is multicultural management more desirable than in the formation of a consortium made up of several corporations, or of representatives from industry, government, and universities. The daunting task of managers is to utilize multicultural skills to create the best in the various organizational cultures and management systems.

As far as a merger is concerned, the parties do not only bring with them a unique organizational history, management, and expertise, but a distinct culture as the merger of Daimler/Chrysler has made obvious. Too often the executives involved in such undertakings ignore these factors to their own detriment, while concentrating on the task (including its financing) at hand. Even within a world corporation, one faces cultural diversity among various departments, divisions, and subsidiaries. In reality, every time a project team is assembled, made up of different disciplines and fields of expertise, the project manager must practice multicultural management. Engineers think differently from manufacturing or finance personnel who, in turn, may differ in perspective from marketing or public relations people; each profession or speciality has a unique subculture, often solving problems differently from one another. When such assemblages of personnel are escalated into an international project team or task force, the management challenges are even greater, for the varying macro- and micro-cultures are participating.

Thus, those experienced in intercultural communication and negotiation are more likely to succeed. Managers who have multicultural proficiency are asked for. But, it is not sufficient to have a good management record in the past. Moreover a multicultural manager has to fulfill a lot of additional prerequisites in order to master the daunting challenges in an international environment that will become increasingly multicultural.

3 The Multicultural Manager

In modifying the managerial task to its cultural context, the managers need to have cross-cultural skills, which means the ability to demonstrate a sequence of behaviour that is functionally related to attaining a performance goal. The true multicultural manager is more „cosmopolitan" – that is, innovative leaders who are effective intercultural communicators and negotiators. These people are comfortable operating anywhere in the world. Whether representing a business, a government, a foundation, an association, or a profession, these are high performers in the world marketplace. They are capable of functioning readily around their own homeland and its regional groupings, or of moving across borders.

Multicultural managers characteristically

- Understand the nature of culture, and how it influences behaviour in the workplace
- Recognizing differences between cultures
- Recognizing which and how cultural factors influence the expression of business structures, systems, and priorities
- Think beyond local perceptions, and transform stereotypes into positive views of people
- Prepare for new mindshifts, while eliminating old mindsets
- Re-create cultural assumptions, norms, and practices based on new insights and experiences
- Reprogram their mental maps and constructs
- Adapt readily to new and unusual circumstances and lifestyles
- Welcome and facilitate transitional experiences
- Acquire multicultural competencies and skills, including foreign languages
- Create cultural synergy whenever and wherever feasible
- Operate effectively in multinational/multicultural environments
- Envision transnational opportunities and enterprises
- Create optimistic and doable scenarios for future.

To fulfil all these different requirements a new job profile has to be created to go in line with this multicultural task. A survey conducted by Töpfer has made clear what the expectations are asked for by the international enterprises.

If multicultural firms are to prosper now and in the future, they must develop managers who can successfully operate in a cross-cultural organization. Working together is different from doing business together as buyer and seller. It requires a deeper understanding of why people from different backgrounds behave the way they do. Without focussing on people, without preparing them for international assignments, the results will be devastating.

Table 1: A Profile of an International Manager

Requirements	Perspective Significance (Percentage)
Proficiency in foreign language	92
Flexibility and adaptability to change	89
Cross-cultural understanding	87
Thinking in global dimensions	83
Marketing knowledge	82
Maturity and emotional stability	81
Initiative and creativity	75
	(N = 482 Manager)

Source: Töpfer: Der lange Weg zum Global Player - Anforderungen an einen international tätigen Manager, UNI 3 (March 1995), p.18

4   Five Dimensions of People Management

People management requires for managers being able to understand and work effectively with people from different cultural, religious, and ethnic backgrounds, as well as the ability to manage teams composed of such cross-cultural members. People management is not to be seen as a function of a specific department (such as personnel or human resources), but as a set of activities any manager in any functional area of a firm must master. Each activity builds upon the others as the process becomes an integrated package.

4.1   Getting the Right People (Recruiting/Selecting)

First, a manager must identify, recruit, and then place individuals in appropriate positions within the organization. Sometimes this process involves people who are already in the company, and sometimes it involves hiring individuals from outside. The first aspect of people management also includes determining the types and numbers of individuals who will be needed in the future for certain positions and examing the existing pool for people who could meet those needs. At the corporate level, this raises such questions as „Are managers with the necessary skills and experience placed in strategic positions throughout the firm's global operations?"

Further questions that can help to optimize this process are:

- What characteristics should be utilized in selecting expatriates?
- Why are expatriates likely to accept/reject international assignments?
- How can a larger pool of potential international assignees be identified and developed?
- Can questionnaires and interviews be used effectively to screen and select candidates who are more likely to be successful abroad?

4.2   Helping People Do the Right Thing (Training)

The jobs that managers are expected to do and the standards by which performance will be judged must be determined, and the necessary training must be provided. This necessity begs the question of whether a firm's manager – who must deal with employees, customers, suppliers, or competitors form different cultures and countries – are adequately trained to understand work successfully with these groups. The most European and the vast majority of U.S. multinational firms fail to prepare individuals adequately to work with individuals from other cultures.

The value of intercultural training is not recognized universally. Different surveys, conducted in Germany as well as in the United States of America, underline the lack of intercultural preparations:

- 85 percent of all German companies send their employees unprepared abroad (Marketing Corporation, Bad Homburg)
- More than 75 percent of all international enterprises do not have any international human resource planning (Institute for Intercultural Management, Königswinter)

- 15 to 30 percent of all international assignments fail (Institute for Intercultural Management, Königswinter/Germany)
- Approximately 70 percent of Americans who must work overseas receive inadequate training or preparation for their international work (Windham International, New York /USA)

Apart from these insufficiencies the damage that will be caused by dissatisfied counterparts, customers or suppliers will have a long-lasting negative impact on the company's overall performance.

Questions that have to be raised in this context are:

- What are the most effective training methods for international assignments?
- What should be the relative mix and content of predeparture and postarrival training?
- Should family members be included in such a training program?
- How can the cost effectiveness of training be calculated?
- How long should a training last and what qualifications should be taught?
- Should the trainer come from within the company or from outside?
- Should the experiences of expatriates being integrated in such a program?

4.3 Determining How People Are Doing (Appraising)

Once an employee has been trained, his or her performance must be measured. However, measuring the job performance of managers who have been sent abroad is tricky. For example, if traditional variables such as profit, sales, and market share are utilized as quantitative measures, should factors that apply to the local business environment (such as movements in exchange rates) be incorporated into the performance evaluation as well? Most firms have little idea about which factors facilitate or inhibit cross-cultural adjustment, organizational commitment, or job performance during an international assignment.

Questions that have to be raised in this context could be:

- How can the expatriate performance be monitored in light of exogenous factors, such as foreign exchange rates, that can dramatically affect the business performance?

- What is the appropriate mix of quantitative and qualitative measures of expatriate job performance?
- To what extent should local nationals be involved in evaluating expatriates?

4.4   Encouraging the Right Things That People Do (Rewarding)

In addition to measuring an individual's job performance, the organization must provide rewards for specific performance behaviour, as well as general compensation and benefits. This aspect of people management raises such questions as „Should all managers receive equal benefits and bonuses, regardless of the country in which they are working?" Most firms complain about the high costs of global assignment, and many firms have cut the total number of expatriates to reduce costs. In the absence of understanding or analysis of the reward systems for global managers, this is unlikely to reduce costs per expatriate or to improve the performance of individual managers.

Necessary questions that should be discussed are:

- To what extent should an expatriate compensation package be utilized to entice employees to accept international assignments versus simply equalizing cost-of-living expenses?
- How should different tax laws for expatriates from different home countries be factored into compensation?
- How should compensation inequities be handled that arise when expatriates of similar level but form different home countries work in the same assignment country?

4.5   Doing Things Right for People (Developing)

Over the long term, a sequence of positions, opportunities, responsibilities, and so forth will be needed to develop the maximum potential of managers. This aspect of management raises such questions as „How should managers sent on international assignments be utilized once they return?", or: „How can employees with successful international experience be effectively repatriated into other organizational units?" or: "How can the immediate task needs in the assignment and the development needs in the individual be effectively balanced?"

There is strong evidence that most German companies do very little planning for the systematic development of global managers. Specifically, most firms do little planning for the return and integration of global managers who have been abroad for some time. Many of these managers are dissatisfied with their jobs and responsibilities after returning to their homecountry.

5 Elements of the Cultural Environment of International Business

Without knowing and handling appropriately the key elements of the cultural environment of business any manager will fail. Assessing the cultural environment of international business depends largely on the type of business and the international activities involved. One practical approach is to break down the broad area of the sociocultural environment into its various elements and to study each element. To describe any of them fully would require a discussion of far greater length and depth than this is possible in this article. Therefore I would like to focus only on those dimensions which have been found to influence international business practices substantially, as shown in the following figure.

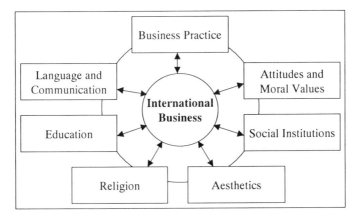

Figure 1: Elements of the Cultural Environment of International Business
Source: El Kahal, Introduction to International Business, 1994, p. 33

5.1   Language and Communication

Of all the cultural elements of the international business environment, language is perhaps the most obvious difference between cultures and probably the most difficult to acquire and understand. There are approximately 3000 different languages in the world with less than 300 nations and 10000 different dialects.

The ability to speak and understand the various interpretation of the language of a foreign country is essential for anyone planning a career in international business. The study of a foreign language should therefore include both the verbal language, or factual knowledge, and the non-verbal language, or interpretative knowledge.

In addition to the formal learning of the verbal language and the ability to speak and communicate effectively in it, business managers must also acquire the competency to recognize the idiomatic interpretations of that language, which are quite different from those, for example, found in a dictionary. Matching words with identical meanings from one language to another, without being aware of the nuances of the local language, double meanings of words and slang and the various interpretations of the cultural terms and concepts, could lead to confusion, embarrassment and expensive mistakes.

Problems faced when conveying a message in another language shows the Pepsi Cola slogan „Come alive with Pepsi". When technically translated in German the message conveyed the idea of coming alive from the grave, and in Asia of bringing your ancestors from the dead. The same problem can arise when companies want to establish a brand name. A couple of years ago, General Motors created the brand name „Chevrolet Nova". After the introduction of its new Chevrolet Nova in Puerto Rico, it found out that although the word Nova means „start" in Spanish, its pronunciation sounded as like „no va", meaning „does not go" , and had to be changed to „Caribe".

Mastering a foreign language is not enough in itself, because not all communication is written or spoken. Non-verbal language, often referred to as the „silent language", can pose serious problems for international business managers. Japanese have been taught to believe that „silence is golden" and to suppress the expression of feelings as much as possible. Silence in communication settings are not empty and to be filled with words, but they should be regarded as important non-verbal means of communication. Silence is such an important part of the non-verbal communication in Japan that it deserves to be addressed on its own. While Westerns usually concentrate on the words that are spoken, Japanese take special note of the pauses between the words. In Japan, people are comfortable with less talk and longer periods of silence than Westerns are. To a Western who is not very familiar to periods of silence during a meeting, five or ten seconds of total quietness can be seen as an eternity. However, it is important to resist the impulse to say something, because it could break an important moment.

Each society has different attitudes towards time. This can have economic consequences for international business relations and be a source of frustration in conducting international business. Punctuality, for example, can cause confusion and misunderstanding in various cultures. In Western societies, arriving late for a business appointment could be interpreted as an insult, while in Arab societies waiting for up to two hours is quite often acceptable, and part of the business culture. But to draw the conclusion, that coming a little bit later to the next meeting would be seen from the Arab point of view as impolite, because their perception of Western culture implies punctuality.

In many Western societies the slogan „Time is money" reflects the attitude towards the time horizon. Any delay in answering a communication could mean, loosing money. This short-term sight can cause many problems. The failure of the former CEO of Daimler-Benz, Mr. E. Reuter, to come to a final agreement with a Japanese car producer within three days underlines the negligence of the language of time. In Asian societies time is more measured by the monsoon than by the clock. This has to be recognized and is essential to successfully conducting international business.

Moreover the body language determines how to behave correctly in a foreign environment. The smallest details of body language can be extremely important to the conduct of international business. It is, however, difficult to generalize about differences in body language across different cultures. The ways in which people move their bodies, stand, sit, cross their legs, touch and walk differ from one country to another. While the traditional handshake in the West is mostly used for greetings and introductions in the East, bowing in front of your partner while placing the hands in a praying position is customary, and kissing on the cheeks is often practised in the Arab world – but between opposite sexes.

Language of space, for example, refers to the size of offices and their location. In most US and Western firms the president and high executives of the company will have the largest offices, usually on the top floor. The Japanese, on the other hand, prefer to work together in an open area. In the Arab world, and in Saudi Arabia in particular, women are not allowed to work in the same offices as men. The Chinese conception of the proper social distance between people in a room, or in an elevator, is somewhat closer than that common to many Western cultures, especially in Germany and America.

5.2 Religion

It is not enough for business managers to know *how* people behave in other cultures and *how* to do business with them. It is also important to understand *why* they behave in the way they do. Religious beliefs shape many kinds of individual behaviour, wether economic, political, legal, or social. Understanding the dominant religion of a particular country, therefore, can provide business managers with a better insight into people's behaviour and cultural attitudes. Ignorance of differences in religious beliefs could lead to frustration and misunderstanding, poor productivity and a drastic reduction in the sales of products, or even cause the ultimate failure of a business.

For example, if a manager working in Saudi Arabia does not know how to behave properly during the time of Ramadan, where drinking, eating and smoking in public is strictly forbidden, he will not only insult his counterparts religious feelings but will - after a while - be very surprised that a well prepared business contract is postponed or will never be signed.

5.3 Aesthetics

Aesthetics refer to the art, folklore, music, drama, myth, legends, sculpture and architecture of a culture. Understanding and interpreting the symbolic meaning of various aesthetics can be problematic for business managers. Use of symbols, for example, could have a distinctive meaning unique to a particular culture. The owl in the United Kingdom symbolizes wisdom, in France it is regarded as an ordinary bird with limited intelligence, while in the Middle East it is considered as a bad omen, or bad luck. A product designer in Saudi Arabia was once arrested because the logo he designed of a snowflake for „Snow White", a local cleaning plant, had six-pointed stars on the label with a strong similarity with the Star of David.

The use and meaning of colour is also of particular importance to international business, because in most cultures colour is used as a symbol that conveys specific messages. Colour perceptions vary greatly from one culture to another. Green, for example, is a very popular colour in Muslim countries, but is also associated with disease in countries with dense, green jungles, while in France green is associated with cosmetics. Black is the colour of death in the America, Europe and the Middle East. In Japan and Asia white is the colour of mourning, and black symbolizes power, luxury, prestige and high quality.

5.4   Education

Education is often restricted to the formal acquisition of knowledge and training within the schools. Broader education takes place outside the classroom, and most people have been educated in this broader sense for the culture in which they live and work.

Understanding the educational environment in foreign countries is crucial to successful international business operations. Looking at the educational background of the foreign country in which a multinational firm is contemplating doing business could provide important information for the personnel manager in determining, for example, the quality of local workforce available for employment. It is not just the level of literacy that is important, but also the nature of the educational systems available in order to determine on-the-job training needs and the development of skills required for the performance of certain business functions. BASF, for example, when recruiting business graduates form Asia, often sends them to the headquarter in Ludwigshafen to attend a six months intensive in-house training programme.

Understanding the level of education can also assist marketers in evaluating and assessing the levels of sophistication of local customers, the nature of the media to be used and the kind of approach to be used in advertising. If, for example, the local consumers are largely illiterate, advertising and package labels would have to be adapted using more visual aids.

5.5   Social Institutions

Social institutions, beliefs and values refer to the ways in which people in different cultures relate to each other. Elements of social organization include, gender, age, family, class structure and social hierarchy.

Those, for example, who are dealing with Vietnamese counterparts should keep in mind the outstanding importance of the „Tinh-Cam-Principle". When a Vietnamese asks another for a favour, he or she usually does it in the name of tinh cam. Even if a manager doesn't speak Vietnamese, it's a key concept. It means, literally, good feelings towards others. If you have it, you are sympathetic, generous and helpful, you do favours which you don't have to, and most importantly, you treat others with respect. A foreign boss of a joint-venture may be perceived as having tinh cam if, for example, he or she attends weddings of a junior employees. If he or she visits a Vietnamese joint-venture partner at home to discuss business and seek advice, and brings a small, appropriate gift, for the children or spouse, then that too can rate highly on the tinh cam scale. And a company which gives gifts to local residents on festival days, or which is seen to contribute to the local community, will also earn tinh cam. But, this being Vietnam, it is not so simple; striving too hard to demonstrate the appearance of tinh cam can be counter-productive. You have to mean it.

5.6   Attitudes and Moral Values

To successfully deal with a new culture, whether with a person from a specific company or a different country, you must make an effort to identify their cultural values and inherent priorities, and how they differ from.

The value American culture places on independence and individual freedom of choice naturally leads to the idea that everyone is equal regardless of age, social status, or authority. Japanese and Arab cultures, however, place more value on age and seniority. The Japanese individual will always give way to feelings of the group, while Arabs respect authority and admire seniority and status.

In examing Table 2, we note that one of the top American values listed is freedom – freedom to choose your own destiny – whether it leads to success or failure. Japanese culture, on the other hand, finds a higher value in belonging. In this culture, you must belong to and support a group(s) to survive. Belonging to a group is more important to Japanese culture than individualism. Arab culture is less concerned with individualism or belonging to a group, concentrating instead on maintaining their own family security and relying on Allah for destiny. Individual identity is usually based on the background and position of each person's family.

Table 2: Cultural Contrast in Value

Americans	Japanese	Arabs
1. Freedom	1. Belonging	1. Family security
2. Independence	2. Group harmony	2. Family harmony
3. Self-reliance	3. Collectiveness	3. Parental guidance
4. Equality	4. Age/Seniority	4. Age
5. Individualism	5. Group consensus	5. Authority
6. Competition	6. Cooperation	6. Compromise
7. Efficiency	7. Quality	7. Devotion
8. Time	8. Patience	8. Very patient
9. Directness	9. Indirectness	9. Indirectness
10. Openness	10. Go-between	10. Hospitality
11. Aggressiveness	11. Interpersonal	11. Friendship
12. Informality	12. Hierarchy	12. Formal/Admiration
13. Future-orientation	13. Continuation	13. Past and present
14. Risk-taking	14. Conservative	14. Religious belief
15. Creativity	15. Information	15. Tradition
16. Self-accomplishment	16. Group-achievement	16. Social recognition
17. Winning	17. Success	17. Reputation
18. Money	18. Relationship	18. Friendship
19. Material possessions	19. Harmony with nature	19. Belonging
20. Privacy	20. Networking	20. Family network

Source: Elashmawi/Harris, Multicultural Management, 1998, p. 72

5.7   Business Practices

First impressions are very important. They way you present yourself during the first encounter may open or close the door to many other opportunities. People from every culture have different procedures the follow and different expectations when interacting with others the first time. These are based on the beliefs of each culture and are additionally derived from the individual value system of each person. This is why the initial meeting with an executive from a different culture must be approached with care and understanding.

To most Americans and Germans alike, for example, the objective of such an encounter is to find out what you do and to add you to a list of contacts. Typically, the Japanese will try to first find out what company you work for, which department you are with, and your individual position within the company. Arabs, on the other hand, will first make an effort to establish personal rapport before discussing any business prospects.

Cultural differences in a business introduction become apparent starting with the exchange of business cards. After receiving someone else's card, most Germans will probably glance briefly at it, then put it away for future reference. Germans often consider the business card exchange a formality, done simply to be able to contact the person again. Conversely, the Japanese consider the business card important to show your company affiliation and your level in the company.

Regardless how you behave at an official welcome, on the telephone, on a banquet, during a business meeting, by presenting gifts, or hosting a foreign delegation, the business etiquette you demonstrate will indicate whether you are crossculturally trained or not with negative or positive consequences for the further business meetings.

6 Summary

Today, more and more managers, besides those employed in already established international firms, are realizing that their businesses cannot be located or conceived of as operating within national boundaries. Domestic firms are increasingly facing external competition within their own domestic markets. Business activities can no longer be considered as external and separate from the global environment within they operate.

To compete successfully, or simply to survive, in such a challenging and dynamic environment, firms are realizing the need for their managers to look for opportunities abroad. A business firm's decision to internationalize its operations does not simply mean expanding into new geographical areas. It involves moving into and operating in different economic, political, legal, sociocultural and financial environments. The ability of the firm to identify these environmental differences, understand their implications for its business and adapt its operations and products accordingly, will be important in determining the success or failure of its international expansion.

Problems encountered during intercultural business interactions lie in the misunderstanding of basic cultural guideline present in each of the world's countries. In order to successfully conduct business across cultures, one must be willing to make the effort to understand and work within these guidelines. Each culture has its own unique way of handling business as well as social interactions. In international business dealings, ignorance of cultural difference is not just unfortunate, it is bad business. Sensitivity to cultural difference is crucial to successful international business operations. Ignorance of cultural differences could end in disastrous business blunders.

References

Black, S., Gregersen, H., Mendenhall, M, Stroh, L. (1999) Globalizing People Through International Assignments, Addison-Wesley, New York

Crane, R. (2000) European Business Cultures, Pearson Education, Essex

Cray, D., Mallory, G. (1998) Making Sense of Managing Culture, International Thomson Business Press, London

Deresky, H. (2000) International Management. Managing Across Borders and Cultures, Prentice Hall, New Jersey

Elashmawi, F., Harris, P. (1998) Multicultural Management 2000, Gulf, Houston

El Kahal, S. (1994) Introduction to International Business, McGraw-Hill, London

Mercado, S., Welford, R., Prescott, K. (2001) European Business, 4th edition, Pearson Education, Essex

Mole, J. (2001) Mind Your Manners. Managing business cultures in Europe, Nicholas Brealey, London

Rothlauf, J. (1999) Interkulturelles Management. Mit Beispielen aus Vietnam, Japan, Russland und Saudi-Arabien, Oldenbourg Verlag, München/Wien

Advertising in Bulgaria
A Nation in Transition

Prof. Dr. Brad Thompson, Ph.D.
Pennsylvania State University

1 Introduction

Bulgaria is in the heart of the Balkans in southeast Europe. It is one of a number of formerly Communist countries in economic and political transition. That seems be the situation not just today for Bulgaria but also for much of its history. The Bulgarian territory was occupied by Thracians, Greeks, Romans, Byzantines, and Slavs before the Bulgarians made it their home. Bulgaria began emerging from 500 years of Ottoman rule in 1878 and after that lands were added and taken away through a progression of battles, wars and treaties. The nation was on the losing side in both World War I and II and then fell after 1945, along with other Eastern European nations, under the domination of the Soviet Union. Bulgaria is generally acknowledged to have been the most loyal of the Soviet Union's European allies. While most Central and Eastern European nations shed communism during the tumultuous year of 1989, Bulgaria was slower to change its socialist heritage even as long-time leader Todor Zhivkov was deposed on 10 November 1989. After a succession of shifts in government, the socialists gave way to a coalition of democratic forces during a disastrous stretch of hyperinflation and public demonstrations in 1996-97. Since then there has been a period of market reforms and privatization of state assets as the country moves toward integration into the European Union and NATO.

Bulgaria's political as well as economic capital is Sofia, a city of about 1.3 million people. Nationwide there are 7.7 million people but the population is declining due to a low birth rate and emigration. Bulgarians make up the largest ethnic group at about 83 percent, followed by Turks (8.5 percent), Roma (2.6 percent) and several others. The Bulgarian Orthodox Church (83.5 percent) and Islam (13 percent) are the largest religions. Bulgarians have a very high literacy rate (98 percent).

The country's gross domestic product in 1999 was an estimated $34.9 billion[1] or $4,300 per capita, although figures may be suspect due to a large underground economy and questionable data. The unemployment rate is reported at around 20 percent. The GDP was estimated in 1997 to be divided by sector as follows: agriculture, 12 percent; industry, 31 percent; and services, 57 percent. The economy has been growing in the 2.5-3.5 percent range since the period of hyperinflation. The nation's currency is the lev, which was redenominated in 1999 by dropping three zeros. It is managed by a currency board and is pegged to the German mark. Bulgaria's biggest trading partners are Russia, Italy and Germany.

With the post-1989 development of a market economy, the Bulgarian advertising market has slowly progressed. By 1999 advertising expenditure amounted to about $56 million. A number of big advertising agencies opened offices in Bulgaria to serve the needs of their clients who opened facilities in Bulgaria. Among those are Saatchi & Saatchi, Amirati Puris Lintas, BBDO, and PBI McCann/Ericsson.

2 Advertising Media

The advertising industry was decimated by the economic collapse in 1996-97. Kamenov (2000) has described the year as "missing" and a "catastrophe" for the advertising industry. Indeed, ad budgets were cut nearly in half that year, although they have now recovered and even exceeded pre-1997 levels. According to the World Association of Newspapers (2000), 1998 advertising expenditures broke down as follows: television, $22.6 million; newspapers, $9.8 million; radio, $6 million; magazines, $2.6 million; and outdoor/transport, $1 million.

2.1 Television

Broadcasting policy in Bulgaria had been controlled since 1990 by the Parliamentary Commission for Radio and Television. Since passage of the Radio and Television Law of 1996, the National Council for Radio and Television has primary oversight, including the appointment of the leaders of the state-owned media. Because the broadcast media are often the subject of intense political debate and struggle there are credibility problems for broadcasting media, especially for Bulgarian National Television and Bulgarian National Radio.

Two licenses are required to broadcast both television and radio. The first is a programming license issued by the National Council for Radio and Television; the second is a broadcasting license is issued by the State Telecommunications Committee. Of particular interest, the National Council for Radio and Television monitors compliance with legal requirements for advertising and program sponsorship, as well as handling other issues. Monitoring can be initiated by the council's own experts or on the basis of citizen or organization complaints.

Bulgaria has three national television channels, the state-owned Channel 1 and Balkan Television, known as bTV, which is owned by Rupert Murdoch's U.S.-based News Corp. There are a total of 33 channels and 3.3 million television sets in use. Television is carried by 100 cable systems, and some television stations broadcast only over cable.

The television market is dominated by Channel 1. Second is bTV, which formerly was the second national channel – Efir 2 – that Murdoch bought in May 2000. It is the first private national television channel.

Third in terms of national audience reach is Nova TV, which began national broadcast coverage in summer 2000. Nova TV features a daily teleshop show, and some of the cable channels have short notices programs. Most channels provide all types of programming, with a stress on entertainment – they show mostly movies, with news programs in the late afternoon and in the evening, morning information blocks, and children's programs in the afternoon. The primary newscast usually starts at 7:30 or 8 p.m.

Cable television viewership is growing. Thirty-six percent of Bulgarian homes have cable TV. Through cable television many channels can be viewed not only in their "home" towns, but also in other big cities that have cable networks. From the channels with largest reach of viewers, Varna-based MSAT and Sofia-based Eurocom, with a 9.7 and a 7.8 percent reach accordingly, are distributed through cable networks.

Until recently, legislation limited the amount of advertising in certain programs. There was not supposed to be advertising on national TV during prime-time hours – from 7 p.m. to 10 p.m. This put a strain on Channel 1, which gets money form the government as well as advertisers. Many of the Channel 1 advertisers whose contracts were breached due to the law removed more advertising, and went to Nova TV, which was the only competitor at that time. The outflow of advertising funds seriously damaged

Channel 1's ability to survive, and the law was revised in 2000. Now there are certain limitations, such as no commercials during children's programs and a maximum of 15 minutes of advertising per hour, of which not more than five minutes may be in a block.

In 1999, Channel 1 received about 50 percent of TV advertising expenditure, with Nova TV coming second with 21 percent. The dramatic reach of bTV since it entered the market is sure to put increasing pressure on Channel 1.

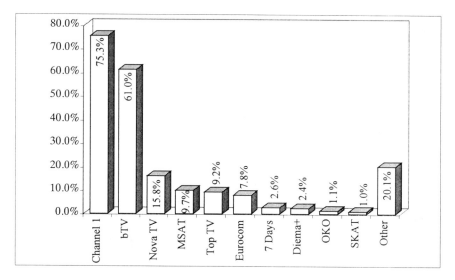

Figure 1: Reach of TV Channels in Bulgaria
Source: Alpha Research, December 2000

2.2 Newspapers

The daily newspaper market is dominated by *Trud* and *24 Chasa*, both run since 1998 by German-owned WAZ Group (Westdeutsche Allgemeine Zeitung). Respectively, they hold 43.9 percent and 23.8 percent of the daily newspaper audience. *Standart* is a distant third with only 2.9 percent of the audience, although its readership has been increasing of late (from 1.5 percent in October 2000 to 4.8 percent in January 2001). This change may be due mainly to the change in format from the typical one-body paper to a segmented approach, where the different sections are bundled together.

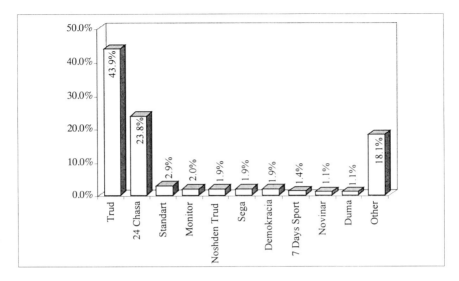

Figure 2: Readership of the 10 Most Popular Daily Newspapers
Source: Alpha Research, December 2000

Circulations in 1999 ranged from 440,000 and 245,000 for *Trud* and *24 Chasa* respectively to 30,000 for *Duma*, according to the World Association of Newspapers. Three-quarters of most papers' circulation is from single-copy sales with the remainder divided almost equally between postal and home delivery. All but one or two papers are tabloid in format. *Dnevnik* was introduced in February 2001 and it is seeking to establish itself as an upscale buy for advertisers. It remains to be seen if it and some of the other smaller newspapers will survive.

Of the newspapers in the above chart, all are news oriented and officially non-partisan, except for *Duma*, the Bulgarian Socialist Party-affiliated newspaper, and *Democracia*, the newspaper of the Union of Democratic Forces. *7 Dni Sport* features only sports news.

Daily newspapers feature mostly small ads. *24 Chasa* and *Trud* offer a two-for-one approach for small ads – advertisers need to submit and pay for their ad in one of the papers and it is run in both.

There is some corporate advertising as well, mainly by the two mobile communications firms in Bulgaria – Mobikom and Mobiltel, and by car dealers and chocolate manufacturers. They are usually printed in color, about a quarter of the page in size.

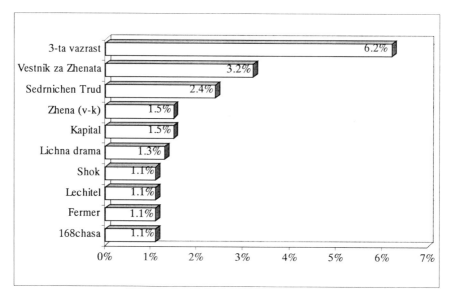

Figure 3: Print Media Audience – Weekly Newspapers, January 2001: 18+
Source: Alpha Research, February 2001

Weekly newspapers in Bulgaria are oriented toward certain audiences rather than the whole population. The one with the biggest audience, *3-ta vazrast* (*Third Age*) is oriented toward elderly people. *Lechitel* deals with health issues; *Fermer* targets farmers. *Lichna Drama* and *Shok* tell the personal stories of ordinary people.

The widely respected *Kapital*, with a readership of 1.5 percent in January 2001, provides analysis of current political and economical events. As with its daily sister publication, *Dnevnik*, it has a rather up-scale readership, reflecting the quality of the publication.

The advertising in weekly newspapers is more particular, targeted more to a differentiated audience than for daily newspapers. For example, *Kapital* publishes mostly advertisements for employment opportunities in foreign companies that operate on the Bulgarian market, and for office equipment and business-oriented services (industrial advertising).

Because of the lower quality of newspapers, weeklies are not as expensive as magazines, and are therefore more accessible to the public. This, together with the high level of segmentation in the audience, makes them attractive to advertisers.

2.3   Radio

The Bulgarian radio market is divided between the state-owned and private radio stations. Horizont, by far the biggest station, is part of the Bulgarian National Radio (BNR) together with the Hristo Botev station. Until 1997 the state-owned stations were the only national ones. A few private stations are now going national, including Darik, FM+, and Express. There are 24 AM stations and 93 FM stations.

The big percentage of Horizont's audience is due to the wide coverage, provided by the state-owned transmitters. It is still the only radio that can be listened to throughout Bulgaria – the private stations, even the ones that are going national, are still available only in big cities and their surroundings.

The radio stations in Bulgaria generally follow four program formats. Darik Radio is using the news-talk show format, with a heavy emphasis on current events and analysis. FM+ and Ritmo are hit radio stations, targeted at audiences who seek entertainment. The national stations, Horizont and Hristo Botev, are a mixed type – they have both hit and talk shows. The rest of devoted to music.the stations are using a format combining both news and music, with a bigger part of the time

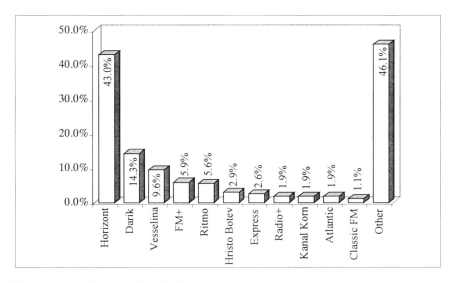

Figure 4: Audiences of Radio Stations
Source: Alpha Research, December 2000

2.4 Magazines

Magazines have highly segmented audiences. The chart below presents the percentages of readership each publication holds, but it is combined for both weekly and monthly magazines.

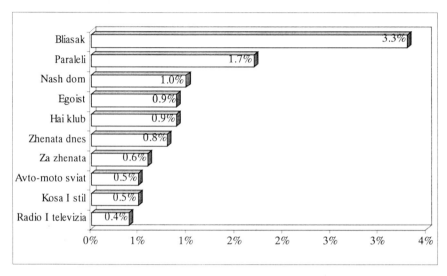

Figure 5: Print Media Audience – Magazines, January 2001; 18+
Source: Alpha Research, February 2001

There were a total of 631 magazines in Bulgaria in 1999 with a total circulation of 13.5 million copies (Petev, 2000).

Most Bulgarian magazines are of high quality, even if the same cannot be said of the content, which is celebrity and gossip oriented. There is no quality social or political magazine in Bulgaria. However, the advertisements that are carried are often full-color and full-page. As in any market, the main problem connected with advertising in magazines is the long lead time required – space has to be reserved at least two or three months prior to publication, and ads have to be submitted at least one month prior to publication. There is lots of competition among magazines for ads, and most magazines do not promise publication in a given issue.

Monthly magazines run mostly product advertising, while services and corporate advertising are predominant in weekly magazines.

2.5   Outdoor/Other

Outdoor advertising, in the form of posters, billboards and signs is becoming more and more widely spread. It has many opponents, usually because of the un-aesthetic effect it has on the towns and because of the possibility of automobile accidents due to inattentive drivers. To account for that, the capital city of Sofia has accepted new regulations that will prohibit the use of billboards in the central part of the city. Since many towns fashion their advertising regulations after those of Sofia, it may be expected that such regulations will appear in other towns sooner or later.

In the meantime, billboards are owned by companies who provide the space to advertising agency, usually for a month at a time with the possibility for extending the time of usage. The leasing companies usually provide the personnel to place and remove the advertisements.

The placement of signs is also limited to some extent. To put up a sign, the advertiser has to submit a project for the sign to the city authorities, who then make a decision on whether to allow it or not. Reasons for turning down a project may include the posing of dangers for the traffic, incompatibility with the architectural plan of the city, or inappropriate contents of the sign.

With only four percent[2] of Bulgarians having access to the Internet, electronic advertising is still not widely used. As Petrova (2000) reported, "The advertising market in Bulgaria has no significant movement towards media transmitted via new telecommunication services." There were a reported 20 Internet Service Providers in 2000, but that number is sure to fluctuate wildly. Nonetheless, the Internet is developing in Bulgaria – together with portal, informational, and newspaper sites, Internet advertising is slowly picking up speed. For now it is mostly banners on various user and information sites. The Bulgarian Banner Exchange network (http://banex.search.bg/) facilitates the usage of banners on Bulgarian sites.

The use of e-mail as an advertising medium is still not widespread among Bulgarian companies.

3   Products

Beer and cosmetics/washing products ads dominate the Bulgarian advertising market. As can be seen from the tables below, beer products account for the biggest part of advertising spending in Bulgaria – 8.3%. Four brands of beer are among the 10 most advertised brands (see Table 2). Two major Bulgarian producers of beer – Inter Brew and Brewinvest, amount for 7.1 percent of the advertising expenditure in 1999. Only Procter & Gamble outspends them with 8.0 percent, which is spread out between their different lines of products – cosmetics, washing powder, and sanitary products.

Table 1: Top Advertisers, 1999

	Company	Gross (000 USD	%
1	Procter & Gamble	4,393.7	8.0
2	Inter Brew	2,112.1	3.9
3	Brewinvest	1,725.5	3.2
4	Mobil Tel	1,653.3	3.0
5	Kraft Jacobs Suchard	1,587.2	2.9
6	Coca Cola Company	1,371.7	2.5
7	Mobikom	1,369.4	2.5
8	Unilever	1,104.7	2.0
9	Wrigley's	885.5	1.6
10	Nestle	834.6	1.5
	Other	37,703.4	68.9
	Total	**54,741.6**	**100**

Source: BBSS Gallup, November 2000

Table 2: Top 10 Brands, 1999. Total TV and Print

	Brand	Gross (000 USD)	%
1	Kamenitza Svetlo	1,167.2	2.1
2	Head & Shoulders	701.6	1.3
3	Zagorka Special	695.2	1.3
4	Ace	643.5	1.2
5	Astika	607.9	1.1
6	Ariel	518.6	0.9
7	Tang	513.2	0.9
8	Ariana	508.0	0.9
9	Safeguard	495.8	0.9
10	Coca-Cola	489.5	0.9
	Other	48,399.2	88.4
	Total	**54,741.6**	**100**

Source: BBSS Gallup, November 2000

Table 3: Top 10 Product Groups, 1999. Total TV and Print

	Product Group	Gross (000 USD)	%
1	Beer	4,511.3	8.3
2	Hair care products	2,120.4	3.9
3	Washing powder	1,494.3	2.7
4	Computer hardware	1,430.2	2.6
5	Carbonated soft drinks	1,275.0	2.3
6	Oral care	1,262.5	2.3
7	Pharmaceuticals	1,222.0	2.2
8	Chocolates & chocolate products	1,168.9	2.1
9	Sanitary products	1,158.1	2.1
10	Alcoholic beverages – hard liquors	1,095.4	2.0
	Other	37,978.1	69.4
	Total	**54,741.6**	**100**

Source: BBSS Gallup, November 2000

4   Ad Agencies

The role of ad agencies is expanding in Bulgaria as in the other nations of Eastern Europe. By at least one estimate, there are thirty full-service companies in Bulgaria. The largest agency is affiliated with Saatchi & Saatchi. Its largest client is Procter & Gamble, which one observer estimates spent about $25 million on advertising in Bulgaria in 2000. The agencies and their associated organizations have tried to bring international norms and ethics to Bulgaria.

The top agencies in terms of gross income in 1996 were:

Table 4: Top Bulgarian Agencies

S. Team Bates, Saatchi & Saatchi	2,622,000
Adia Young & Rubicam	1,000,000
Ogilvy & Mather	451,000
P.B.I. McCann-Erikson	438,000
Lowe GGK Sofia	280,000
Olympic DDB Bulgaria	237,000
Grey	102,000
Leo Burnett/Sofia	100,000

Source: Advertising Agency International, April 1997

Media & Reklama magazine publishes media consumption data of use to ad agencies and others. In addition, the National Center for Public Opinion Surveys gathers data on readership of the national dailies and its segmentation (Petev, 2000). Another publication of interest to media observers is *Balkan Media*, which is published in English.

5   Legal Issues

Several laws affect advertising in Bulgaria. The most general regulation of advertising comes under the Law on the Protection of Competition. It prohibits misleading ads or those that disparage the reputations of competitors.

Other laws regulate the advertising of specific products. For example, the Law on Tobacco and Tobacco Products prohibits some advertising of cigarettes and other tobacco products, except for point-of-sale ads and brand name promotion. For example, depictions of smoking are not permitted. Advertising of alcoholic spirits products is voluntarily limited to evening hours on television. Beer can be advertised at any time on television on radio. Another law of interest is the Pharmaceutical Law, which prohibits advertising of pharmaceuticals not registered with the National Institute for Control of Pharmaceutical Products. Ad content for registered pharmaceuticals must be approved in advance of its appearance. Only over-the-counter drugs may be advertised; advertising for prescription drugs is prohibited.

6   Conclusion

While it is difficult to make general observations about Bulgarian media and advertising because of the transitional nature of both the political and economic situation in the country, one factor stands out: It is a growing marketing tool and there is increasing segmentation in the media that is being reflected in advertising. The title of Kamenov's (2000) article neatly sums up the situation: "On the Edge of Optimism." Indeed, that could be said for the country in general, for while the Balkans have not been particularly stable over the past ten years, Bulgaria is the most stable of the post-Communist countries in the region. Such stability will, over time, make Bulgaria a place in which business plays an important role and advertising becomes an increasingly significant part of the nation's economic development.

References

Alpha Research, http://www.aresearch.org. Site accessed: Feb. 2, 2001
Bulgarian Parliament, http://www.parliament.bg. Site accessed: Feb. 1, 2001
CIA World Factbook, 2000. Washington: Government Printing Office.
Gallup BBSS, http://www.gallup-bbss.com. Site accessed: Jan. 29, 2001
Kamenov, Kamen.(2000). "Advertising in Bulgaria: On the Edge of Optimism." *The Global Network*, Bucharest, pp. 57-70
Petrova, Teodora. 2000. "A brief look at the digital changes in the media field and the development of the Web pages in Bulgaria," *The Global Network*, Bucharest, pp. 71-83
World Press Trends, 2000, World Association of Newspapers, Paris

Useful Address

Association of Advertising Agencies - Bulgaria
02 943 46 44 fax
02 43 28 13
ara@astratec.net
1544 Sofia
Veliko Turnovo St. 13

The author was a Fulbright lecturer at American University in Bulgaria in 2000-01. He would like to thank Sofia Panayatova for her help in preparing this chapter.

Notes

[1] All amounts are given in dollars even if originally reported in other currencies.
[2] "The Bulgarian IT Market – in the Shadow of the State." *Kapital*. Dec. 6, 2000.
  http://www.capital.bg/2000-50/35-50-1.htm

Advertising in China

Prof. Stella Lai Man So

Dept. of Marketing, The Chinese University of Hong Kong

1 Background

The Economic reform implemented in China during the last two decades has significantly improved the living standards of the Chinese Mainland. The rapid pace of economic development has brought about an increasing purchasing power of the Chinese population who is more willing to spend. Until the economic reform, the Chinese Mainlanders had largely been isolated from foreign goods and services. However, changing from a socialist economy to a planned economy supplemented by market forces, China as a huge potential consumer market is flooded with a tremendous number of foreign imported goods for consumers to choose from. As the market becomes competitive, it is crucial for companies to be able to quickly create product awareness among the potential consumers in order to secure a share-of-mind of the consumers and subsequently influence their choice decision among competing brands. Advertising is an effective marketing element to assist companies to make their brands known to the market.

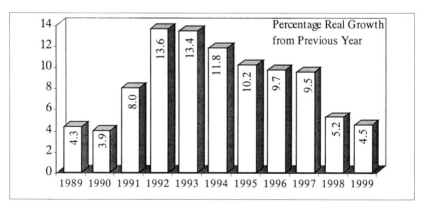

Figure 1: Real GDP Growth in China, 1989-1999
Source: China Statistical Yearbook, 2000

China is one of the few markets in the world which combine a vast size with huge development potential. Its economy has been growing at an average rate of 9-10% over the last ten years, and it is expected to maintain rapid growth in the future. The GDP is 8,042 billion yuan in 1999 compare to 225 billion yuan in 1970. The per capita GDP reached 6,534 yuan in 1999 comparing to 275 yuan in 1970 (Figure 1).

2   Advertising - Market Overview

During the Cultural Revolution, advertising, as the symbol of capitalism, was labeled as evil, deceptive and reflective of the practices of capitalist businesses, and was officially prohibited in China. The limited advertisements in those days were mainly used for the purpose of political propaganda.

Starting from 1979 when the reforms began, the Chinese advertising industry has experienced three phases of development (HK Trade Development Council 1998):

- *Starting phase (1979-1991)*
  During this period the advertising market was largely dominated by limited state-owned advertising. Foreign participation in the advertising industry was very limited. Most of the local advertisers had to follow the government's instructions and use only appointed advertising agencies.

- *Fast Growth and Development Phase (1992-1993)*
  Dramatic increase in advertising turnover, number of advertising agencies and number of professionals. The central government implemented a very liberal policy on the advertising industry which allowed foreign advertising agencies to set up joint ventures in China.

- *Control and Implementation Phase (1994-present)*
  Although most of the largest international advertising agencies have joint ventures or representative offices in China, the approval of advertising agencies has higher requirements as under the control of the central government. The central government has tight control on the creative of advertising.

3   Advertising Industry

3.1   Advertising Expenditure

In the past two decades following the economic reform and open door policy, advertising has been flourishing again in China along with the influx of foreign imported goods. Advertising is one of the fastest growing industries in China for the past decade. Advertising volume represented 0.46% of the total GNP in the country in 1966, and it employed more than 477,000 people (Advertising Yearbook, 1996). The Chinese mainland's rocketing advertisement market grew to be Asia's largest in 2000, outranking even Hong Kong and Taiwan in both volume and growth rate. According to the statistics from *Asian Advertising and Marketing*, the advertising expenditure in Mainland China in 2000 were US$ 9,692 millions, which represented the highest growth rate (208%), and the highest adspend in the region (Table 1).

Table 1: Asia Pacific Adspend Totals (USD millions)

	1996-97 % change	1997-98 % change	1998-99 % change	1999-00 % change	1999 AdEx	2000 AdEx
China	208.4	45	15	58.0	6133	9692
Taiwan	56.8	19	-26	unknown	1875	unknown
Hong Kong	20.1	2	14	16.3	3043	3539
Vietnam	7.8	0	4	32.9	76	101
Singapore	4.5	-7	3	17.0	730	854
Malaysia	-11.9	-17	16	22.2	663	810
Philippines	-14.8	7	15	-4.3	1290	1234
Thailand	-47.0	-24	31	5.3	1093	1151
South Korea	-52.5	-26	33	21.5	4240	5150

Source: Asian Advertising And Marketing, April 1997/March 1998/July 1999
ACNielsen Media International

Regions in China can be broken down into three tiers based on the relative adspend of each tier (Figure 2). The first tier consists of the most prosperous cities: Shanghai, Beijing and Guangdong. They make up just 8% of the population, but over 50% of the total adspend in the country.

The second tier consists of five provinces - Zhejiang, Jiangsu, Sichuen, Liaoning and Shandong. They make up 30% of the population, and 25% of the total adspend. Once the top-tier region matures and its growth slows down, the second-tier region will grow faster as the government will concentrate on its development. This region has a very large potential in growth.

The third tier consists of the other 23 provinces. They are still relatively underdeveloped, and account for just under a quarter of the total adspend.

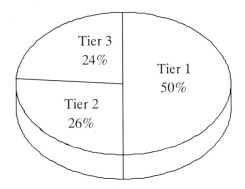

Figure 2: Adspend Breakdown by Tier

Table 2: Chinese Provinces by Tier

Region	Provinces Included
First Tier	Shanghai, Beijing, Guangdong
Second Tier	Zhejiang, Jiangsu, Sichuan, Liaoning, Shandong
Third Tier	Other 23 provinces

Source: China Advertising Yearbook, 1999

This pattern of adspend also reflects the different consumption patterns in the different regions in China (Figure 3). Currently, more than half the advertising expenditure is for consumer goods, including food, household appliances, cosmetics and pharmaceuticals (Figure 4).

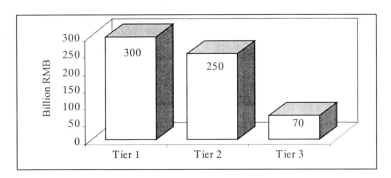

Figure 3: Average Wholesale And Retail Sales in Different Tiers (1995)
Source: Chinese Statistical Yearbook 1996, BA&H analysis

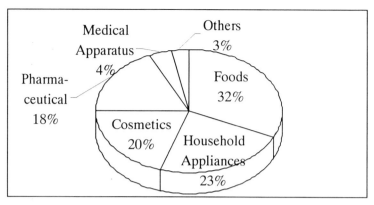

Figure 4: Adspend for Consumer Goods (1995)
Source: China Advertising Yearbook, 1996

3.2 Advertising Agencies

Many foreign advertising agencies have offices in China. Dentsu was the first to open offices in Beijing and Shanghai in 1972. Interpublic-Jardin, J. Walter Thompson, Saatchi and Saatchi, Advertising, and Ogilvy and Mather were among the pioneers.

The increase of advertising billings was partly fueled by multinational advertisers' continued expansion in China. There were 48,000 advertising agencies in China as of the beginning of 1996, an increase of 12% from the year before, and over 180 Chinese-foreign joint venture agencies (South China Morning Post, 1996). Since international agencies are still required to have a local joint venture partner before they can directly purchase media, locally hired people now make up 80 to 90% of staff at international agencies. However, most of the international advertising agencies have already established offices or joint venture partners in the Mainland (Table 3).

In 1999, Saatchi & Saatchi Great Wall ranked number one among the foreign advertising agencies in terms of its advertising billings. International advertising agencies specialize in providing full service and nationwide coverage. Although small in market share, they are growing very rapidly in China. The key success factors of international advertising agencies are their worldwide client base, financial strength and nationwide planning. However, international advertising agencies are not perceived as flexible as compared to local advertising agencies. They have higher operational cost then local firms, concentrate on higher budget projects and their client focus has been largely limited to multinational corporations.

Table 3: 1999 China 4 As Agency Ranking (USD millions)

1999 Ranking	Name of Agency	1999 Billings	1998 Billings	% change	1998 Ranking
1	Saatchi & Saatchi Great Wall	135.99	133.14	2.1	1
2	Ogilvy & Mather China	108.71	108.92	-0.2	2
3	J. Walter Thompson China	93.97	74.09	26.8	5
4	Leo Burnett – China	92.55	100.10	-7.5	3
5	Bates China	89.77	84.90	5.7	4
6	Grey China	72.44	65.94	9.9	6
7	Euro RSCG	51.54	50.50	2.1	8
8	D'Arcy	40.77	46.50	12.3	7
9	DDB China	32.75	26.47	23.8	10
10	* FCB China	25.99	28.62	-9.2	9
11	BBDO/CNUAC	14.85	19.22	-22.7	11
	TOTAL	**514.64**	**496.33**	**2.8**	
*FCB and Bozell merged in September 1999 reported jointly as FCB China					
# FCB and Bozell billings combined for comparison purposes					

Source: Media, 31 Mar. 2000

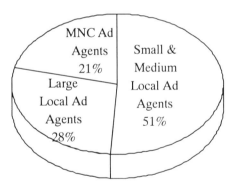

Figure 5: Total Billings Break Down by Different Types of Ad Agents
Source: China Advertising Yearbook, International Advertising, BA&H Analysis

Many large and small size local advertising agencies are emerging in the market. The local advertising agencies are enjoying good relationship with the media due to long term cooperation. They are still the key clients to local media and usually enjoy privileges in terms of payment, priority and urgent services. Comparing with the international advertising agencies, the local agencies have better competitive advantages, such as lower operating cost and being more flexible since they can serve as subcontractors to international advertising agencies. The local agencies, therefore, represent more then 50% of the total billings (Figure 5).

4 Chinese Consumers and the Market

Although the income level is still relatively low, it has risen dramatically in recent years and Chinese consumers are more willing and afford to pay for various products and services. The mean total household income of the Mainland consumers in 1997 was RMB 10,400 (US$11,250), a 74% gain over the mean household income of RMB 5,960 (US$690) in 1994 (The Gallup Organization 1997).

4.1 Advertisers and Brands in China

In China, there are three segments of advertising users with important differences in buying factors and demand for advertising services.

1. Multinational advertisers
2. Emerging local advertisers
3. Traditional local advertisers

In the 90s, China advertising market was mainly driven by multinational advertisers and the emerging local advertisers. In recent years, the confidence and assertiveness shown by local enterprises are especially encouraging. As the local marketers have more experience in marketing, they have come out of the shadows of foreign brands. All top 10 advertising products are local brands (Table 4). Together they account for 7 per cent of total advertising in China. As for foreign products, an international brand leader Coca-Cola ranked 20th among the most advertised products in 2000.

Since the emerging local advertisers are competing with multinationals, they are becoming increasingly quality conscious. They also focus on building brands and improving packaging, positioning and advertising. Many of them have their own in-house advertising departments or agencies. Additionally, the local advertisers have a lower operating cost and therefore they represent a more competitive advantage over the foreign competitors.

Table 4: China AdEx – Top 10 Products, 1998 (USD millions)

Wahaha AD calcium milk	19.9
Sunrise ice tea	17.7
Intel Pentium II processor	17.6
Nokia mobile telephones	17.6
China Telecom	15.1
Backbest	14.8
Yanghengtang Duoer capsules	14.7
Crest toothpaste	13.9
Nokia 6110 mobile telephones	13.4
Pepsi Cola	13.2

Source: ACNielsen

Across all industry sectors, pharmaceuticals remained the leader, accounting for three of the top 10 product categories (Table 5). Furthermore, among the top 10 product categories, only a few products are not related with medicine and product health care. Advertising on tonic and vitamin products alone accounted for more than 10 billion yuan (US$ 1.2 billion), or 12.5 per cent of all advertising in China.

Table 5: China AdEx – Top 10 Advertising Categories, Jan-Sep 2000

Rank	Category	Total (USD millions) (2000 media coverage)	% change (Media coverage comparable to 1999)
1	Tonic & Vitamin	105.90	221
2	Chinese OTC	42.44	171
3	Residential Estate-Sale/Rental	27.95	45
4	Communication Equipment & Service	20.26	118
5	Shampoo & Conditioner	18.33	17
6	Computer	16.67	168
7	Chinese Wines & Spirits	15.38	18
8	Skin Care	15.26	16
9	Cough & Cold Prep	15.13	109
10	Mobile Phone & Accessories	13.59	33

Source: ACNielsen Media International

The majority of the top advertisement expenditures are spending on similar products. Top advertising categories like tonic and vitamin, OTC drugs, computer and communication services have one thing in common. They all improve the quality of life. Heavy advertising in these categories reflects the growing lifestyle expectations among Chinese consumers.

Advertising in health-related categories increased dramatically compared to 1999. Following the new government regulation allowing distribution in supermarket, advertising in Chinese OTC drugs grew 171%,
while cough and cold drugs increased 109%. Computer advertising grew
168% while communication equipment and service grew 118%.

4.2 Consumers

The consumer way of life has taken off in China and is spreading fast. A
low base of consumer goods ownership coupled with strong growth in
buying power has given sustained momentum to the phenomenal growth
and tremendous opportunities in the consumer market. Family income levels have risen sharply in both urban and rural China, medium income levels have risen from RMB 4,380 to RMB 8,000. The medium income level
of urban residents (RMB 10,000) remains considerably higher than that in
rural China.

The Gallup Organization in 1997 conducted an in-depth consumer survey in China to study the consumer attitudes and lifestyle trends of the
People's Republic of China. The findings indicated that adults rate the
quality of their life a being nearly a third better than it was five years ago
(29%), and expect its quality to improve by a further 32% over the next
five years.

Many global brands are already widely known in China. Half of the
twenty best-known foreign brands among Chinese consumers are Japanese, especially the electrical home appliances. However, 73% respondents
said they prefer to purchase Chines-made goods. Despite growing exposure to Western culture and technology, consumers remain faithful to traditional, core Chinese values, while occasionally practicing with Western
values. In general, it was argued that comparing with other Asian counterparts, the Chinese consumers are more open-minded, more willing to take
risk, with less brand loyalty and more optimistic about the future of their
country.

A consumer purchasing survey of over 1,000 household in Beijing,
Shanghai and Tianjin was conducted in 1998 (China Business Times) re-
vealed that advertising is growing in influence and beginning to affect the
buying habits of China's consumers (Tables 6 & 7). Additionally, store
location and store type were also found to influence consumer behavior.

Table 6: Advertising's Influence on Product Types

Product	% Respondents Influenced By Advertising
Laundry detergent	61%
Air conditioner	61%
Fast foods (e.g. ramen)	60%
Microwave oven	52%
Soap	52%
Cosmetics	47%
Refrigerator	32%
Television	29%

Source: 1998, Zhonghua Gongshang Shibao (China Business Times)

Table 7: Store Preference For High-end Shopping

29%	Traditional shopping centers
27%	Retail stores
24%	Specialty stores
17%	Luxury stores

Source: 1998, Zhonghua Gongshang Shibao (China Business Times)

4.3   Regional Differences

To enter the vast market of China, foreign advertisers should understand the importance of regional disparities for marketing operations in the market. Geographical segmentation of China based on location, economic development, and local culture. In order to produce a good advertising campaign, we cannot treat the consumers in China as one whole homogenous group. There are many heterogeneous groups in China. Based on economic development and consumer purchasing power, there are seven regional markets in China: South, East, North, Central, Southwest, Northwest, and Northeast (Figure 6).

Based on average annual household income, these regional markets fall into three distinctive levels of market development. South China and East China, both with average annual household income more than 20,000 yuan represent the "growth markets" (Table 8). Then the next three regions including North China, Central China and Southwest China, they are the "emerging markets" of China. Each region differs in terms of their individual demographic variables.

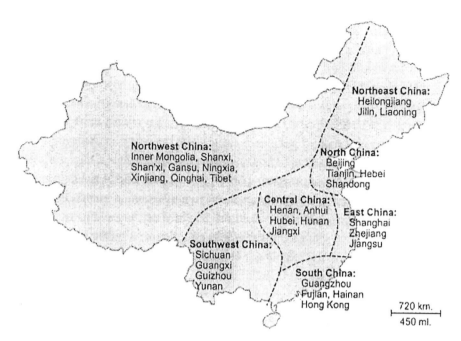

Note: The regional boundaries are simplified, thus do not reflect the actual demarkations

Figure 6: China's Seven Regional Markets

The most prosperous and dominant cities in China are Beijing, Shanghai and Guangzhou as most of the investors are well aware of and interested in putting their investment into. It is because of the high chasing power of the people. However, many household goods marketers are now recognizing that China's true commercial potential is not primarily the urban centers, rather, it is the rural consumers who account for the bulk of China's consumption. The affluence is increasing and communications are improving in the rural areas. In the long term, it will be the rural markets that account for the majority of sales. Policy directives are also enhancing the potential of the rural markets, such as the recent expansion plan of Northwest China. This region remains the "untapped market", waiting to be explored by foreign investors.

It is important for foreign advertisers to understand the overall market potential of China as well as regional differences. Each regional market is unique, and consumers have different perceptions of foreign goods.

Table 8: Demographic Data of China

Region	South China	East China	North China	Central China	South-west	North-east	North-west
Sample size	12	39	398	226	553	226	70
Demographics							
Household income*	27,481	24,659	12,993	13,831	14,008	8,683	7,770
Age*	41	43	40	39	42	42	38
Education*							
Elementary/less (%)	16.6	7.7	10.7	12.2	28.1	19.0	41.7
High school (%)	66.7	69.3	62.8	69.5	56.2	69.0	46.3
College and beyond (%)	16.6	23.1	26.4	18.3	14.8	12.0	2.8
Occupation*							
Professionals (%)	18.2	12.5	9.3	12.8	12.0	4.8	2.9
Factory workers (%)	18.2	27.5	27.8	34.8	15.2	20.2	5.7
Office workers	9.1	10.0	3.3	3.2	8.4	2.6	1.4
Government officials	0.0	10.0	23.8	6.4	6.3	9.7	0.0
Service	9.1	5.0	2.3	4.8	2.9	5.3	0.0
Other large group	9.1	5.0	3.8	4.8	8.0	15.4	70.0
	(Student)	(Retail)	(Retail)	(Retail)	(Agri-business)	(Home-maker)	(Agri-business)
Note:* Significant at 0.001							

Source: Journal of Consumer Marketing, Vol. 17 No. 1 2000 P. 62

5 Media in China

5.1 TV

Television and newspapers are the most important media in China in terms of advertising revenues. Television is by far the most popular medium for information and entertainment among Chinese consumers (Table 9). There is only one nationwide television station, CCTV (China Central Television), but cable satellite stations are growing fast. Yet, advertising at prime time on television currently remains a supplier's market.

From the above table, 83.3 percent of audiences in South China are watching cable TV. Consumer products are dominating the TV advertising market (Tables 10 and 11).

While television remains the most popular medium, especially among foreign and joint venture companies, newspapers, radio and magazines are preferred for more focused efforts because of their niche target segments. Outdoor billboards and neon signs are also becoming increasing popular.

Table 9: Media Usage

Region	South China (%)	East China (%)	North China (%)	Central China (%)	South-west (%)	North-east (%)	North-west (%)
Broadcast TV*	25.0	52.5	31.3	38.0	43.4	71.6	53.5
Cable TV*	83.3	69.2	68.3	68.9	68.8	28.3	14.3
Radio*	8.3	5.1	24.9	46.8	40.7	23.0	20.0
Newspaper*	75.0	82.1	54.8	50.8	46.1	29.6	16.9
Magazine*	25.0	30.8	40.1	44.7	36.7	32.9	9.9
Note:* Significant at 0.001							

Source: Journal of Consumer Marketing, Vol. 17 No. 1 2000 P. 64

Table 10: 1998 First Quarter China AdEx – Top 5 Categories (USD millions)

Advertiser/Products	TV AdEx	% change*
Haircare	35.75	60
Chinese wines & spirits	32.85	-31
Video machines & accessories	24.8	341
Skin Care	23.9	-26
Toothpaste & oral hygiene	18.9	-4
*Trent data not available due to increased media monitoring in 1997		

Source: ACNielsen SRG China

Table 11: 1998 First Quarter China AdEx – Top 5 Advertisers or Products (USD millions)

Advertiser/Products	TV AdEx	% change*
Nokia mobile telephone	7000	N/a
Elegbacae Depigment Cream	6053	81
Olive 100 Year Shampoo	4179	N/a
Tide Washing Powder	3697	N/a
Rejoice Deep Moist 2-in-1 Shampoo	3510	375
*Trent data not available due to increased media monitoring in 1997		

Source: ACNielsen SRG China

Mainland China has nearly 300 million households with TV sets and 900 TV stations. Majority of the advertising media spending was spent on TV (67%) versus Newspapers (31%) and Magazine (2%) (Figure 7). Since TV entertainment is popular among most people, advertisers choose this medium for promoting their products.

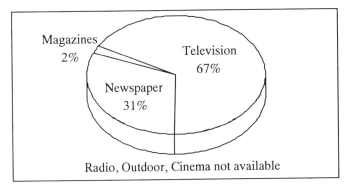

Figure 7: Total Gross Adspend 1998
Source: ACNielsen Media International

The eight channels of CCTV, the only network with a national audience, lead the field of by reaching an astonishing 87% of the entire population. With an audience of about 300 million households, the 15-second slot following the CCTV national evening news is the most expensive of all.

China's TV industry is rapidly developing. By August 2000, 59.3 percent of families had access to satellite TV programs via cable TV (China Business 2000). Similar to the other TV stations, consumer products are dominating the Satellite TV advertising. (Table 12)

Table 12: China AdEx – Top 10 Advertising Categories, First Quarter 1998

Rank	Category	Satellite Adspend (USD millions)	% change
1	Retail	9.3	2
2	Leisure	9.3	11
3	Corporate	6.7	7
4	Travel	5.6	83
5	Entertainment	5.1	87
6	Finance	4.6	61
7	Automotive	4.5	39
8	Foodstuffs	4.2	96
9	Liquor	4.2	74
10	Cosmetics & toiletries	4.1	3

Source: ACNielsen SRG

5.2 Prime Media and Prime Time

Most advertising agencies and advertisers are interested in buying prime media at the prime times or prime locations, as there is a huge different in readership/audience viewership ratings. Thus, commercials need to be aired adjacent to quality programs. However, Mainland China is an extremely controlled environment when it comes to advertising and promotion, media buying becomes a complicated issue that caused considerable dissatisfaction in the industry. Although media practices have greatly improved in the past couple of years with the removal of the multi-tier price system, media outlets as vehicles for advertising placement still cannot be freely chosen by advertising agencies.

Getting access to prime slots is essential to improve the visibility of the advertisement. There are some common channels for accessing prime media, such as contact media directly; provide the TV stations with free programs in exchange for free air time; buy air-time via media brokers; buy media via in-house advertising agencies of the media etc.

5.3   Print

In 1979, the entire mainland boasted just 186 newspapers. By 1986, there were 1,500. Today (2001), there are more than 3,000. Many publications are growing in size and publishing supplements to attract advertisers (Table 13). Publications such as the Beijing Youth Daily, Beijing Evening News, and Guangdong's Southern Weekly have won widespread popularity by expanding news coverage. Penetration rates in urban areas are high for such papers: the Beijing Evening News has a daily circulation of 1 million according to unaudited PRC estimates.

Although newspapers are widely read in China, a common incentive against advertising in them is their unstimulating content and their unattractive print quality. Advertising space is also limited by regulations. No more than 15% of the space in newspapers is allowed to print advertisements. Limited advertising space in key newspapers translates into booking lead times of anywhere from 4 to 8 weeks. An Economist Intelligent Unit survey has found that offices generally subscribe to morning newspapers, and evening papers and weeklies tend to be bought more at home. Thus, the morning papers are preferred more by advertisers of luxury goods, while consumer products are advertised more in the evening papers and weeklies.

Similar to the television advertisers, consumer products, such as telecommunication services, health products, computers etc., are the major advertising spenders in newspapers (Table 14 and 15).

Table 13: China AdEx – Top 10 Newspaper 1998

Rank	Newspaper	AdEx (USD millions)
1	Guang Zhou Daily Newspaper	94.84
2	Xinmin Evening Newspaper	94.10
3	Beijing Daily Newspaper	58.97
4	Shenzhen SAR Newspaper	49.10
5	Xinhua Daily Newspaper	39.78
6	Today Evening Newspaper	33.33
7	Jiefang Daily Newspaper	28.49
8	Shenzhen commercial Newspaper	27.74
9	Beijing Youth Newspaper	26.55
10	Nanfang Daily Newspaper	26.15

Source: China Advertising Yearbook, 1999

Table 14: China AdEx - Top 10 Advertising Categories, 1999

Rank	Categories	AdEx (USD millions)
1	Residential Estate-Sale/Rental	163.08
2	Computers	86.92
3	Mobile phones	58.59
4	Tonic & Vitamin	47.69
5	Shopping centers	41.67
6	Telecommunication Companies	36.28
7	Air conditioners	34.62
8	Buildings	28.46
9	Computer peripheries	26.92
10	Computer manufacturer	25.64

Source: Guangdong Hang Sai (269 newspapers)

Table 15: China AdEx - Top 10 Advertisers/ Products, 1999

Rank	Categories	AdEx (USD millions)
1	Motorola Auto-dual band Chinese Mobile phone	163.08
2	China Renmin Bank	86.92
3	Nokia mobile phone	58.59
4	Intel Pentium III Micro-processor	47.69
5	Motorola all-band commercial mobile phone	41.67
6	China Telecom Guangdong Worldwide service	36.28
7	China Unicom 130 phone network	34.62
8	Audi	28.46
9	Santana	26.92
10	Shanghai General	25.64

Source: Guangdong Hang Sai (269 newspapers)

5.4 Circulation

Newspapers need to measure their audiences to assess their performance. The Auditing Bureau of Circulations (ABC) is an independent auditing group that represents advertisers, agencies, and publishers. This group verifies statements about newspaper circulation statistics and provides detailed analyses of newspapers. In China, all the newspapers are unaudited. There is no ABC office in China. Newspapers' circulation data are measured or audited by local audit firms.

5.5 Magazines

PRC editions of regional titles of foreign magazines, such as BusinessWeek China and Elle China, and Chinese language editions of other English-language magazines imported from Taiwan, Hong Kong, and Singapore, such as Esquire and Marie Claire, have also been successful. These magazines, which have excellent print quality and more color pages than their PRC-based counterparts, target well-educated, higher-income PRC consumers. Local glossy fashion magazines such as Look and How are setting new trends for the local magazine industry. However, advertisers interested in magazine are also facing with long booking times. Actual circulation figures are also unknown.

5.6 Radio

Radio is quite inexpensive and easy to access. One radio station usually has 6-10 channels broadcasting 15-18 hours each day, meaning there is plenty of time available. It takes just about two weeks from the time advertisement is created to air it. Compared with television, air time is inexpensive. There are around 1,300 radio stations in China and are increasing offering foreign syndicated radio programs that permit corporate sponsorship. Musical programs in particular are attracting large number of advertisers.

5.7 Outdoor Advertising

Outdoor advertising has grown tremendously over the past few years. Billboards, rooftop neon signs, buses, taxis, subways, video walls, bus shelters, lamp posts, and street side "light boxes" are becoming widely available in most urban areas (Table 16 and Table 17). In recent years, major streets in Beijing and Shanghai, for example, have seen a profusion of light boxes-standalone street side, electrified advertising signs.

There is no central control over outdoor advertisement. Advertising agencies have to contact a variety of organizations and related government organizations for the source of outdoor media.

Table 16: China Top 10 Categories, 1999

Rank	Categories	Number of billboards
1	Carbonated drinks	1011
2	Tonic & vitamins	660
3	Residential Estate-Sale/Rental	473
4	Banks	448
5	Cigarettes	447
6	Refrigerators	386
7	Electronic Appliances	380
8	Beers	366
9	Air-conditioners	323
10	Credit Cards	292

Source: Guangdong Hang Sai (limited in main roads and streets in urban area)

Table 17: China Top 10 Advertisers, 1999

Rank	Categories	Number of billboards
1	Pepsi Cola	1011
2	Yongsheng Refrigerators	660
3	Lu A natural alga pills	473
4	Coca Cola	448
5	7-Up	447
6	Chingtao Beers	386
7	Weiwei soy milk powder	380
8	Marlboro	366
9	Er Yuan Beast Cream	323
10	Coconut Tree cigarettes	292

Source: Guangdong Hang Sai (limited in main roads and streets in urban area)

5.8 Internet Advertising

According to ACNielsen, Internet usage has doubled in Beijing, Shanghai and Guangzhou in the past two years, although the usage rate of 4% is still low by international standards (Table 18). In Nanjing, usage surged from 2 percent to 7 percent between 1997 and 1998.

Table 18: China Adspend on Internet Web Site

Period	Adspend (USD millions)	% change
4th quarter 1999	8.2	-
1st quarter 2000	10.7	29.8
2nd quarter 2000	23.3	117.9

Source: ACNielsen

The proportion of advertising on the Internet is less than 0.1 percent of the total advertising in China. Limited access to Internet is the largest obstacle to the development of Internet advertising.

5.9 Sponsorships and Promotions

Store promotions, such as free samples, do satisfy the Chinese desire for a bargain. Cross-reference promotions, where a different related items is offered free with the item being sold, have become very popular marketing tools, e.g. offering a free soap with a hair shampoo, or a toothbrush with a toothpaste. Foreign firms have also engaged in active sponsorship of sporting events, concerts, exhibitions and education funds to build up their corporate image in either the community as a whole, or in specific sectors.

6   Advertising Research

6.1 Development

China's market research industry has expanded rapidly in recent years (Figure 8). This growth has been partly fuelled by the entry of multinational firms into China, increasing competitions significantly and the need for accurate market information.

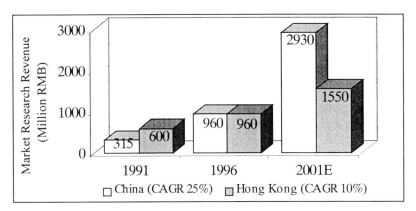

Figure 8: Revenues For Market Research Firms in China
Source: BA&H interview & analysis

6.2 Media Research Data

Although market research has been developing quickly, it still lags behind international standards. Media planning in China is complicated by the fact that syndicated surveys on media habits have been available for only 18 cities through the AC Nielsen China Media Index. Foreign firms tend to be interested in at least 20-30 cities, however, and some want to sell in as many as 200 PRC cities. Sample sizes of other market research firms' surveys are often too small to make accurate projections. As a result, some foreign firms regularly send their own media buyers into local markets to talk directly to local TV stations, newspapers, and consumers.

The research market in China is dominated by multinational market research agencies (Figure 9, Table 19). The services they offer are quite diverse, being customized as well as syndicated. The dominance of the multinational players is due to a relatively early market entry, sophisticated analytical capabilities, nationwide coverage, and in some cases, global client alignment. However, they have disadvantages in local understanding and high cost structure.

In recent years, there are few emerging large local research agencies in China that are carrying out major research surveys used by advertisers to determine their media planning. The large local research firms have competitive advantages in good networks in the major cities, lower cost structure, local client contact, media connections and better understanding of local market and culture.

Table 19: 5 Dominant Types of Media Research Data

	Media Measurement	Conducted by Research Firm/ Surveys
Readership Data	Print	Central Viewer Survey Consulting Centre (CVSC) --- Research: - China National Readership Survey (CNRS) - China Media Market Survey (CMMS) AC Nielsen AC Nielsen China Media Index
TV Rating	TV	AC Nielsen, CVSC
Ad Expenditure	Ad spending for all media	AC Nielsen, CVSC
Retail Audit	Audit newsstand readership data and behavior	AC Nielsen, CVSC
Consumer Studies	Consumer behavior and attitude	AC Nielsen, CVSC

Source: Data collected from in-depth interview with Media Director of Grey Advertising Agency (2001)

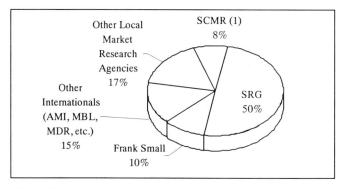

Figure 9: China Market Research Industry (1996)

7   Advertising and the Law

Advertising in China also faces with a problem of censorship, with many types of advertising practices that are common in other countries might be banned in China. The PRC Advertising Law, enacted in February 1995, lays out uniform rules on advertising through all media, and is enforced by the Sate Administration of Industry and Commerce (Appendix). The law was designed to combat the rampant problem of exaggerated or unsubstantiated claims, with the objective of maintaining a healthy media environment. The law intends to ban advertisements that hinder the social public order or violating the social customs. New rules issued in 1977 by Ministry of Radio, Film, and Television (MRFT) further state that TV and radio commercials must not contain anything that encourages children to take up unhealthy habits, nor present women in "improper" ways.

Procedures for advertising content approval are still quite vague and can be costly and time-consuming. Advertisers need to be very careful so as not to break any of the advertising rules. Usually, the media undertakes the responsibility to censor itself and ensure the legality of the advertisement content. However, other government units might also get involved in the censorship and placement of advertisements. Therefore, advertisers must devote significant resources to locating the correct authority.

On the other hand, the advertising message should preferably be simple and direct. Because advertising campaigns that are approved in one city could be disapproved in another.

From March 1996, the commissions that advertising agencies can charge their clients have been standardized by SAIC and State Planning Commission to 15% of the production costs.

References

Advertising and Market Research in Chinese Mainland: Opportunities for Hong Kong, (March 1998), Research Department, Hong Kong Trade Development Council

Geng Cui and Quiming Liu, *"Regional market segments of China: opportunities and barriers in a big emerging market"*, Journal of Consumer Marketing, Vol. 17 No. 1 2000. Pp. 55-72

The Gallup 1997 Nationwide Survey of Consumer Attitudes and Lifestyles in The People's Republic of China, The Gallup Organization

Appendix:

NEW PRC ADVERTSING LAW
OVERVIEW AND HIGHLIGHTS

Promulgated October 27, 1994
Effective February 1, 1995

WHO IS AFFECTED?

Article 2:

Advertisers:	Legal persons, economic organizations or individuals that design, produce and disseminate advertising for their own account or that commission others to do so [i.e., clients].
Advertising Operators:	Legal persons, economic organizations or individuals that provide advertising design, production and agency services on commission [i.e., advertising agencies].
Advertising Disseminators:	Legal persons or economic organizations that disseminate advertisement for and advertiser or advertising operator commissioned by an advertiser [i.e., the media].

WHAT ARE THE BASIC REQUIREMENTS FOR ADVERTISEMENTS?

Article 3:

Must be "truthful and lawful and meet the requirements for the development of socialist spiritual civilization." [You've come a long way, baby: 1987 State Council regulations provided that the purpose of advertising was "to serve the needs of socialist construction."]

Article 4:

Must not contain false information or deceive or mislead consumers.

Article 5:

Principles of fairness, good faith and trustworthiness must be observed.

SOME SPECIFIC PROHIBITIONS

Article 7 provides that advertisements may not:

   (1)   Use the national flag, emblem or anthem of the PRC;
   (2)   Use the names of State authorities or personnel;
   (3)   Use terms such as "State level," "top level" of "best."
   (4)   Jeopardize public stability, endanger personal or property safety or damage the public interest;
   (5)   Obstruct order or act against good social customs;
   (6)   Contain obscene, superstitious, terrifying, violent or repulsive contents
           [Note: 1987 State Council regulations also prohibited "absurd" advertising];
   (7)   Discriminate on the basis of nationality, race, religion or sex;
   (8)   Obstruct the protection of the environment and natural resources; or
   (9)   Contain other contents prohibited by laws or regulations.

MORE DO'S AND DON'TS

Article 12:

Advertisements may not disparage competitors' products and services. [Note:; This is generally interpreted to restrict, if not prohibit, comparative advertising.]

Article 13:

Advertisement can't be disguised to look like something else, such as news reports.

Article 8:

Advertisements may not be harmful to the physical and mental health of minors or disabled persons.

Article 9:

Descriptions of performance, origin, use, quality, price or promises must be clear and explicit.

Article 10:

> Data, statistical information, survey findings, digests and quotations must be truthful and accurate and sources identified.

Article 11:

> For patented products, patent numbers and classifications must be stated. Non-patented products or those for which applications have not been granted or patents that are terminated, cancelled or invalid can't be advertised as patented.

Article 25:

> No use of a person's name or portrait without his or her advance written consent.

SPECIAL RULES FOR PHARMACEUTICALS AND MEDICAL APPARATUS

Article 14:

> No unscientific claims or claims as to rate of successful cure or efficacy.

No comparative advertising.

> No use of names or portraits of research units, academic or medical institutions, experts, physicians or patients.

Article 15:

> Pharmaceutical ads must be approved by State Council or provincial/autonomous region or large municipal public health administrative department.

> If a prescription is required, the ad must state it must be used only under a physician's guidance.

Article 16:

> Anaesthetics and psychotropic, toxic and radioactive drugs may not be advertised at all.

SPECIAL RULES FOR AGROCHEMICALS

Article 17:

> May not claim to be absolutely non-toxic or harmless; claim unscientific assertions or warranties; contain text, language or pictures in violation of safe use rules; contain other prohibited contents.

SPECIAL RULES FOR TOBACCO PRODUCTS

Article 18:

> May not be advertised on radio, movies, television, newspapers or periodicals, or in public places such as waiting halls, auditoriums, conference rooms and halls, stadiums and gymnasiums for sports competitions, etc.
> All advertising must state: Cigarette smoking is hazardous to health.

SPECIAL RULES FOR FOODS, ALCOHOL AND COSMETICS

Article 19:

> Advertising must comply with public health requirements.
>
> Medical terms or terms likely to cause confusion with pharmaceutical products may not be used.

WHO IS RESPONSIBLE FOR ADMINISTERING THE LAW?

Article 6:

> Administrations for Industry and Commerce above the county level. [Note: because of the joint and several liability of advertisers, advertising operators and advertising disseminators, media outlets often exercise censorship as well.]

CENSORSHIP, DOCUMENTATION AND CONTROL

Article 34:

> Television, radio, movies, newspaper, periodical or other media advertisements for pharmaceuticals, medical apparatus, agrochemical, veterinary drugs, etc. must be censored prior to dissemination by advertisement censorship authorities.

Article 35:

> When applying for clearance of and advertisement requiring censorship, the advertiser must submit any required supporting documents.

Article 24:

> To place an ad, an advertiser must produce its business license and other documents supporting its right to engage in business, quality inspection documents (if quality is mentioned in advertisement), and censorship approval documents if required.

Article 27:

> Advertising operators and disseminators must inspect and verify the supporting documents and the content of the ads. Advertising operators and disseminators are forbidden to support or disseminate ads that are untrue or don't have required documentation.

Article 32:

> Outdoor advertising is prohibited: (1) on traffic signs or traffic safety facilities; (2) if it would affect municipal public facilities, traffic safety facilities or traffic signs; (3) where production, people's livelihood or appearance of a city will be harmed; (4) in construction control zones, protected cultural relic units, historical sites or scenic sites; or (5) where placement of outdoor advertisements has been prohibited by People's Government units at or above county level.

LIABILITY AND PENALTIES

Article 37:

> Remedies include: cessation of advertising and spending and equal amount of money to run corrective ads; payment of fines equal to one to five times the advertising fees.
>
> Fees earned by advertising operators and disseminators shall be confiscated, and a fine of one to five times the fee imposed.
> In a serious case, the offending business can be shut down. If the activities constitute a criminal offense, criminal liability will be imposed according to law.

Article 38:

> If the lawful rights and interests of consumers are harmed by false advertising that deceives or misleads them, the advertiser has civil liability. If the advertising operator or disseminator knew or should have been aware of the false advertising but still carries on, the operator or disseminator is jointly and severally liable.
> If the advertising operators and disseminators can't provide real names and addresses for the advertisers, the operators and disseminators are civilly liable.
> Social or other organizations that recommend commodities or services to consumers in false advertisements are jointly and severally liable.

Article 39:

> Penalties for violating Article 7: Cessation of dissemination and public rectification. The advertising fees will be confiscated and a fine of one to five times the fees imposed. In a serious case, the offending business can be shut down. If the activities constitute a criminal offense, criminal liability will be imposed according to law.

Article 40:

> Penalties for violating Articles 9 to 12: Cessation of dissemination and public rectification. The advertising fees will be confiscated and a fine of one to five times the fees may be imposed.
> Penalties for violating Article 13: Public rectification and imposition of fines of RMB 1,000 to 10,000.

Article 41:

> Penalties for violating Article 31 or for advertisements for pharma-
> ceuticals, medial apparatus, agrochemicals, food, alcoholic bever-
> ages or cosmetics violating Articles 14 to 17 or 19: Rectification or
> cessation of dissemination, confiscation of advertising fees, and im-
> position of fines of one to five times the fees. In a serious case the
> business can be shut down.

Article 42:

> Penalties for violating Article 18 by appearance of tobacco adver-
> tisements in ratio, movies, television, newspapers or periodicals or
> by placing tobacco advertisements in public places: Cessation, con-
> fiscation of advertising fees and possible imposition of fines of one
> to five times the advertising fees.

Article 43:

> Penalties for violating Article 34 by not submitting advertisements
> for censoring where required: Cessation, confiscation of the adver-
> tising fees and possible imposition of fines of one to five times the
> advertising fees.

Article 44:

> Penalties for an advertiser submitting false supporting documents:
> Fines of RMB 10,000 to 100,000. This also applies to forging or al-
> teration of censorship approval documents. If the activities constitute
> a criminal offense, criminal liability will be imposed according to
> law.

Article 47:

> Advertisers, advertising operators and disseminators will have civil
> liability for: (1) advertisements that harm the physical or mental
> health of minors or the disables; (2) forging a patent; (3) disparaging
> the competition;(4) using another person's name of portrait without
> consent; or (5) other infringements of civil rights and interests of
> others.

Article 48:

> Appeals from an adverse administrative decision can be made either
> to a higher administrative level or to the People's Court.

[Note: Civil and criminal liability may be imposed pursuant to other law
and regulations as well, such as the Anti-Unfair Competition Law, Consumer Protection Law and Product Quality Law.]

Useful Addresses

1. Media-Related Organization

Ministry of Culture
A83 Donganmen
Beijing
Telephone: 6401-2255

State Press and Publication Administration
85 Dong Si Nan Da Jie
Beijing
Telephone: 6512-4433

The State Administration of Radio, Film & TV
2 Fuwaidajie
Beijing 100866
Telephone: 6609-3114

All China Journalists Association
Xi Jiao Min Xiang, Beijing
Telephone: 6603-3862

2. Newspaper Organizations

Renmin Ribao (People's Daily)
2 Jin Tai Xi Lu
Beijing. 100733
Telephone: 6509-2121
Fax: 6500-3109

Jingli Ribao (Economic Daily)
277 Wang Fu Jin Da Jie
Beijing. 100746
Telephone: 6512-5035

Gongren Ribao (Worker's Daily)
An Ding Men Wai, Liu Pu Kang
Beijing, 100718
Telephone: 6421-1561

3. Electronic Media Organizations

China Central Television
No. 11 Fuxing Rd.
Beijing, 100859
Telephone: 6850-0114

Central People's Radio Station
2 Fuxingmenwai Dajie
Beijing 100866
Telephone: 6851-5522

Advertising in Greece

Dr. Betty Tsakarestou
Panteion University of Social and Political Sciences, Athens

1   Background and Development of Advertising in Greece

The advertising sector has carved for itself a leading role in the modern Greek economy during the last fifty years. The first agencies set up functioning in the 1870s. But it was in the post war era, between the 1950s and 1970s that we experienced the first stage of institutionalization and professionalization of advertising. Advertising messages made their way in a hostile ideological context, capturing the attention not only of the desired target audiences but of political parties, activists and intellectuals as well. The common claim against advertising was its so-called "hidden persuasive power" to control the mind and the consciousness of people and even more the cultural and media production.

The advertising agencies were well aware of that negative perception and they tried to self regulate their methods and practices in order to gain social acceptance. From 1970 to 1980 is the phase of internationalization and consolidation of the Greek advertising industry.[1]

American multinational networks collaborate with successful local agencies and open their Greek subsidiaries (e.g. BBDO Athens, Spot/Thompson, Bold Ogilvy & Mather, McCann Erickson, etc.). The 1980s and the first five years of the 1990s are characterized as the "golden" age of the Greek advertising market. The adspend as percentage of GDP rises from year to year (see Fig. 1) and reaches 1.86% in 1995. The advertising agencies and their people prosper investing in new buildings, high salaries, in-house research tools and opening new departments offering new services to their clients, such as public, direct marketing and promotion. At the same time advertising agencies set up specialist media-buying companies, which accumulate negotiating power pressing media for important detours of money.

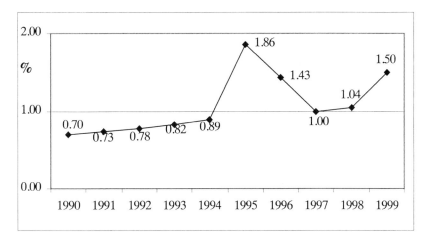

Figure 1: Adspend as Percentage of GDP
Data Source: Magazine EPILOGI

1995 is a landmark year for the industry, the media and the communication professionals. The economic recession is *ante portas* and coincides with a crisis of reliability and trust among advertising agencies, advertisers and the media. The opacity of media buying negotiations gives rise to a big issue: the transparency of the tariffs. The debates under the self- regulation umbrella fail to conclude in mutual understanding and agreement between the interested parties. As a consequence the Hellenic Ministry of Press and Mass Media enforced a law to regulate and control the advertising practices.

Five years on we can trace the repercussions of the new law on advertising industry. In 1996 and 1997 the adspend as percentage of GDP falls to 1.43% and 1.00% respectively compared to 1.86% in 1995. Newspapers are the big losers. Advertising agencies see a 15% cut to their gross income. Staff lay-offs, reengineering and takeovers of small agencies are the direct response of CEOs.

Meanwhile the economic and organizational upset creates opportunities for the newcomers in the market. A bunch of independent local advertising agencies, direct marketing, sponsoring and web communication companies come to the fore. "Excellence in creativity", "branding", "relationship marketing", "cause-related marketing", "web advertising", "strategic communication", "reputation management", "total communication" and "experiential marketing" are the emerging buzz words of the most sophisticated companies.

It sounds like a paradox that the crisis occurred at a time of public acceptance and legitimization of advertising. According to a recent survey conducted by Panteion University in collaboration with research companies Focus and MRB Hellas on behalf of the Hellenic Association of Advertising Communication Agencies (HAACA), the public image of advertising and advertising profession is surprisingly better than ten years before. Furthermore career in advertising is quite an attractive choice among ambitious young people.

2   Institutions, Self-Regulation and Legal Restrictions

2.1 The Hellenic Association of Advertising Communication Agencies (HAACA)

The Hellenic Association of Advertising-Communications Agencies, a non-profit organization founded in 1968, is recognized by the authorities and other public sector organizations with which it cooperates regularly in order to promote the advertising and communication profession as the representative body of the industry in Greece. At present, HAACA's membership totals 46 advertising agencies, 12 public relations agencies, 10 media specialists and 9 direct and/or interactive marketing agencies.

The HAACA maintains excellent relations with national advertising agencies associations around the world and has been a member of the European Association of Communications Agencies (formerly European Advertising Agencies Association) since 1969 and a founding member of the European Advertising Standards Alliance (EASA).

Apart from its institutional role, the other major field of activity for HAACA is the organization of industry events. The Advertising Conference, which has contributed significantly in promoting the industry, was established in 1986. Also, in 1989 the Advertising Festival was the first established with the purpose of rewarding advertising creativity in Greece. March 2000 saw the first Effie Hellas Awards, which reward advertising efficiency and effectiveness and in March 2001, AD DAYS –an event targeting younger professionals and students- was organized with great success.[2]

The HAACA is also an institution promoting the self-regulation of Advertising. The Greek Code of Advertising was announced in 1977 and it has been recognized by all agencies-members of HAACA, the Greek Adverting Association, the Association of Greek industries, the Professional Association of all media and the Institute of Consumers. Recently, it has been recognized by the Greek law as well.

The Code arose in purpose to maintain public criticism of the advertising industry and to fear of even greater government interventions in the future. The main rules of the Code read as follows:

- **Decency**
  Advertising shall be free of statements, illustration or implications, which are offensive to public decency.

- **Honesty**
  Advertising shall avoid the use of exaggerated or claims that cannot be approved and shall not take advantage of consumers' fears, prejudices, ignorance or lack of experience.

- **Truth**
  Advertising shall tell the truth, and shall reveal significant facts (product characteristics, price, etc) the concealment of which would mislead the public.

- **Comparisons**
  Comparative advertising shall not break the rules of fair competition. Advertising agencies and advertisers shall be willing to provide substantiation of claims made.

- **Testimonials**
  Advertising containing testimonials shall be limited to those of competent witnesses who are reflecting a real and honest choice based on their personal experience.

- **Respect**
  Advertising shall respect private life and shall avoid showing to children risky activities.

The Code also contains four sections setting standards concerning advertising to children, tobacco advertising and promotion, political campaigning and environmental issues in communication.

Complaints are received or initiated more frequently by competitors or consumers associations and rarely by individual citizens. The HAACA in case of a justified complaint asks the advertiser to withdraw the objectionable ad or to modify it. It also asks the media to ban the ad from their program.

HAACA has gained public respect and praise for its devotion to good practice enforcing self-regulation. Nevertheless, as mentioned earlier, the tariffs transparency issue justified state intervention in advertising industry. Since 1995 the Greek State issued several laws and decrees in order to protect personal data and to restrict the advertising of cigarettes, alcohol and drugs. Another law controls the appropriate use of the symbols of Olympic Games by the Olympic sponsors. In the beginning of 2001 a constitutional reform took place. The new Constitution settles matters of media ownership, it defines the limits of the freedom of the press and it empowers the National Council of Radio and Television to observe and regulate the functioning of the media.

2.2   The Greek Advertisers Association (GAA)

The Greek Advertisers Association, a non-profit organization founded in 1978, is the representative body of industrial, commercial and services companies whose products and services are nationally advertised. The GAA is member of the World Federation of Advertisers. GAA's mission is to promote the interests of its members and to provide information, education and guidance to them in order to maximize the benefits of their advertising spending. The GAA organizes events, seminars and conferences that contribute in building excellent relations with the industry, the state, the media and other opinion leaders.

According to a recent survey conducted by Research International on behalf of GAA, the advertisers choose their advertising agency according to its creativity records and its negotiating power with the media. They also expect their agencies to have a good knowledge and a genuine interest in their brand. And last but not least, the agency should respect the deadlines of delivery. These findings confirm the embedded mistrust between advertisers and their agencies.

This year the GAA launched the "Social Awards" in order to praise advertisers for their contribution in the fields of social and environmental responsibility and culture. This initiative takes place in a moment where social corporate responsibility (CSR) has become a major political issue within EU in the context of its social cohesion policy.

2.3   Consumers

Consumers' rights are protected by the General Secretariat of Consumers founded in 1997 by the Ministry of Development, and by several NGO's (e.g. The Institute of Consumers) whose mission is to inform public on corporate malpractice and to call them for action.

3   The Greek Advertising Market

The Greek economy has a good record of achievements the past few years: low inflation, faster growth than the EU average and an acceptably low budget deficit, hoping of emulating Portugal and Spain.

The Greek advertising industry is a rapidly growing sector of the national economy. Furthermore, it plays a key role in the expansion of local, international and multinational agencies in the emerging markets of southeastern Europe. The major advertising groups are well established in the Greek market:

Adel/Saatchi & Saatchi, Bates Hellas, BBDO Group, Bold/Ogilvy, Carat, D' Arcy Athens, Euro RSCG Athens, Geo/Young & Rubicam, Gnomi/ FCB, Grey Athens, Leo Burnett, Lowe Lintas, McCann-Erickson, Olympic DDB, Publicis Athens, Scholz & Friends, Spot/J.W. Thompson, TBWA Athens.

It is estimated that 3,000 people approximately work in advertising and communication agencies, 60% of them are women and 40% of them are men with an average age of 30-35 years old. The majority of young professionals hold a university degree or a Master's either in Economics or Marketing & Management or Communication. Of course, creative people come from different backgrounds: Arts, Design, Computer Graphics, and Philosophy. They are considered, together with media people as a professional elite renowned for their prominent role in shaping public taste, preferences and opinions.

3.1   Information Services in Greek Media Planning

In the Greek market various tools are available which give valuable information on both consumer purchase behavior and level of viewership/listenership/readership of media and measurement of the advertising expenditure in the Greek media.

There are four major companies active in this industry, namely, FOCUS, AGB Hellas, Media Services and AC Nielsen.

FOCUS

BARI FOCUS is a national readership and listenership survey offered to the Greek market since 1986. It provides continuous information related to media consumption habits, consumers' lifestyles and product ownership.

Data is collected through personal interviews every 12 weeks and sample size is about 80,000 individuals.
Age clusters are as follows: 13-17, 18-24, 25-34, 35-44, 45-54, 55-70.

All data are available within socio-economic breakdowns, e.g. upper/middle/lower class and educational background and reported 3 times a year.
BARI FOCUS clients are advertising agencies, advertisers, television and radio stations, newspapers and magazines.

AGB Hellas

AGB Hellas is responsible for the quantitative measurement of television audiences' behavior to a metered system.
Research procedure consists of:

- An establishment survey, representative of all Greek households and it has a dual purpose:

- To provide the best possible estimate of the television scene in Greece.
- To provide the basis for panel recruitment. (1,200 households participate in the panel, 3,500 persons approximately, reference population: 9,081,315).

- Meter installation and maintenance, data retrieval, editing and processing.

The panel is disproportionate and sampled, both geographically and with respect to key demographics.

AGB Hellas also offers an audience targeting based on lifestyle preferences. The theoretical assumption is that media consumption is based both on demographics and lifestyle habits.

To provide better sample sizes for important reporting demographics AGB Media Services has also designed two products.
- TELEMONITOR analyzes television behavior in detail for a wide range of target audiences.
- TELESPOT evaluates advertising campaigns and advertising expenditures.

AC Nielsen

AC Nielsen media measurement research includes audience estimates for television, magazines, newspapers, radio and cinema. ACNielsen also offers advertising expenditure measurement and customized media research. The sample population is distributed in all major Greek cities, in semi-rural and in rural areas as well. The methodology used is based on day-after-recall personal interviews.

It can correlate combined information on media and product consumption. All data is available within demographic breakdowns and are reported twice a year.

3.2   Media Shops – Media Specialists

Media shops and media specialists are leading companies in media buying and planning. They have heavily invested in creating in-house research tools as a unique advantage offered to their clients. Most of them belong to big advertising/communication groups.

There are many international and local agencies active in the Greek market like:

- BGM Media Direction (BBDO Group)
- The Media Corp (BBDO Group)
- Zenith Media
- GMG Media Group
- International Media
- Maxi Media
- The Media Edge
- MindShare Hellas
- Open Media
- Optimedia
- Place Media
- Starcom (Leo Burnett)
- Tempo/Optimum Media
- Universal McCann Hellas
- Initiative Media

3.3   Advertising Expenditures

Since 1997 the total adverting spending shows a steady and healthy growth until the end of 2000. Regarding 2001 the first indications are that the adspend will remain at the levels of 2000 showing a small increase, about 1% (Data source: Media Services).

TV has a dominant share of 38% followed by magazines with 27%. The advertising spending at TV have exceeded the 620 thousands dollars in 2000. Newspapers and outdoor advertising have moderate percentages 17% and 14% respectively. Radio has the smallest share of the total adspend with 4% targeting at more niche audiences.

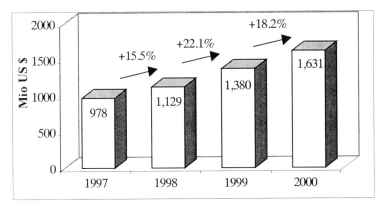

Figure 2: Total Advertising Spending 1997-2000
Data Source: Media Services
1 US$ = 365.4 GDR (Source: Bank of Greece, Bulletin of Conjunctural Indicators, No 46, Jan 2001)

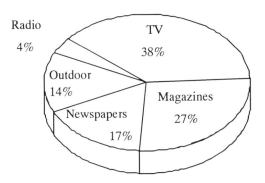

Figure 3: Share of Media Expenditure 2000
Data Source: Media Services

Table 1: Advertising Expenditures per Advertising Medium 2000

Advertising Medium	2000 ('000 US$)	Share of total, %
TV	621.1	38.1
Magazines	438.6	26.9
Newspapers	281.9	17.3
Radio	65.7	4.0
Outdoor	224.0	13.7

Data Source: Media Services

Table 2: Top Advertising Branches of Business (2000)

		Advertising Expenses ('000 US$)	Share of total, %
1	Automobiles	121.3	7.4
2	Tobacco Products	89.3	5.5
3	Beverages	72.5	4.4
4	Public Sector	71.4	4.4
5	Banks	67.0	4.1
6	Mobile Telecommunications	60.7	3.7
7	Beauty Care Centers	43.9	2.7
8	Automobile Dealers	41.9	2.6
9	Dairy Products	38.9	2.4
10	Cosmetics	33.2	2.0

Data Source: Media Services

The big spenders in 2000 are the automobile industry and the tobacco companies followed by the beverages, the public sector and the banks.

Table 3: Top Advertisers (1999)

		Advertising Expenses ('000 US$)
1	Bodyline (Beauty Care Center)	24.6
2	Procter & Gamble	23.2
3	Unilever Hellas	21.8
4	Panafon (Telecommunications)	20.2
5	Stet Hellas (Telecommunications)	18.2
6	OPAP (Lottery)	15.1
7	Greec ministries	13.4
8	United Distillers	12.4
9	Delta (Dairy Products)	12.2
10	Cosmote (Telecommunications)	11.9
11	Anelor (Cosmetics)	11.9
12	DOL (Publishing company)	11.3
13	Automobile Dealers	11.0
14	Nestle	10.5
15	Sky (Media)	10.1
16	Kosmocar (Automotives)	9.9
17	PASOK (Political party)	9.3
18	Fiat Auto Hellas	9.2
19	Nethold Mediterranean	8.5
20	Hyundai	8.5

Data Source: Media Services

In 1999 the top ten of advertisers included both local and international companies. Beauty care centers, fast moving consumers goods and telecommunications are the adspend champions. It is also interesting that the Greek government during the last years has realized the importance of advertising in promoting the public sector programs and investments.

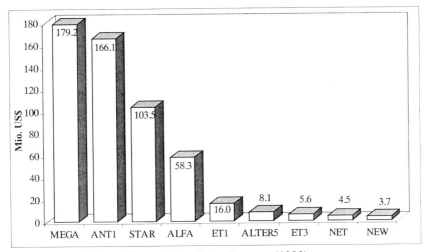

Figure 4: Television – Gross Advertising Income (1999)
Data Source: Media Services

The Greek TV industry is dominated by the private TV stations which have the biggest share of the adspend adding up to 95%. This is the result of the prevalence of the private owned channels which have a total share of viewing of about 85% (Fig. 5).

In 2000 the number of spots in TV showed a small decrease compared to 1999 of 4.3% (2000: 946,160, 1999: 988,445). However, the total airtime of spots increased by 4.6% (2000: 20,457,972, 1999: 19,563,485), (Fig. 6).

The state owned channels, namely ET1, NET and ET3 hold a minority share in adspend. However, in terms of content they are considered as the quality TV channels.

Cable TV has a minor presence in Greece yet.

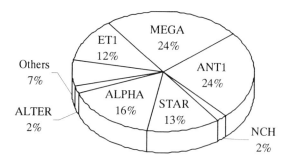

Figure 5: Television – Share of Viewing – Channel Reach (2000)
Data Source: Media Services

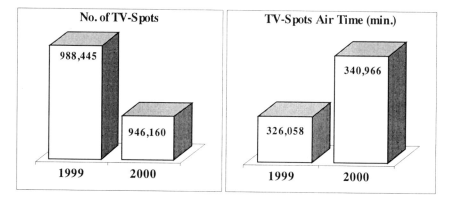

Figure 6: Television – Spot and Air Time (2000 vs. 1999)
Data Source: Media Services

The magazine sector is a fast moving industry where many acquisitions take place and a lot new magazines appear each year. Usually only a few survive and many of them have only a short-term life cycle. The biggest share of adspend is invested in weekly magazines and magazines targeting at women. TV magazines and the rest of the titles which target smaller and better-defined market segments follow.

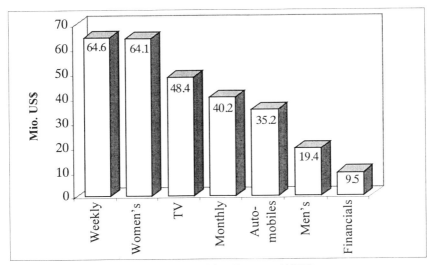

Figure 7: Magazines – Gross Advertising Income (1999)
Data Source: Media Services

Newspapers in Greece have lower circulation numbers compared to other European countries. Sunday and evening newspapers hold the lion share of the adspend followed by financial newspapers. The latter have high growth with a lot of titles launched during the last five years.

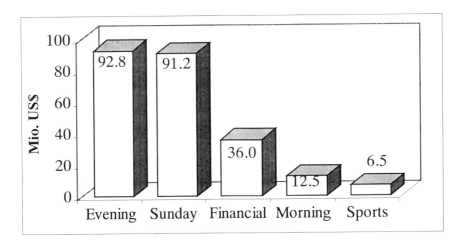

Figure 8: Newspapers – Gross Advertising Income (1999)
Data Source: Media Services

Despite the fact that radio is a minor advertising medium there is a pro-liferation of radio stations targeting niche target groups. In the beginning of 2001 many radio stations, among them some very popular ones, have lost their broadcasting permit after the reinforcement of a stricter law re-garding the distribution of bandwidth.

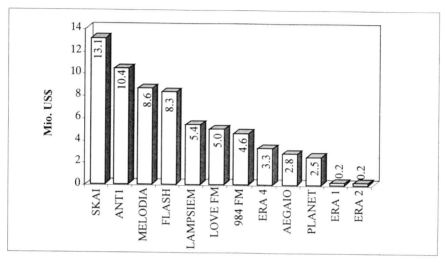

Figure 9: Radio – Gross Advertising Income (1999)
Data Source: Media Services

News radio stations, like SKAI and ANT1, are mainly preferred by ad-vertisers and music radio ones, like MELODIA and LAMPSI, follow. The state owned radio stations, i.e. ERA1 and ERA2, have a very low adver-tising income.

References

Mattelart, A. (1989). *Advertising International*, Routledge
Tsakarestou, B. (2001). *Advertising in Fordist and Post-Fordist Era*.
    Kastaniotis editions, Athens (to be published)

Useful Addresses

1. The Hellenic Association of Advertising Communication Agencies
    (HAACA).
    7 Iperidou Str.
    105 28 Athens
    Greece
    tel. +30 1 324 6215 – 8
    fax. +30 1 324 6880
    email: admin@edee.gr
    http://www.edee.gr

2. The Greek Advertisers Association (GAA)
    17 Mousson Str.
    115 24 Athens
    Greece
    tel. +30 1 698 3917 - 8
    fax. +30 1 698 4129
    email: sde@otenet.gr
    http://www.sde.gr

www.acnielsen.com
www.agb.gr

4   Internet Advertising in Greece

George Frigkas
Researcher, Panteion University, Athens

4.1   The Greek Internet Advertising Market

The Greek Internet Advertising is still lacking behind the European Average. Very few are the advertising companies that have invested in creating the needed infrastructure for promoting an on-line advertising campaign. On the other hand the expansion rate of the Greek Internet advertising is very high and predictions show that the advertising expenditure is doubling every year.

According to data given by Eurisko, a Greek company specializing at web ad campaigns management, in 2000 approximately 1,500,000 USD was spent for banner ad campaigns in Greek sites. This accounts to only 0.1% of the total ad expenditure. The predictions for 2001 are over 5,000,000 USD, which is normal, as the Greek Internet advertising market will sooner or later reach the global average (predictions of Zenith Media account 4.5-5% of the total ad budget to Internet by 2003).

Another study conducted by the Athens University of Economics shows that Internet users represent 10% of the Greek population, 2/3 of whom are men, usually between 17 – 34 years old, most of them of a higher educational level. The Greek surfer visits almost equally Greek and foreign sites, the most popular being in.gr, yahoo.com, flash.gr and altavista.com[3].

4.2   Problems

The main problems of the Greek Internet advertising are:
- The penetration of Internet is relatively lower than the European average, even though the number of the Greek Internet users is growing rapidly.[4]

  Most of the studies concerning Internet penetration in Greece assume that Greek Internet users are not more than 10% of the population. This is a small number compared to 40% - 50% of the northern European countries.

- There is no common way of calculating the traffic of a web site[5]
  The last year there has been serious discussions about the need of establishing a commonly accepted way of calculating the web site traffic. This is a very serious factor for the advertising industry, but the major Greek players have not yet concluded neither on a third party that could complete this task, nor on the main principles and techniques.

- The e-commerce is still limited[6].
  Internet advertising, especially the first years, is closely tied to the expansion of e-commerce. The first and largest ad spenders are dot-com companies, or e-shops. Thus, the relatively low acceptance of e-commerce in Greece is another major problem, even though the next few years are expected to show an increasing e-commerce spending for the Greek consumer.

- The Greek advertising agencies (or even the branches of the multinational advertising companies) are not adequately prepared for performing an on-line advertising campaign. There is an obvious lack of specialized personnel that can fulfill an ad campaign and even fewer executives that are able to propose the use of Internet as an advertising medium and convince the big ad spender.

4.3   Most Important Web Sites

The last years the sites of the .gr domain have invested a lot in producing on-line Greek content that could attract Greek-speaking audience. Thus, nowadays there are many interesting (at what concerns advertising) web sites that cover various areas of interest.

1) Portals
   - In.gr: The most important Greek web site, with a vast directory, an adequate search engine and the best news coverage by far. According to various studies more than 85% of Greek users visit In.gr and for about 40% it's the site they visit most often.
   - Flash.gr: It is said to be the second player of the Greek Internet. 20% of the Greek audience prefers this site.
   - e-one.gr: Focusing more on specialized news, especially concerning arts and politics.

- e-go.gr: A new portal, with good news coverage and very modern layout.
- Pathfinder.gr: Based on Crete, it supports a very powerful search engine and provides competitive services.
- Thea.gr: One of the oldest Greek sites, it seems to have lost the biggest number of its audience, focusing nowadays on lifestyle content.

2) Vortals
  i) Economy
   - Naftemporiki.gr: By far the most important Greek vortal, a sub-division of the daily economic newspaper Naftemporiki. It covers an extensive range of economical and political news but mainly offers daily on-line live coverage of the prices of the Greek stock market, having built a huge database of news, stock prices, announcements etc. for practically every Greek enterprise.
   - Reporter.gr: Maybe the only successful web site based on a subscription model.
   - Eco2day.gr: An online newspaper with many new features, such as video coverage of events, modern design etc.

  ii) Sports
   - Supersport.gr: Probably the best sports vertical portal, with a big database of every sport, it belongs to the unique Greek pay TV sports channel.
   - Sport.gr: A sports vortal with various sections, such as sports, Athens 2004, Sports Cyprus etc.
   - Contra.gr: Focusing on the opinions of its editors, it resembles to the style of writing of the sports newspapers.

  iii) Health
   - In.health.gr: It is a part of in.gr and focuses on medical and healthy life subjects
   - Doctors.in.gr: A site belonging as well to in.gr, it is addressed to doctors.
   - Care.gr: The same idea with in.health, but belongs to flash.gr

  iv) Music
   - Avopolis.gr: Vertical portal focusing on rock music.

- Babylon.gr: Another important player with rich content about rock music.
- Virginmega.gr: The biggest music e-shop, it belongs to Virgin Music
- Sonymusic.gr: Vortal about Greek music and musicians, with much news, as well as a series of smaller sites with info about many Greek singers.
- Mad.gr: Music vortal about Greek music, it belongs to Mad TV, a TV channel focusing on music and lifestyle. Many new and interesting forms of advertising.

3) e-shops
   - Plaisio.gr: The most successful Greek e-shop, a subsidiary of Plaisio shops
   - Agora.gr: A shopping mall that belongs to Hellas On Line, it has not yet created an adequate e-shops network.
   - Oops.gr: Another shopping mall, with a big investment and a serious network of retailers.
   - Opensop.gr: Another effort of Otenet.gr the largest (and public) Greek ISP

B2B marketplaces
- Yassas.com: Focusing on tourism B2B transactions
- Cosmoone.gr: The first and largest generic B2B marketplace.
- Be24.gr: The second big player in B2B e-commerce.

4.4 Pricing[7]

In general, there are three ways of pricing web advertising in Greece:
- Pay per view
- Flat fee
- Barters

The most widely used is pricing the ads base on flat fee depending on the page and the time. On the other hand many sites are proposing pay per view model, with a CPM (Cost per Thousand Impressions) ranging from 13–23 USD. It is relatively easy of course to make arrangements based on barters, especially between sites, or even press and sites.

4.5   Advertising Companies

- Eurisko: A company specializing in web advertising planning and management, uses DART of Doubleclick (www.eurisko.gr)
- Forthnet – Engage: Forthnet, one of the leading Greek ISPs uses the web ad management tools of Engage (www.fothnet.gr)
- NMS: It is the interactive branch of the BBDO Group in Greece, specializing in creating and promoting products and services in Internet (www.nms.gr)
- Yellow net road: Recently acquires by J. W. Thomson in Greece, it produces interactive ads. (www.yellownetroad.gr)
- Opticom: an independent web advertising company, with a good reputation in web design and developing (www.opticom.gr)
- Zentropy: the interactive advertising company of McCann Erickson Worldwide is present in Greece as well. (www.zentropy.gr)
- Zenith Media: Belongs to Adel Saatchi & Saatchi advertising company.
- Media Shop – Otenet: A newly created web advertising management company, owned by the largest Greek ISP, Otenet. (www.otenet.gr)

---

[1] Armand Mattelard (1989). *Advertsing International*. Routledge 1989.

[2] Source: HAACA

[3] "The greek internet consumer", survey conducted by ELTRUN and Rota

[4] Data provided by a survey conducted by Focus (Focus WebID)

[5] E-Market, December 2000, "The need for trustworthy ad traffic measurement" p. 34

[6] "The greek internet consumer", survey conducted by Heltrun and Rota

[7] E-Market, June 2001, "Internet Advertising", p. 50

Advertising in Hong Kong

Prof. Stella Lai Man So
Dept. of Marketing, The Chinese University of Hong Kong

1   Background

Hong Kong, once a British colony, has been handed back to the Republic of China in 1997 after 150 years under British rule. It became a special administrative region (SAR) of China as stipulated in the Sino-British Joint Declaration of 1984 and the subsequent Basic Law. These legal instruments allowed Hong Kong to enjoy a high degree of autonomy, and China agreed to implement the principle of "one country, two systems". Thus, Hong Kong has continued to maintain its free and open economic system.

Asiaweek (December 11, 1998) ranked Hong Kong as Asia's seventh best city on a "quality of life" index. 92.4 percent of its 6.8 million people are literate, while 95 percent live in urban areas. Most of the Hong Kong people are living in the busy city environment.

Hong Kong is a meeting point of the cultures of the East and West. Although 95 percent of the population is of Chinese descent, its population composition also includes residents from other Asian nationalities. Cantonese is the most commonly used Chinese dialect, but many people also speak English and Mandarin.

Free trade and low taxation, coupled with the rule of law and an efficient civil service, enabled Hong Kong economy to take off in the early 1970s. With an estimated real GDP growth of 10.5%, Hong Kong was the fastest growing economy in Asia in 2000 (Table 1). Growth figures were boosted by the sharp rise in China trade coupled with price deflation. China, as a major driver of growth, is a big potential market that is ready and eager to buy Western goods. Hong Kong, one of the Four Tigers of Asia, serves as a middleman for information and goods to this big market and generates a large amount of economic activity in the region. As much as 90% of Hong Kong's total exports are now re-exports from China compared with less than 40% in the 1980s. On the other hand, it is the most important entre-port for the Chinese mainland as about 40% of the mainland's foreign trade are handled via Hong Kong.

As one of the most service-oriented economies in the world, in 1999, the service sector contributed to 85.3% of Hong Kong's GDP and employed about 85% of workers. Exports of services revived and grew strongly by 13.7% in 2000, leading to a surplus of more than US$19 billion. It is ex-pected that demand for services offered by Hong Kong should remain strong as China's dealings with the international community increase upon World Trade Organization accession.

Table 1: Major Economic Indicators

	1998	1999	2000	2001
Population(mn)	6.69 (1)	6.76 (1)	6.86 (1)	6.86 (3)
Gross Domestic Product (US$bn)	161.4	157.4 (2)	162.4 (2)	166.3 (4)
Real GDP Growth (%)	-5.3	3.0 (2)	10.5 (2)	3.0 (4)
GDP Per Capita (US$)	24,294	23,419 (2)	23,897 (2)	24,240 (4)
% Change in Consumer Prices (CCPI)	2.8	-4.0	-3.7	-1.8 (5)
Unemployment Rate (%)	4.7	6.2	5.0	4.6 (6)

(1) End-period figures (resident population), (2) Revised estimates (May 2001), (3) End-2000 figure, (4) Projection, (5) Jan-Apr 2001, (6) Feb-Apr 2001
Source: tdctrade.com

2   Advertising Industry

There are 4,074 advertising and related agencies in Hong Kong employing 18,184 people. The annual revenue for the sector is more than US$2.1 bil-lion (Table 2).

Table 2: Advertising and Related Services

Number of establishments (March 2000)	4,074
Number of persons engaged (March 2000)	18,184
Business receipts and other income (1998, US$ million)	2,149
Value-added (1998, US$ million)	517
Exports of advertising and market research services (19998, US$ million)	598
Contribution to total services exports (%)	1.7

Note: Advertising and related services include: advertising companies and agen-cies; public relation services; market research companies; and other advertising services.
Source: Census and Statistics Department

2.1   Advertising Expenditure

Hong Kong is the advertising capital of Asia. It ranked second in the world and first in Asia in terms of per capita adspend. Hong Kong's total adspend amounted to US$ 3,539 millions in 2000, up 15% from US$ 3,0 43 millions in 1999 (Table 3).

Advertising is one of the fastest growing services industries in Hong Kong, in line with the development of Hong Kong into a high-income economy and the rapid rise of the Chinese mainland as a big market for consumer products and other goods and services. Hence, Hong Kong is widely regarded as the gateway to the mainland's opportunities.

Table 3: Asia Pacific Adspend Totals (USD millions)

	1996-97 % change	1997-98 % change	1998-99 % change	1999-00 % change	1999 AdEx	2000 AdEx
China	**208.4**	**45**	**15**	**58.0**	**6133**	**9692**
Taiwan	56.8	19	-26	Unknown	1875	Unknown
Hong Kong	20.1	2	14	16.3	3043	3539
Vietnam	7.8	0	4	32.9	76	101
Singapore	4.5	-7	3	17.0	730	854
Malaysia	-11.9	-17	16	22.2	663	810
Philippines	-14.8	7	15	-4.3	1290	1234
Thailand	-47.0	-24	31	5.3	1093	1151
South Korea	-52.5	-26	33	21.5	4240	5150

Source: Asian Advertising And Marketing, April 1997/March 1998/July 1999
ACNielsen Media International

2.2   Advertising Agencies

The advertising market in Hong Kong is dominated by the major international agencies (Figure 1, Table 4). The major associations are association of Association of Accredited Advertising Agencies (4As) and the Hong Kong Independent Advertising Agents Association (HiA). Most of the Hong Kong 4As members are major multinational agencies and account for more than 50% of the market. There are 20 4As members in Hong Kong.

In general, advertising agencies initiate, manage and implement advertising campaigns. The full-service agencies are traditionally providing three major types of services, namely account management, creative services and media planning. Now, some bigger multinational agencies also provide related services such as sales promotion, Internet advertising services and public relations. A recent industry trend is for advertising agencies to spin off their media planning department as specialist companies. MindShare is leading the market share of the specialized media planning market (Table 4).

Table 4: Asia Media Agency Ranking (Asia-Pacific – 1999/2000)

Rank	Agency	Total (US$m)	Share of Market
1	MindShare	2,558	19.1%
2	Universal McCann	2,313	17.3%
3	OMD	2,094	15.7%
4	Media Edge TME	1,550	11.6%
5	Bcom3/Mediavest/Starcom	1,333	10.0%
6	Zenith Media	1,199	9.0%
7	Initiative Media Worldwide	823	6.2%
8	Medicom	494	3.7%
9	TN Media/FCB	343	2.6%
10	Optimedia	240	1.8%
11	CIA	205	1.5%
12	Carat	164	1.2%
13	Eurolab	56	0.4%

Source: Recma Report

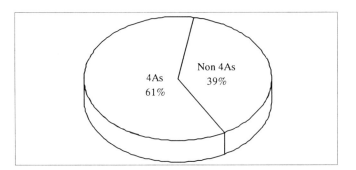

Figure 1: Hong Kong Advertising Industry, % Revenues (1996)
Source: Cable and Satellite Asia (November/December 1996)

Hong Kong has a highly developed consumer market, with several major multinational players competing with each other for market share. Hong Kong advertising agencies are generally perceived as professional in all respects by Chinese Mainland advertisers and advertising agencies. They have the reputation of being able to deliver high-quality services and have advanced technology in production and management capabilities.

Ogilvy & Mather has topped the Hong Kong billings ranking for the third year in a row. For 1999, the agency raked in billings worth HK$ 1.148 billion, up about three percent from the year before. DDB jumped one place to second with a 12 percent increase in billings to HK$1.047 billion (Table 5).

Table 5: 1999 Hong Kong 4As Agency Ranking (All figures in HK$ millions)

1999 Ranking	Name of Agency	1999 Billings	1998 Billings	YOY % change	1998 Ranking
1	Ogilvy & Mather Hong Kong	1,147.93	1,111.68	3.3%	1
2	DDB Worldwide	1,047.00	935.81	12.0%	3
3	J. Walter Thompson	944.63	968.09	-2.4%	2
4	* FCB Hong Kong	830.00	878.04	-5.5%	4
5	McCann-Erickson Guangming	744.68	826.23	-9.9%	6
6	Leo Burnett – Hong Kong	731.77	835.29	-12.4%	5
7	Bates Hong Kong	687.70	733.77	-6.3%	7
8	Grey Hong Kong	646.04	533.92	21.0%	8
9	Euro RSCG	492.44	514.44	-4.3%	9
10	Dentsu, Yong & Rubicam	470.20	510.22	-7.8%	10
11	BBDO Hong Kong	379.46	320.44	18.4%	11
12	Publicis Ad-Link	315.06	-	-	-
13	D'Arcy	270.91	301.97	-10.3%	12
14	Saatchi & Saatchi	255.39	278.73	-8.4%	13
15	TBWA Hong Kong	170.94	219.46	-22.1%	15
16	Lowe & Partners/Live	152.12	114.59	32.8%	17
17	Dentsu Inc., Hong Kong Branch	145.55	192.72	-24.5%	16
18	Ammirati Puris Lintas	144.11	231.89	-37.9%	14
19	Fortune	85.04	103.20	-17.6%	18
	TOTAL	**9,661.97**	**9,610.49**	**0.54%**	

* FCB and Bozell merged in September 1999 reported jointly as FCB China
# FCB and Bozell billings combined for comparison purposes
Source: Media, 31 March, 2000

3   Consumer Behavior in the Hong Kong Market

In Hong Kong, consumption seems to have been legitimized as a "daily" goal. Shopping, going to movies, and dining out are some of the territory's favorite leisure activities. The craze for a luxurious life is also found among the younger generation. Therefore, advertisements in Hong Kong, as an indicator to reflect a society's value system, were found emphasizing "hedonic consumption" and "price value". In contrast, advertisements in the PRC emphasized "product performance" and "performance assurance". In Hong Kong, "work hard and play hard" is well accepted as a guiding principle by many people. Therefore, Hong Kong people often use material possessions as a primary base for normative judgements and value brand names as symbol to reinforce their social identity.

As a well developed and westernized cities, advertising budgets in Hong Kong are mostly spent on consumer products or services (Table 6). Among the top ten advertising categories, telecommunication services are dominating the advertising market. Heavy advertising in these categories reflects the growing importance of telecommunications and the modern life style in Hong Kong.

Table 6: Adspend in Hong Kong 1999 Top 10 Categories

Category	Million US$	Million HK$	Growth
Communication equipment & services	130	1014	+108%
Mobile phone service & equipment	122	950	-11%
Supermarkets	111	862	+184%
Overseas travel	109	849	+20%
Residential estates – sales/rental	107	837	-23%
Newspapers/books/magazine/radio/TV	106	829	+19%
Mainland China Properties	98	765	+86%
Restaurants/clubs	88	689	+28%
Records and tapes	729	565	-16%
Credit cards	68	527	-5%

Source: ACNielsen Media International, 2000

As for the top twenty brands in terms of advertising expenditure, all of them are consumer products and services (Table 7). Telecommunication services, banking services and travel agencies have dominated the top twenty brands that reflect the importance of service industry in Hong Kong.

Supermarket advertising spending has the highest growth rate. Due to the direct selling method has been newly developed and the new wet market concept has been brought into the supermarket business, the two major supermarket chains Park'N Shop and Wellcome have their adspend increased by 152% and 129% respectively.

Table 7: Adspend in Hong Kong 1999 Top 20 Brands

Brand	TV Adspend		Total Adspend		Growth
	Million US$	Million HK$	Million US$	Million HK$	
HK Telecom CSL and One2free	16332.3	2093.9	46728.0	5990.8	+17%
Park'N Shop	11645.4	1493.0	36477.7	4676.6	+152%
Hutchison Telecom	14430.2	1850.0	30048.7	3852.4	+39%
SUNDAY Network	19678.4	2522.9	25405.3	3257.1	+88%
Wellcome Supermarket	4178.8	535.7	24665.4	3162.2	+129%
Tierra Verde (Gr)	21589.1	2767.8	22133.0	2837.6	+115%
Admart	1780.3	228.2	18682.4	2395.2	-
McDonald's	17353.3	2224.8	17987.3	2306.1	+24%
HSBC	7402.3	949.0	15515.8	1989.2	-3%
Smartone and EXTRA	8031.3	1029.7	15132.4	1940.1	-1%
Hong Thai Citizens Travel Services Ltd.	4449.8	570.5	14483.0	1856.8	+22%
Fortune Pharmacal Co. Ltd.	13882.8	1779.8	4197.0	538.1	+87%
Standard Chartered Bank	7690.4	985.9	10032.3	1286.2	+27%
Chase Bank	3740.3	479.5	13344.8	1710.9	+71%
Morning Star Travel	5126.7	657.3	12071.6	1547.6	+56%
New World Mobility	6427.1	824.0	11754.1	1506.9	+20%
Wing On Travel	3396.3	435.4	11570.7	1483.4	+16%
Hang Seng Bank	7453.7	955.6	11483.8	1472.3	- 20%
Johnson & Johnson	8793.9	1127.4	10099.8	1294.8	- 13%
Cathay Pacific	6118.8	784.5	9868.5	1265.2	+102%

Source: ACNielsen Media International, 2000

4 Culture and Advertising

Because of the strong western influences, Hong Kong's advertising has been characterized as combining both Western and Chinese culture. Although many ads in Hong Kong use Chinese language, either wholly or in part, they appeal to many Western values. It was found by a research that Hong Kong is the most westernized of the three Chinese markets: Taiwan, Hong Kong and Mainland China.

The fact that mixed English and Chinese is still the dominant form of language used reflects Hong Kong consumers' language habit of mixing English and Chinese. Therefore, mixed language is the unique character of Hong Kong advertising and it enhances the association of the Hong Kong local audiences with the content of the ads. Comparing with the advertising content in the Mainland China, Hong Kong advertising creative emphasizes less on the traditional Chinese culture whereas more Western culture can be observed in the creative style.

5   Media

The media industry in Hong Kong is very prosperous and competition is keen. As a city with six million people, it has the largest number of newspapers in the world.

Television and newspaper are two major media that attract advertising expenditure in Hong Kong. Over 80% of the total advertising spending spent on these two media (Table 8).

Table 8: Advertising Revenue by Media, 1972-97

Year	TV	News-papers	Maga-zines	Radio	Others	Totals %	Annual Ad-spend in HK$ millions
1972*	34.0	54.7	3.7	5.5	2.1	100	222
1974*	41.0	49.1	3.3	4.6	2.0	100	239
1976*	53.8	39.2	3.0	2.7	1.3	100	280
1978*	58.5	31.8	5.4	3.4	0.9	100	460
1980*	49.0	38.4	7.7	4.6	0.3	100	939
1985**	60.2	23.5	9.6	3.7	3.0	100	2,871
1987**	57.4	26.4	10.4	2.5	3.3	100	3,865
1989**	50.5	28.7	12.9	3.8	4.1	100	5,529
1991**	50.4	27.7	12.8	4.7	4.4	100	7,532
1993**	42.9	36.3	10.8	6.0	4.0	100	11,395
1995**	49.2	28.9	11.9	6.5	3.5	100	15,116
1997**	46.9	32.9	11.9	5.3	3.0	100	20,400
1999**	45.2	36.4	11.6	3.9	2.9	100	23,651

Source: *Marketing Research Department, HK-TVB Ltd; **HK Adex, SRG

5.1   The Press

Under the Basic Law, China is obliged to let Hong Kong keep its present way of life, including press freedom for at least 50 years. In 1997, 30 Chinese-language dailies, 10 English-language dailies, one bilingual daily, and four dailies in other languages had registered with the Hong Kong government. The background, circulation and readership data of some popular dailies in Hong Kong are listed in Table 9. Some have distributed networks and print editions overseas, particularly in the United States, Canada, the United Kingdom, and Australia. Some regional and international publications such as the Asian Wall Street Journal, Asiaweek, the Far Eastern Economic Review, and the International Herald Tribune have chosen Hong Kong as their base or location for their headquarters. Hong Kong has its competitive advantage of advanced telecommunications infrastructure, the availability of the latest technology, and its strategically important location in Asia.

Table 9: Press

Title	Established	Nature	Circulation	Readership
Oriental Daily News	1969	Mass	*	2,551,000
Apple Daily	1995	Mass	406,666	1,780,000
The Sun	1999	Mass	*	*
Ming Pao Daily News	1959	Elite	85,699	285,000
Sing Pao Daily News	1939	Mass	*	241,000
South China Morning Post	1903	Elite, English	117,563	206,000
Hong Kong Daily News	1959	Mass	*	157,000
Tin Tin Daily News	1960	Mass	*	158,000
Sing jTao Daily	1038	Elite	59,338	118,000
Hong Kong Economic Times	1988	Elite, business	68,123	101,000
Hong Kong Economic Journal	1973	Elite, business	63,120	62,000
Wen Wei Po	1948	Mass	*	*
Ta Kung Pao	1938	Mass	*	*
Hong Kong Commercial Daily	1952	Business	*	*
Hong Kong Standard	1949	Elite, English	*	*

Source: Hong Kong Audit Bureau of Circulation (ABC) Ltd (July-December 1998 figures). Those marked by an (*) were either not members of ABC or did not report figures; *ACNielsen media index Hong Kong mid-year report (1999)*. Those marked by an (*) were below one percent average issue readership (aged 9+) which was the cutting point adopted by ACNielsen.

The Sun claimed that its readership just surpassed 1 million one week after its launch and ranked third among all newspapers. The scenario was obviously a result of its price-cutting strategy to sell at HK$2 per copy. *Apply Daily* and *Sing Pao Daily News* correspondingly slashed their regular retail price from $5 to $3. *Oriental Daily News*, its parent company also owns *The Sun*, followed suit and reduced its price from $4 to $3.

The two top dailies in Hong Kong are Oriental Daily News (ODN) and Apple Daily (Table 10). According to ACNielsen, Oriental Daily News' readership drops from 2.5 million in the July 1998/June 1999 period to 2.2 million in 1999/2000. The figure for Apple Daily also edged lower from 1.7 million to 1.6 million.

The third popular newspaper, The Sun, launched by Oriental Press Group in 1999 is a sister title to ODN has taken away some of the readership from the two major dailies. Now, Apple, ODN and The Sun dominate 80% of the market in Hong Kong. These three major dailies are targeting at the mass market and therefore the editorial standard is designed to attract the largest possible number of readers by offering market-driven content.

Table 10: Newspapers (read yesterday)

	2000 Mid-year Report (Jul 1999-Jun 2000)		1999 Mid-year Report (Jan-Dec 1999)		1999 Mid-year Report (Jul 1998-Jun 1999)	
	('000)	%	('000)	%	('000)	%
Oriental Daily News	2,236	36	2,412	40	2,551	42
Apple Daily	1,615	26	1,642	27	1,780	30
The Sun (1)	777	13	-	-	-	-
Ming Pao	326	5	288	5	285	5
South China Morning Post	308	5	303	5	206	3
Sing Pao	216	3	236	4	241	4
Sing Tao Daily	145	2	133	2	118	2
Hong Kong Daily News	122	2	157	3	158	3
Hong Kong Economic Times	120	2	107	2	101	2
Tin Tin Daily News	100	2	127	2	157	3
Base: All aged 9+	6,176,000		6,105,000		6,011,000	

(1) The Sun was monitored from April 1999 onwards.
Source: Media, 2000

Table 11: Weekly Magazines (read in past week)

	2000 Mid-year Report (Jul 1999-Jun 2000)		1999 Mid-year Report (Jan-Dec 1999)		1999 Mid-year Report (Jul 1998-Jun 1999)	
	('000)	%	('000)	%	('000)	%
Next Magazine	568	9	610	10	667	11
Sudden Weekly	499	8	569	9	621	10
Easy Finder	368	6	406	7	459	8
East Week	329	5	371	6	482	8
TVB Weekly	266	4	288	5	326	5
East touch	254	4	282	5	316	5
Yes	165	3	197	3	250	4
Eat & Travel Weekly	151	2	130	2	115	2
Ming Pao Weekly	129	2	144	2	176	3
Cable Guide Weekly *	119	2	-	-	-	-
Oriental Sunday	110	2	151	2	193	3
PC Market	99	2	119	2	100	2
Base: All aged 9+	6,176,000		6,105,000		6,011,000	

* Cable Guide Weekly was originally named Cable Guide which was a monthly magazine. It has changed its name to Cable Guide Weekly and was monitored from May 1999 onwards.
Source: Media, 2000

South China Morning Post, the most dominant English daily, together with the Chinese daily, Ming Pao Daily News, represent the most prestigious dailies in Hong Kong. The English-language South China Morning Post serves the small but powerful constituencies of the expatriate community and the Chinese elite.

On the magazine side, Next's readership is the highest among all the other local magazines. However, its readership also fell from 667,000 to 568,000. Media specialists said that the declines were mostly due to new niche publications flooding into the market, including Weekend Weekly, a leisure travel title; New Monday, which covers leisure and lifestyle issues; plus a whole host of new entertainment magazines (Table 11). These new titles are target-oriented and the fact that people find them attractive represented a psychographic shift in readership habits.

5.2 Broadcasting

Commercial television in Hong Kong began in 1957, when Rediffusion introduced a closed-circuit bilingual TV channel. In 1967, the first wireless TV broadcaster, Television Broadcasts Ltd., was introduced. Each of the two major TV broadcasters, TVB and ATV (former Rediffusion), carries one Chinese- and one English-language channel. TVB Jade, the Cantonese channel, has come to dominate the local TV industry ever since its inception, has consistently secured 70 percent to 90 percent of the prime time rating share (Table 12).

Table 12: Weekday Prime Time TV Rating (TVRs)

Year	TVB Jade ratings	ATV Hong Kong ratings
1985	43	8
1987	45	4
1989	36	8
1991	31	10
1993	29	9
1995	24	12
1997	30	9
1999	26	11

Note: In 1998, one TVR=1% of total TV audience (aged 4+) = 60,450 individuals.
Source: SRG ACNielsen

Virtually all Hong Kong households have access to television (99%) (Table 13)- about 2 million TV households, constituting 6.3 million viewers aged 4 or above. More than 35 percent of TV households own more than one TV set. In late 1995, more than 78 percent also had a videocassette recorder. Although the average time people spent on daily TV viewing has decreased from 4.2 hours in 1990 to 3.5 hours in 1994, TV viewing remains Hong Kong's most popular leisure activity.

Table 13: Household Media Equipment

Households with TV sets	99%
Households with VCR	73%
Households with cable TV	20%
Households with satellite TV	19%
Households with home computer	36%
Households with Internet connection	16%
Number of mainline telephones per 100 people	56.5
Number of cellular telephones per 100 people	54.4 (November 1999)

Note: Other surveys put the figures of households with home computer, as well as Internet connections much higher. For example, some studies estimate that over 50 percent of Hong Kong households had computers at home in 1998. The Office of the Telecommunications Authority puts the number of personal computers in Hong Kong at 1.5 million in 1998.
Source: ACNielsen 1998 Establishment Survey; Howlett, 1998; OFTA

Altogether, the TV industry in Hong Kong provides more than 38 channels (Table 14). It consists of two commercial TV broadcasters, a quasi-public broadcaster, a cable television operator, an interactive TV service, and a number of regional satellite TV broadcasters. Hong Kong is also the home of some regional TV broadcasters, including Satellite Television Asian Region Ltd. (STAR TV), Chinese Television Network (CTN), and Chinese Entertainment Television (CETV).

Table 14: Broadcasting

Number of TV stations	3 (ATV, TVB, HKCTV [formerly Wharf Cable])
Number of TV channels	4 (terrestrial), 35 (cable)
Number of radio stations	3 (CR, MR, RTHK)
Number of radio channels	13 (3 by CR, 3 by MR, 7 by RTHK)

As a communication hub of the Asia-Pacific, Hong Kong has the world's largest Chinese TV program library. It is also an important exporter of audiovisual products.

As far as radio is concerned, Hong Kong has two commercial radio broadcasters, Commercial Radio (CR) and Metro Radio (MR), as well as a quasi-public radio, Radio Television Hong Kong (RTHK). CR and MR each has three channels, two of which use Chinese, while the third uses English. RTHK is organizationally a government department but editorially independent.

5.3 New Media

The development of information technology in Hong Kong has been very rapid in the past decade. It is estimated that there are about 125 Internet Service Providers (ISPs) - including major ones like HKT -IMS, Star, HKNeT, and CTInets, - were in operation in mid-1998 serving 25 percent of Hong Kong's households. More than half of all households had personal computers and thee estimated number of Internet users stood at 850,000 (ACNielsen, 1998).

The average home users access the Internet three to four times a week for e-mail and for surfing the Web. In 1996, only 4.5 percent of the households had their personal computers connected to the Internet, but the figure more than doubled to 10.6 percent in 1997 and then to 16 percent in 1998. The number of Internet users in Hong Kong increased rapidly from 271,000 in 1996 to 500,000 in 1997. The current number of Internet users is believed to be more than 1 million (ACNielsen, 1998).

Online media is a new choice for media planning, advertisers are increasingly adopting the online concept into their media schedule. While campaign optimization on the fly stands out as one of the saving graces of online advertising, dotcoms themselves are looking to less cyber-based avenues to get their message out. In Hong Kong, dotcom advertising expenditures increased nine-fold to US$176 million, but took a sharp turn in the June quarter and saw the second half of the year finishing one-third lower than the first (Table 15).

Table 15: Hong Kong Dotcom AdEx, 2000

	Dotcom AdEx US$ million	Share %
Quarter 1	48	27
Quarter 2	59	34
Quarter 3	39	22
Quarter 4	30	17
Total	176	100

Source: ACNielsen

Newspaper ranked the first in terms of media used by dotcoms, Chinese television ranked second garnering HK$238 million (Figure 2).

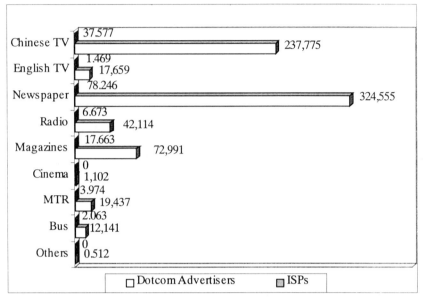

Figure 2: Dotcom Ad – Media Breakdown (HK$ '000)
Source: ACNielsen AdQuest (Jan-May 2000)

The online financial service providers and the telecoms players continued to be the strongest spenders (Table 16). Topping the adspend bill was CASH online, tagged by Sunday.com and HongKong.com.

Table 16: Top 20 Dotcom Advertisers (Jan-May, 2000)

Rank	Website	HK'000
1	CASH	41,532
2	Sunday.com	34,270
3	Hong Kong.com	33,207
4	C&WHKT Broadband Netvigator	28,718
5	C&WHKT Netvigator	28,577
6	House18.com	25,171
7	Propertystreet.net	24,177
8	Tom.com	13,779
9	Ecesay.net	13,716
10	Red-dots.com	13,338
11	e-finance.com.hk	12,802
12	Sunevision.com	12,614
13	Pandaplanet.com	12,456

Table 16, continued

14	Stareastnet	12,248
15	Comicinema.com	12,242
16	Andylau.com	12,183
17	SCMP.com	11,895
18	KGI Asia	11,635
19	Smartone I-Smart	11,418
20	Leonstareastnet.com	11,225
	Top 20 Total	377,203
	Top 20 Total vs Jan-May Total	43%

Source: AC Nielsen AdQuest

6 Market Research Industry in Hong Kong

The market research industry in Hong Kong has shown steady growth over the past few years, and can be expected to do so in the future especially with the increasing interests of foreign investors in the Chinese Mainland market. There are about 45 market research firms in Hong Kong. Of these, about 10 are full service firms that conduct fieldwork and data collection by themselves. The Hong Kong market research industry is dominated by multinational agencies, which comprise about 60-70 % of the total.

Useful Addresses

1. Media-Related Organization

The Association of Accredited Advertising Agents of Hong Kong (4As)
1702 Mcdonald's Building 45-54 Yee Wo Street
Causeway Bay, Hong Kong
Telephone: 852-2882 8151
Fax: 852-2880 5083
E-mail: hk4as@netvigator.com
URL: http://www.aaaa.com.hk

The Broadcasting Authority (Secretariat)
Television and Entertainment Licensing Authority
39/F, Revenue Tower 5, Gloucester Road
Wanchai, Hong Kong
Telephone: 852-2594 5721
Fax: 852-2507 2219
URL: http://www.hkba.org.hk/

2. Newspaper Organizations

Apple Daily
No. 8 Chun Ying St.
TKO Industrial Estate West
Tsueng Kwan O, Hong Kong
Telephone: 852-2990 8388
Fax: 852-2741 0830
URL: http://www.appledaily.com.hk

Oriental Daily News
Oriental Press Center
7 Wang Tai Road
Kowloon Bay, Kowloon, Hong Kong
Telephone: 852-2595 3111
Fax: 825-2898 3783
E-mail: odn@oriental.com.hk
URL: http://www.orientaldaily.com.hk

South China Morning Post
29/F, Dorset House
979 King's Road, Quarry Bay, Hong Kong
Telephone: 852-2565 2222
Fax: 825-2516 7478
URL: http://www.scmp.com

3. Electronic Media Organizations

Asia Television Ltd. (ATV)
Television House
81, Broadcast Drive
Kowloon Tong, Kowloon, Hong Kong
Telephone: 825-2992 8888
Fax: 825-2338 6469

Cable Television, Wharf Cable Ltd.
4/F Wharf Cable Tower
9 Hoi Shing Road
Tsuen Wan, N.T., Hong Kong
Telephone: 852-2112 5541
Fax: 852-2112 7844
URL: http://www.cabletv.com.hk

Television Broadcast Ltd. (TVB)
TV City
Clearwater Bay Road
Sai Kung, N.T., Hong Kong
Telephone: 852-2335 9123
Fax: 852-2358 1300
URL: http://www.tvb.com.hk

Radio Television Hong Kong (RTHK)
Broadcasting House
30 Broadcast Drive
Kowloon Tong, Kowloon, Hong Kong
Telephone: 852-2339 7774
Fax: 852-2794 1137
URL: http://www.rthk.org.hk

Advertising in Hungary

Dr. Szabó D. Tamás, Marketing Department
Budapest University of Economic Sciences and Public Administrations

1   Advertising Infrastructure

Hungary has an emerging economy, producing a gross domestic product (GDP) of 44005 million USD for a population of 10 million. Within the Central European countries, Hungary has quite developed an advertising industry and the total ATL media expenditure raised from 35 million USD (1991) to 794 million USD (2000)[1] which is equal to a share of 1.8% of the Hungarian GDP.

The Hungarian media industry has a wide range of media vehicles including terrestrial, fringe and cable TV, radio, magazines, newspapers, billboards, city lights, cinema and more and more web sites too.

Hungary has quite well developed an advertising industry with sophisticated media research information systems and expenditure monitoring systems too. In Hungary only the ATL media expenditure is measured officially by a monitoring firm. There is no official information for the total advertising industry. The media expenditure is monitored on ratecard basis, all the main advertising media is monitored by the advertising monitoring company. All firms have the opportunity to create competitive media analysis using this advertising monitoring database. The Hungarian advertising scene is rather transparent, each advertiser knows exactly what, how, where and how often its competitors advertise. In the case of TV research, advertisers know as soon as the day after a particular commercial is broadcast how many people watched it and even how they break down socio-demographically.

As in other countries, Hungary has some problems with the advertising, mainly the advertising overflow and regulation systems.

---

[1] 1 US $ = 282,27 HUF as of 2000. Source: Hungarian National Bank

1.1 Advertising Expenditures

Hungary has a highly multiplex offer in terms of advertising media (cf. Table 1) and, because of this, has the ideal conditions for modern market communication aiming both at the mass market and at specific target groups.

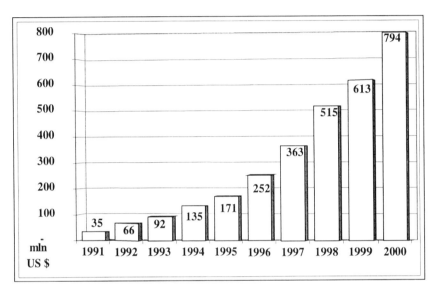

Figure 1: Advertising Media Expenditures in Hungary
Source: MEDIAGNOZIS, 2001

Table 1: Advertising Media Expenditure 1992-2000; in '000 USD

	1992	1993	1994	1995	1996	1997	1998	1999	2000
Terrestrial TV	27,992	41,889	58,655	66,580	89,008	121,510	196,150	277,563	443,124
Fringe Cable TV	0	0	0	0	14,569	54,638	89,348	58,182	15,235
Dailies	22,710	27,406	33,238	43,774	62,766	79,182	90,161	103,627	116,676
Magazines	13,974	17,891	24,842	33,011	39,491	53,943	75,385	93,149	112,078
Radio	0	0	10,557	14,810	22,355	24,768	26,926	36,358	42,587
Outdoor	1,504	4,605	7,175	11,696	21,745	26,214	34,408	39,979	58,991
Cinema	104	133	359	432	988	1,822	1,620	2,914	3,806

Source: MEDIAGNOZIS, 2001

TV has the dominant share of 59% (cf. Figure 2), and the most dominant are the two commercial terrestrial TV channels launched in 1997. The second largest media is the print media with share of 29%. There are some thousands of publications in the country that are used for advertising, but the most dominants are not more than six hundreds.

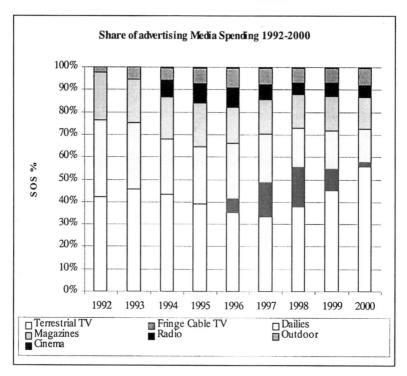

Figure 2: Share of Advertising Media Expenditure 1992-2000
Source: MEDIAGNOZIS, 2001

TV as the main national medium is in the first position with a share of 59% or 458 million $ of the total media expenditure (cf. Table 1). Its development is highly dynamic, and its advertising turnover grown rapidly after the launch of two terrestrial private TV station, TV2, and RTL Klub. During the last 5 years more and more TV stations, Radios, and magazines appeared, the number of national and rural newspapers was not increased. Cinema and outdoor advertising could not increase their share of the media expenditure during this period.

The list of top advertising media in the year 2000 was lead by the private commercial TV stations followed by the main public TV channels, the main nationwide daily newspapers and the largest outdoor operators.

Table 2: Top Advertising Media 1998 (on rate card price)

		Gross advertising media income 2000 (000 US $)
1	TV2 /MTM-SBS	240,479
2	RTL-KLUB	169,552
3	MTV 1	33,241
4	NÉPSZABADSÁG	21,623
5	MULTIREKLÁM	16,470
6	DANUBIUS RÁDIÓ	15,579
7	HVG VILÁGGAZDASÁG	15,041
8	EUROPLAKÁT	10,780
9	NŐK LAPJA	8,961
10	SLÁGER RÁDIÓ	8,753
11	PESTI EST	7,798
12	NAP KELTE - ATV	7,458
13	MAGYAR HÍRLAP	7,007
14	JUVENTUS RÁDIÓ	6,958
15	OUTDOOR	6,591
16	METRO	5,936
17	AKZENT MEDIA	5,716
18	INTERMEDIA	5,627
19	MAI NAP	5,618
20	MAGYAR NEMZET	5,538

Source: MEDIAGNOZIS, 2001

Table 3: Top Advertisers 2000

	Advertiser	Gross advertising media income 2000 (000 US $)
1	UNILEVER MAGYARORSZÁG KFT.	32,420
2	HENKEL BUDAPEST KFT.	24,311
3	PROCTER & GAMBLE KFT.	24,022
4	PANNON GSM	19,632
5	WESTEL 900 RT.	17,570
6	NESTLÉ HUNGÁRIA KFT.	13,828
7	L'OREAL	13,754
8	COCA-COLA MAGYARORSZÁG	12,901
9	BORSODI SÖRGYÁR RT.	9,595
10	BENCKISER KFT.	9,084
11	MASTER FOODS HUNGARY	9,028
12	BEIERSDORF KFT.	8,880
13	MAGYAR DANONE KFT.	8,370

Table 3, continued

14	DREHER SÖRGYÁRAK RT.	8,315
15	KRAFT JACOBS SUCHARD	7,717
16	BRAU UNION HUNGÁRIA KFT.	7,475
17	FERRERO	7,197
18	WRIGLEY HUNGARIA KFT.	7,024
19	SZERENCSEJÁTÉK RT.	7,004
20	MAGYAR TÁVKÖZLÉSI RT.	7,000

Source: MEDIAGNOZIS, 2001

Table 4: Top Advertising Branches of Business, 2000

	Sector	Gross advertising media expenditure 2000 (000 US $)
1	FOOD	106,843
2	BEAUTY CARE	87,174
3	COMPUTERS, OFFICE TECHNOLOGY, TELE	80,796
4	DRINKS	67,330
5	HOUSEHOLD GOODS	54,229
6	PUBLISHING, MASS MEDIA	50,843
7	TRANSPORT VEHICLES	50,327
8	LEISURE, ENTERTAINMENT	42,614
9	BANKING, INSURANCE COMPANIES	42,071
10	MEDICINAL PRODUCTS	41,496
11	SERVICES	39,811
12	TRADE	28,964
13	CLASSIFIED	15,659
14	FURNITURE AND FURNICHINGS	13,487
15	TRAVELLING, TOURISM	13,148
16	TOBACCO AND SMOKING ITEMS	10,733
17	ENERGY, FUELS	8,450
18	HOUSEHOLD APPLIANCES	7,729
19	CLOTHES AND ACCESSORIES	5,522
20	CONSTRUCTION	5,145
21	EDUCATION, TRAINING	4,955
22	COMPANY REPORTING	3,075
23	REAL ESTATE	2,531
24	AGRICULTURE	2,513
25	PACKAGING INDUSTRY	1,713

Source: MEDIAGNOZIS, 2001

Unilever, Henkel, Procter &Gamble, Pannon GSM (mobile) and Westel 900 (mobile), are the main advertisers in Hungary (cf. Table 3). Tables 4 and 5 show the top advertised products and branches of business.

Table 5: Top Advertised Brands

	Brand	Gross advertising media expenditure 2000 (000 US $)
1	PANNON PRAKTIKUM TELECOMMUN.	6,231
2	PANNON GSM PROM. TELECOMMUN.	5,447
3	PRIVAT LOAN	3,504
4	BORSODI BEER	3,351
5	AMSTEL BEER	3,268
6	DOMINO PROM. TELECOMMUN.	3,147
7	WESTEL 900 TELECOMMUN. IMAGE	2,967
8	COCA-COLA CRB.S.DRNK.	2,913
9	WESTEL 900 PROM. TELECOMMUN. PRODUCT	2,858
10	ISDN TELECOMMUN.	2,552
11	STELLA ARTOIS BEER	2,493
12	PERSIL GREEN POWER W.PW.LQ.	2,472
13	CENTRUM VITAMIN	2,462
14	TOMI KRISTÁLY W.PW.LQ.	2,427
15	PANNON GSM TELECOMMUN.	2,389
16	FANTA CRB.S.DRNK.	2,381
17	TESCO HYPERM.	2,357
18	MOMENTUM PROM. TELECOMMUN.	2,348
19	HEINEKEN BEER	2,280
20	ORBIT CH.GUM	2,237

Source: MEDIAGNOZIS, 2001

1.2   Institutions of the Hungarian Advertising Industry

The Hungarian advertising industry is well organized. Most of the main advertisers, agencies and media are members of the **Hungarian Advertising Association** [*Magyar Reklámszövetség*, (MRSZ)]. The top agencies formed the **Association of Hungarian Communication Agencies** [*Magyar Kommunikációs Ügynökségek Szövetsége*, (MARS)]. In the late '90s, the industry formed, its selfregulation association, **Advertising Expert's Professional Tool** [*Önszabályozó Reklám Testület* (ÖRT)], that helps the everyday operation of the advertising industry.

The **Audit Bureau of Circulations** [*Magyar Terjesztés Ellenőrzési Szövetség* (MATESZ)]] is a neutral institution for self-regulation of advertising media. It has more than 80 members, made up of advertisers, media and advertising agencies. The objective of the MATESZ is to prepare and provide comparable circulation of advertising media - both print and on-line -, in order to support fair and objective competition. The MATESZ audits the distribution of daily and weekly newspapers, consumer magazines, business publications, advertising papers, business directories and manuals and websites.

Each publisher member prepares and submits a quarterly report to the MATESZ. This report contains the average circulation per issue for the past quarter referred to the separate circulation terms. The MATESZ issues quarterly "Circulation Reports," (see: www.matesz.hu) each appearing as a bound volume. This report provides information on press runs, paid subscriptions, single copy sales, total paid, returns, free distribution and total distribution.

1.3   Information Services in Hungarian Media Planning

Basically media research has two principal goals: a contact survey and the description of target groups. On the one hand, media research attempts to survey how many people had what number of contacts with an advertising medium within a certain period of time. On the other hand, it attempts to describe these people with reference to certain socio-demographic and psychographic criteria.

The relevant sources of information for media planning can be classified as follows:
- Advertising expenditures
- Structure of media users

1.   Advertising Expenditures

In Hungary there is only one source of information on advertising expenditures. MEDIAGNOZIS reports gross data obtained from its observations of print, radio and TV advertisements, and self report from outdoor companies. Advertisements in these media are recorded and extrapolated on the basis of actual rate card price lists. This company publishes monthly reports in database format.

2. Structure of Media Users

Concerning the investigation of media users respectively the reach of media there are some main sources of information available: the National Media Analysis and the AGB Hungary People Meter.

The **National Media Analysis** (NMA) is conducted by the Szonda Ipsos and GFK Hungary, as a syndicate research.

The purpose of the NMA is to gather and supply data for media audience measurement. The population covered by the NMA is made up of Hungarian population aged 14 and over and living in private households in Hungary. Sample size is approximately 24,000 interviews for print media and 12,000 self filled questioner for radio.

The question of who watches what and when on TV is answered by the **AGB Hungary Panel**. This panel consists of a representative sample of all private Hungarian households with at least one TV set. Sample size is 840 households, accounting for approximately 2 400 people.

In order to record viewing habits, a so-called **AGB meter** is connected to all TV sets in the recruited households. Each person in the households registers when he or she is watching TV by pushing the appropriate person-button on the remote control of the AGB meter. The data thus collected contain information on

➢ How many households/people are watching TV
➢ What socio-demographic groups are watching TV
➢ What program(s) is/are being viewed
➢ How long each viewing session lasts

These data are referred to as "reach" or "rating."

TV Audience Measurements[2] are based on a "panel" (sample) which reports continuous watching behavior during a long time period. Behavior of such panel is considered as the typical behavior of the "region" which this panel represents. For this reason, panel selection is the most important phase of the research. For creating the panel, a research company (selected by way of a tender) initially carries out the database research with the questionnaire method. The demographic picture of the region to be measured is identified through the Establishment Survey. This picture gives information about sex, age, education, occupation and family size of the people living in that region. In its selection, AGB Hungary ensures that the sample families whose

---

[2] Source: AGB Hungary, www.agb.hu

viewing behaviors shall be measured, reflect this picture. If, for example, 20 percent of the population of a certain city is constituted of females, are above the 20 age-group, are housewives and primary school graduates, the sample family members with these features will also be 20 percent. Those families who accept to work with AGB Hungary and match the structure of the panel to be created, are selected from among those who have been included in the Establishment Survey. 20 percent of families working with AGB are replaced every year. One reason for this replacement arises out of natural causes (moving of the family to another area, leaving the panel by own will, etc.) and the other reason is the completion of cooperation with AGB, starting with the first families included in the panel. Thus, a single family remains in the AGB Hungary panel at a maximum for three years and during the fourth year this family is replaced with another family of the same features. Families in the panel are presented with a gift (from AGB catalogue) every year. These small gifts are not in the nature of influencing the television viewing behavior of families.

3. **Media Databases and Directories**

There are online and offline media databases that contain the most important Hungarian advertising media. The traditional media directory is published three times a year, called MÉDIA ÁSZ. From 2000 there is an online advertising media service that contains media prices, news and other important information too, the site can be found at www.mediainfo.hu

2   The Hungarian TV Market

Since the early 1997s, private broadcasters have dominated the advertising market (cf. Figure 3), while the public stations have taken the leading positions in the viewer market shares (cf. Figure 4).

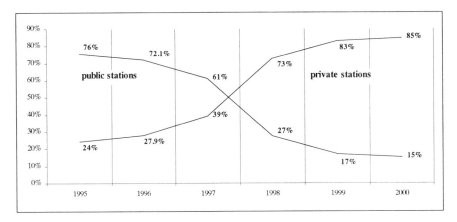

Figure 3: Development of Share of Viewing, Hungarian TV
Source: AGB Hungary, 1995-2000

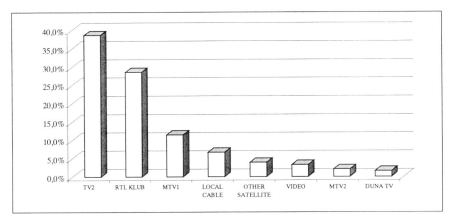

Figure 4: Viewer Market Shares in Hungarian TV
Source: AGB Hungary 2000

3   The Hungarian Press Market

From 1990 the Hungarian press market changed dramatically. The number
of publications increased more than ten times within ten years. The most
significant changes were made in the magazine market. By 2000 most of
the international magazines has been published in Hungarian. 1997-1998
were the years of woman magazines, 1999-2000 were the years of male
life style magazines, when its magazine market changed a lot.

3.1   Newspapers

Newspapers are one of the most important advertising media in Hungary. They are classified into daily and weekly and into regional and nationwide newspapers. Metro is the most popular daily newspaper (it turned to nationwide in the first half of 2001), followed by the largest traditional nationwide daily paper, Népszabadság. On the third place is Vgasárnap Reggel, which is a weekend newspaper as a nationwide publication of regional (county) newspapers. Regional daily newspapers are an advertising medium used mainly by local and regional advertisers.

Table 6: Important Daily and Weekly Newspapers Q4, Y2000

		Circulation (000)
Metro	Daily	219.6
Népszabadság	Daily	204.9
Vasárnap Reggel	Weekly	126.5
Blikk	Daily	115.5
Nemzeti Sport	Daily	90.2
Mai Nap	Daily	86.9
Kisalföld	Daily	82.6

Source: MATESZ 2001

3.2   Consumer Magazines

Although consumer magazines principally address the total population, a classification is made with regard to the textual focus:

1. **Radio and TV program magazines** (RTV) address the total population with a range of topics of general interest. (*TVR-Hét; Színes RTV*). RTV magazines have high circulation figures and high reaches, so that the readership is structured similarly to the population.
2. **Family and Women magazines** generally reach the audience in a valuable condition of reading,
   - Women magazines (*Kiskegyed, Story, Nőklapja*)
   - Family magazines (*Reader's Digest*)
   Although family and women magazines have a comparably low circulation, they do have a high reach within the respective target groups.

3. **Special interest magazines** are characterized by a single editorial focus and by low circulation figures and low reach, but distinct focuses within their own readership.
   - Housing and living (*Lakáskultúra, Otthon*)
   - Lifestyle magazines (*Max, Playboy*)
   - Motor press (*Auto2, Autó Motor*)

Table 7: Hungarian Consumer Magazines 2000

	Circulation (000)
Radio and TV magazines	
TVR-Hét	432.6
Színes RTV	384.6
RTV program magazines	123.5
HVG	117.7
Family and Women magazines	
Story	396.6
Nők Lapja	350.9
Kiskegyed	268.4
Tina Extra	179.6
Special interest magazines	
Házi Praktika	103.0
Lakáskultúra	73.4
Otthon	67.1
Gyöngy	55.1

Source: MATESZ 2001

References

AGB Hungary: Telemonitor, Budapest, 2000
MATESZ, www.matesz.hu
MEDIAGNOZIS: Advertsing media expenditure riports 1992-2000
Szabo, D. T.: Médiatervezés a reklámban, AULA, Budapest, 2000
www.agb.hu

Useful Addresses:

- MEDIAGNOZIS
  H-1054, Budapest, Alkotmány u. 10
  Tel.: +36 1 302 4282

- Szonda Ipsos
  1096 Budapest, Thaly Kálmán utca 39
  Tel.: +36 1 476 7600,
  Internet: http://www.szondaipsos.hu

- AGB Hungary
  1146 Budapest, Hermina út 57/59
  Tel.: +36 1 461 7050,
  Internet: http://www.agb.hu

- GFK Hungaria
  1146 Budapest, Hermina út 57/59
  Tel.: +36 1 461 7050,
  Internet: http://www.agb.hu

- Magyar Reklámszövetség (Hungarian Advertising Association)
  1074 Budapest, Dob utca 45
  Tel.: +36 1 322 0640; Fax: +36 1 322 7841,
  Internet: http://www.mrsz.hu

- Association of Hungarian Advertising Agencies (MARS):
  1062 Budapest, Bajza utca 31
  Tel.: +36 1 342-4929, Fax: +36 1 322-1024
  Internet: http://www.mars.hu

- Advertising Expert's Professional Tool (ÖRT)
  1132 Budapest, Borbély u. 5-7.
  Tel.: +36 1 349-2717, Fax: +36 1 239-9866
  Internet: http://www.ort.hu

- Kreatív (professional advertising magazine)
  1037 Budapest, Bojtár u. 64-66
  Tel.: +36 1 4366-123, Fax: +36 1 4366-135
  Internet: http://www.kreativ.hu

- Mediainfo.hu -Media Information Service
  (professional ATL advertising media database and online magazine)
  1146 Budapest, Stefánia út 16
  Tel.: +36 1 468-2333, Fax: +36 1 220-8353
  Internet: http://www.mediainfo.hu

Advertising in Ireland

Prof. Dr. Tony Meenaghan, Department of Marketing
Graduate School of Business, University College Dublin

1   Introduction

The Republic of Ireland represents one of the smaller economies of the European Union, of which it has been a member since 1973. This is indicated by its population of just 3.75 million and a territory size of 70,300 square kilometers. The Republic of Ireland is a particularly open economy being hugely dependent on external trade as the basis for its economic prosperity. Some two-thirds of its exports are to other economies within the EU.

Recent years have seen major economic prosperity in the Irish economy. Government economic policy initiatives based on low inflation, wage moderation and prudent budgetary policy combined with Ireland's access to the vast European market, have resulted in a dramatic turnaround in Ireland's economic performance. High annual growth rates have made the Republic of Ireland the fastest growing economy in the industrialized world, earning the label the 'Celtic Tiger'. This economic prosperity has in turn led to a buoyant advertising market with total advertising expenditure increasing 36% between 1999 and 2000 (IAPI Adspend 2000).

The year 2001 has seen some evidence of a slow-down in the Irish economy, a consequence of changes in the information technology/ telecommunications sector and indeed a down-turn in the US economy on which Ireland is dependant. This has been particularly reflected in advertising for categories such as property and recruitment as well as the IT and Telecommunications sector.

Advertising expenditure in the Republic of Ireland as a percentage of GDP was .95% in 1990, however this declined to .83% in 1999 before recovering to 1% in 2000 (WARC 2001). In terms of per capita advertising expenditure (including classified/display advertising) the Republic of Ireland increased from $116.4 in 1990 to $206.5 in 1999 and $250.2 in 2000 (WARC 2001).

2   Analysis of Advertising Expenditure

Total advertising expenditure for the Republic of Ireland (ROI) was £611.2m in 2000. (IAPI - Adspend 2001). The full breakdown by media is shown in Table 1. Total press (including national and regional newspapers as well as magazines) accounted for 57% of total advertising expenditure. Television which accounted for 26% of expenditure in 2000 represented the second most important advertising medium.

Table 1: Profile of Media Expenditure - Jan - Dec 2000 (in IR£s)

Medium	Expenditure Jan - Dec 2000 (IR£m)	Profile %
PRESS	351.1	57
TELEVISION	157.2	26
RADIO	43.3	7
OUTDOOR	54.8	9
CINEMA	4.81	1
TOTAL	**611.2**	**100**

Note: These figures do not include classified/display advertising.
Exchange Rate: IR£1 = €1.27, IR£1 = $1.17
Source: IAPI Adspend 2001

Table 2: Adspend in Local Currency at Current Prices (Million IR£)

Year	Total	Press		Magazines		TV		Radio		Cinema		Outdoor	
1990	175	82	47%	12	7%	50	29%	20	11%	n/a		13	7%
1991	180	83	46%	12	7%	55	31%	20	11%	1	1%	12	7%
1992	198	92	46%	12	6%	63	32%	21	11%	1	1%	12	6%
1993	214	97	45%	13	6%	70	33%	23	11%	1	0%	13	6%
1994	225	96	43%	15	7%	77	34%	24	11%	2	1%	14	6%
1995	259	117	45%	16	6%	85	33%	26	10%	2	1%	16	6%
1996	284	121	43%	15	5%	92	32%	28	10%	3	1%	19	7%
1997	324	157	48%	14	4%	99	31%	29	9%	3	1%	24	7%
1998	356	169	47%	11	3%	110	31%	34	10%	4	1%	30	8%
1999	410	190	46%	9	2%	132	32%	38	9%	4	1%	38	9%
2000	554	288	52%	13	2%	152	27%	43	8%	5	1%	55	10%

Note: The figures quoted in Table 2 do not include classified/display advertising. The total for 2000 differs from Table 1 as WARC data, although based on IAPI estimates, have been subject to discounting by WARC.
Source: World Advertising Research Center (WARC), 2001

Table 2 shows the profile of advertising media used in the Republic of Ireland over the period 1990-2000. As expected there are no hugely dramatic changes in market share by media. However it is noteworthy that Press advertising increased from 43% in 1994 to 52% in 2000. This strong performance can in part be attributed to the recruitment and property sectors as well as general economic climate. However it would be incorrect to interpret the strong performance of Press advertising as meaning that other media sectors are in decline. This point is underlined by the fact that while Television advertising fell from a high of 34% in 1994 to 27% of total advertising expenditure in 2000, Television advertising revenues increased three-fold over the period 1990-2000.

3   The Irish Media Market

Despite its relatively small scale, the Republic of Ireland is nonetheless a vibrant media market. As is the case in other markets, technological changes have been a major influence on media developments. The issue of 'overspill' media, principally from its nearest neighbor, the United Kingdom has also had a profound effect on the Irish media market. While this chapter focuses on the Republic of Ireland market, it is increasingly common for advertisers and agencies to plan advertising campaigns on an All-Ireland basis which includes both the Republic of Ireland and Northern Ireland. Media inflation is also a significant feature of the Irish advertising landscape, with such inflation varying considerably by medium. Media inflation on RTE Television increased 91% between 1994 and 2000 against a consumer price index increase of 21% for the period. Similarly media costs on RTE radio increased 59% and on Sunday newspapers by 35% over the period (MCM Communications 2001). Production costs for advertising are also significantly higher in the Irish market than elsewhere due to several factors including the high costs of labor, the scale of the market and the high production values demanded. Each of the major sectors of media in Ireland is now examined in turn.

3.1   Press

The press sector can be sub-divided into two distinct sub-categories, the indigenous Irish owned press sector (represented by the National Newspapers of Ireland, NNI) and overspill press (largely from the UK).

Table 3 below indicates the readership of the Irish national newspaper titles. (Note newspapers of UK origin and non-NNI members are not covered by this source.) Particularly noteworthy is the share of market held by Independent Newspapers Group which is estimated to now own 65% of the Irish newspaper market, including nationals and regional press (Media Week 2001). National titles owned by the Independent News and Media Group include the *Irish Independent*, the *Evening Herald*, the *Sunday Independent* and the *Sunday World*. This group is also a significant shareholder in *The Star* and *The Sunday Tribune*.

Table 3: Readership of National Newspapers

	2000
Morning Titles	
Irish Independent	644 (22%)
Irish Times	311 (11%)
Examiner	238 (8%)
Star	443 (15%)
Any Morning Title	1455 (49%)
Evening Titles	
Evening Herald	357 (12%)
Evening Echo	87 (3%)
Any Evening Title	444 (15%)
Any Daily Title	1718 (58%)
Sunday Titles	
Sunday Independent	1085 (37%)
Sunday Tribune	258 (9%)
Sunday World	981 (33%)
Sunday Business Post	156 (5%)
Any Sunday Title	2018 (68%)
Irish Farmers Journal	267 (9%)
Any NNI	2392 (81%)

Based on readership by any adult
Source: Lansdowne Market Research/JNRR Survey 2001

Given that the United Kingdom represents Ireland's nearest neighbor and that both countries share a common language the Republic of Ireland is an obvious market for overspill in the case of all media originating from the UK. This is particularly obvious in the Press sector. For example Table 4 shows that UK Newspaper imports account for 32% of the total Sunday newspaper market.

Table 4: Origin of Republic of Ireland Newspapers – Sunday – 2000

	Irish	UK	Total
*Tabloid	308,786	268,762	577,548
**Mid-Market	67,101	15,746	82,847
***Quality	455,192	107,195	562,387
Total	831,079	391,703	1,222,782
	67.97%	32.03%	

Read: *Tabloid   - Irish - Sunday World
                      - UK - Sunday Mirror
      **Mid-Market - Irish - Ireland on Sunday
                      - UK - Mail on Sunday
      ***Quality   - Irish - Sunday Tribune
                      - UK - Sunday Times

Source: National Newspapers of Ireland 2001

This overspill phenomenon is represented in all sectors of the Sunday newspaper market. In the tabloid end of market UK imports account for 46% of the total market but the penetration of UK titles in the quality segment of the Sunday newspaper market is only 19%. Important factors influencing the penetration of UK Press titles have been lower cover prices (particularly in the tabloid sector) and a trend toward special Irish editions of UK titles, an obvious example in this regard is the *Sunday Times* which now sells 85,000 copies of its Irish edition in the Irish Republic. Moreover, the overspill phenomenon is also apparent in other sub-sectors of the press, namely daily newspapers and magazines.

Table 5 shows the top twenty advertisers by category in press for the year 2000. While the top 4 categories of advertiser, Appointments, Small Advertisements, Personal/Special notices and Government Departments are traditionally heavy users of Press advertising, it is noteworthy that 6 Property/Auctioneering companies appear in the Top 20 advertisers, a fact which underlines the strength of that sector which has itself been fuelled by a strong national economic performance, though now immediately vulnerable to economic down-turn.

Table 5: Press - Top Advertisers/Categories - Jan - Dec 2000

1	Appointments	£49,851,410
2	Small Advertisements	£49,678,640
3	Personal / Special Notices	£22,361,060
4	Government Depts. (R.O.I)	£9,474,260
5	Sherry Fitzgerald	£8,419,990

Table 5, continued

6	Eircom (Telecom Eireann)	£6,937,620
7	Hamilton Osborne King	£5,003,460
8	Misc. Concerts	£4,197,370
9	Gunne Auctioneers	£3,989,170
10	Electricity Supply Board	£3,156,370
11	Esat Digifone	£2,637,990
12	D.I.D.	£2,580,670
13	Ross McParland	£2,466,970
14	Lisney Auctioneers	£2,328,770
15	Power City	£2,157,600
16	Currys	£2,051,960
17	Dixons	£1,955,840
18	Douglas Newman Good Auctioneers	£1,782,980
19	Dunnes Stores	£1,782,350
20	Compustore	£1,728,280

Source: IAPI Ad-Spend

3.2 Magazines

The magazine market in the Republic of Ireland is relatively small though highly competitive. This sector has seen its share of total advertising revenue decline from 7% to 2% between 1990 and 2000 (Table 2). The overspill phenomenon indicated in the newspaper market is particularly evident in the magazine market and indigenous Irish magazine titles complete with strong magazine brands (mainly of UK origin) in the various sub-segments of the magazine market such as Celebrity (*Hello, OK*), Fashion, Home and Garden, Food and Drink, etc. Unlike their newspaper counterparts UK magazine titles have not to date published 'Irish' editions for the Irish market, however special Irish editions of *Hello* and *Sky* are expected in Autumn 2001.

It is estimated that 160 different magazine titles are available in the Irish market, with almost all of these in the consumer magazine sector as opposed to the business-to-business sector. A vibrant Irish economy has led to the introduction of many new magazine titles in all sectors of the magazine market in recent years.

On average advertising revenue accounts for 27% of title revenues with copy sales contributing 73% of total income. Distribution is largely by retail sales (95%) with magazine subscriptions only accounting for 5% of distribution (FIPP/Zenith Worldwide Magazine Trends 2001/2002).

Table 6 below shows the Top 10 magazine advertisers while the Top 10 advertiser categories are shown in Table 7.

Table 6: Top Ten Magazine Advertisers (2000)

Advertiser
L'Oreal
Laboratoires Garnier
Phonovation
Kellogg's
Eircom
Lancome
Government
Ivenus
Icommerce
Esat

Source: IAPI 2001

Table 7: Top Ten Magazine Advertising Categories (2000)

Category
Personal Hygiene
Industry
Food
Unclassified
Theatre
Retail
Tourism
Drinks
Finance
Clothing

Source: IAPI 2001

3.3   Television

Television advertising accounts for 26% of total advertising revenue in the Republic of Ireland with expenditure increasing three-fold between 1990 and 2000. The television market in Ireland has been affected both by the emergence of new domestic channels, namely TV3 and TG4 and overspill from channels broadcasting from the UK, namely ITV, Channel 4 and Sky

Television. BBC channels which are also available in the Republic of Ireland are not commercial channels. RTE which is the dual funded state broadcaster, (i.e. license fee and advertising revenue) has traditionally dominated the Irish television market with three separate channels, namely RTE 1, Network 2 and TG4. This dominance is increasingly challenged and Table 8 below indicates the relative penetration of the different television channels now available in the Republic of Ireland market. For example the information in Table 8 shows that RTE control some 48% of total peak time daily viewing throughout the three channels of RTE (35.5%) Network 2 (10.7%) and TG4 (2.7%)

Table 8: Television Station Penetration – Republic of Ireland

ADULTS 15+ 01/01/01-17/06/01		RTE1	Net-work 2	TG4	TV3	UTV	Chan-nel 4	Sky One	Sky News	BBC 1	BBC 2	All Other	Total TV
Mon-Sun	Av TVR	3.9	1.5	0.3	1.7	1.4	0.7	0.3	0.2	1.1	0.6	1.2	12.9
0300-	Index	113	86	106	107	109	110	90	95	110	107	86	103
2359	000s	113	42	9	48	40	20	10	7	33	16	35	373
All Day	Share	30.3	11.3	2.3	12.9	10.6	5.5	2.6	1.8	8.8	4.3	9.5	100
	Av Mins	394	147	30	168	138	71	34	23	115	57	124	1301
		RTE1	Net-work 2	TG4	TV3	UTV	Chan-nel 4	Sky One	Sky News	BBC 1	BBC 2	All Other	otal TV
Mon-Sun	Av TVR	12	3.6	0.8	4.2	4.1	1.6	0.9	0.4	2.6	1.2	2.4	33.9
1800-	Index	113	97	111	106	111	111	91	91	111	110	96	107
2329	000s	348	105	22	123	118	46	26	12	75	36	70	980
Peak-Time	Share	35.5	10.7	2.2	12.5	12.1	4.7	2.6	1.3	7.6	3.7	7.1	100
	Av Mins	278	84	18	98	95	37	20	10	60	29	56	784

Source: RTE 2001

TV3 which was originally formed as an Irish owned station funded solely by advertising revenue is now largely owned by Canadian media group CanWest Global Communications and the UK group, Granada. This latter linkage has resulted in a flow of strong programming which has considerably boosted market share. UTV (the Northern Ireland based ITV operator) is increasingly focused on an all-Ireland basis and is now available in 67% of Republic of Ireland homes. Sky Television now sells specific Republic of Ireland advertising on its services.

It is currently estimated that 50% of Irish households have cable subscriptions, mainly with cable supplier NTL. Cable subscription provides access to an increasing array of foreign channels leading of greater competition between broadcasters and facilitating increased levels of available commercial airtime.

While all television networks have benefited from a buoyant Irish economy the slow-down in the Irish economy will pose serious challenges for all television broadcasters in the ROI market. Table 9 shows the Top 20 advertisers on RTE Television for the year 2000.

Table 9: RTE Television Top Advertisers (Client Group) Jan – Dec 2000

1	Unilever
2	Eircom
3	Masterfoods Ltd
4	BT ESAT Group
5	C&C Group
6	Procter & Gamble
7	Cadbury Ireland Plc
8	L'Oreal Ltd
9	Kellogg Co. of Ireland
10	Irish Biscuits Ltd
11	National Lottery
12	Nestle Ireland Ltd
13	Musgrave Ltd
14	Beecham of Ireland Ltd
16	Reckitt & Coleman
17	Kraft Jacob Sucard
18	National Dairy Council
19	Smiyh & Nephew Ltd
20	CPC Ireland Ltd

Source: RTE 2001

3.4   Radio

Radio in Ireland is responsible for 7% of total media spend (see Table 1) however while radio advertising revenue in the sector has doubled between 1990 and 2000, its share of the total advertising market has been in decline in recent years. As a medium radio has been little affected by the overspill phenomenon which affects other media e.g. television, press, however this is expected to change albeit slowly with the availability of digitalized streaming. Radio costs in Ireland are relatively cheap at a cost per thousand of $2.72 which compares favorably with countries such as Spain and Denmark with radio cpt rates of $5.26 and $4.62 respectively (Carat International 2001).

The radio stations attached to the national broadcaster RTE, namely Radio One, 2FM and more recently Lyric FM dominate the radio market however the advent of national radio competitors such as Today FM and particularly a network of local radio stations have served to reduce the dominance of RTE radio stations. The emergence of a number of strong Sales Houses representing the independent radio sector has seen local radio become a significant option for national advertisers. As can be seen from Table 10 the recently established Today FM now holds 15% of the national weekday audience while the major RTE radio station Radio One has lost 5% market share over the period 1995-2000 according to the most recently available radio JNLR estimates. Of particular note is the scale of listenership for local radio.

Table 10: Radio – National Weekday Listenership

	1995	2000
Radio 1	35%	30%
2 FM	29%	29%
Lyric FM	-	3%
Today FM	-	15%
Any Local	51%	55%

Source: Carat/JNLR 2001

Table 11 shows the top 20 Radio Advertisers for RTE for the year 2000.

Table 11: RTE Radio Top Advertisers (Client Group) Jan - Dec 2000

1	Eircom	11	MBNA Ireland
2	BT ESAT Group	12	Brennans Bakery Dublin Ltd
3	Bank of Ireland	13	C3 - Imagine
4	Unilever	14	Automobile Association
5	National Lottery	15	Irish Times Ltd
6	Allied Irish Banks	16	RTE Guide
7	Independent Newspapers	17	Ryans Tourist Group
8	C&C Group	18	Hyundai Cars
9	Motor Distributors	19	Knorr Best Foods
10	E.B.S.	20	Golden Pages

Source RTE 2001

3.5   Outdoor

As indicated in Table 1 outdoor advertising currently accounts for 9% of total media expenditure in Ireland and this sector has witnessed an increase in its share of market in recent times. Site saturation and strict environmental controls limit capacity with media owners upgrading the quality of sites in order to maintain competitiveness with other media. Carat International estimate the cost per "large" site (adjusted for common size) at $82.59 for outdoor advertising in Ireland. Similarly costs for outdoor advertising are estimated as follows: Italy $40.41, France $47.33, UK $63.58, and Netherlands $55.99 making Ireland relatively expensive for outdoor advertising.

Significant changes to outdoor advertising include a decline in large billboards, the emergence of both electronic sites and ambient media as well as the growth of smaller sized outdoor sites and 'street furniture' opportunities.

Table 12 shows the top 10 advertisers for outdoor advertising for the year 2000.

Table 12: Outdoor Top Advertisers Jan - Dec 2000

1	Eircom / Eircell	£3.9m
2	Guinness Ireland Group	£2.1m
3	Showerings	£1.7m
4	Edward Dillon	£1.4m
5	Murphy Breweries	£1.4m
6	Nestle	£1.3m
7	UDV	£1.2m
8	Pepsi	£1.0m
9	Irish Distillers	£0.9m
10	McDonalds	£0.8m

Source: O.M.A. 2001

3.6   Cinema

The Republic of Ireland has the highest proportionate cinema going population in Europe with attendances increasing from 7.5m admissions in 1990 to 14.9m in 2000. This considerable growth has been driven by a doubling of numbers of cinema screens over the period 1990-2000 and the changing demographic structure of the population which has a considerable proportion of its population in the youth category who are heavy cinema users. Cinema screen growth is set to continue, but overall cinema revenue is expected to come under some pressure from home entertainment opportunities driven by technological convergence.

Table 13 shows the top 20 brands of cinema advertising for the year 2000.

Table 13: Top Brands in Cinema Advertising 2000

1	Guinness	11	Pantene
2	Bulmers	12	Eircell Emerge
3	Eircom	13	Coors Light
4	Budweiser	14	Tia Maria
5	Eircell	15	Feria
6	Nike	16	Esat Digiphone Online
7	Tayto Crisps	17	Maltesers
8	Red Bull	18	Siemens M35
9	Eircell Wap	19	Aero
10	Cadbury Masterbrand	20	Ritz

Source: Carlton Screen Advertising

3.7   Internet

While significant re-evaluation of the Internet is taking place following the dot.com collapse of 2000/01, the position of the Internet as a communications medium in Ireland is that penetration and usage is considerably behind the USA and is perhaps average for Europe. Figure 1 below indicates the trend in Internet penetration in Ireland. Currently it is estimated that some 30% of Irish adults are on-line.

Nielsen net ratings suggest that in 2000 Internet penetration in Ireland was 27% compared to 19% in Germany, 28% in Holland with Norway and Sweden having penetration levels greater than 40%. Nua Internet Surveys suggest that Internet penetration in 2000 was 46% in the USA and 36% in Australia. In terms of the location of usage it is suggested that home users as a percentage of all users is 53% in Ireland as against 72% in the UK and 96% in the USA. Irish consumers are reasonably active in terms of eCommerce activity, with some 50% of Irish on-line purchases taking place with suppliers outside the Irish market. (Amarach Consumer Trendwatch 2001)

In line with international experiences Irish on-line users have reduced their usage of other media, particularly television in order to spend time on-line. (Irish Internet Association www.iia.ie). In common with the expe-

rience in other economies, Internet usage is concentrated among the com-
puter-related, educational, professional and managerial occupations with
low rates of usage among the less privileged.

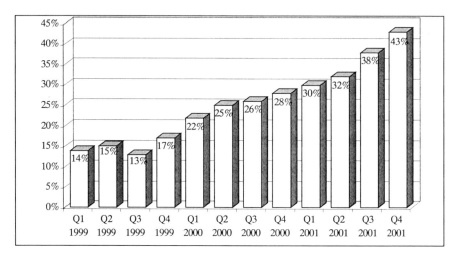

Figure 1: Internet Penetration in Ireland (ROI)
Source: Amárach Consumer Trend/Watch and Amárach Forecast

4 Analysis of Advertisers

Table 14 outlines total advertising expenditure in the Republic of Ireland
by product group. As can be seen the product group retail outlets accounted for £56.5m or 9.2% of total advertising expenditure.

Table 15 outlines the Top 30 Advertisers in the Republic of Ireland for
the year 2000. The top four advertisers – Appointments, Small Advertisements, Personal/Special Notices and Government Departments, while col-
lated under this heading do not properly constitute brands in the traditional
marketing sense. Eircom (the recently privatized telecommunication company, Telecom Eireann) alone accounted for £18m expenditure (or some
3% of total). Much of this expenditure can be linked to the corporate re-
branding of that recently privatized entity. While FMCG companies such
as Kelloggs and Cadburys, and Drinks companies, (both alcohol – e.g.
Guinness, Gilbeys etc. and non-alcoholic e.g. Coca Cola) are traditionally
major advertisers, as stated earlier the presence of four Property/ Auction-
eering companies, Sherry Fitzgerald, Hamilton, Osborne King, Gunne
Auctioneers and Ross McPartland on this list gives an indication of the

extremely buoyant Republic of Ireland property market, itself born out of the 'Celtic Tiger' phenomenon. As stated earlier this sector is vulnerable to any down-turn in the Irish economy.

Table 14: Expenditure by Product Group - Jan - Dec 2000

	CATEGORY	SPEND (£m)	S.O.V.
1	Retail Outlets	56.5	9.2%
2	Construction	51.7	8.5%
3	Industry	49.9	8.2%
4	Food	46.0	7.5%
5	Beverages	39.3	6.4%
6	Theatre / Culture	37.2	6.1%
7	Personal Hygiene	31.8	5.2%
8	Motor Trade	29.6	4.8%
9	Financial	23.6	3.9%
10	Tourism	21.7	3.6%
11	Office Equipment	14.9	2.4%
12	Household Equipment	14.4	2.4%
13	TV/Video/Audio Recordings	8.9	1.5%
14	Cleaning Agents	7.9	1.3%
15	Leisure / Sport	5.3	0.9%
16	Fuel	4.3	0.7%
17	Agriculture	3.2	0.5%
18	Tobacco	3.1	0.5%
19	Clothing	2.5	0.4%
20	Instruction	2.5	0.4%
	Unclassified	154.6	25.3%
	TOTAL	611.2	100%

Source: IAPI AdSpend 2001.

**Table 15: Top 30 Advertisers in ROI – Year 2000 –
(All Media Advertising in IR£000s)**

	Advertiser	Expenditure	% SOV	Accum SOV
1	Appointments	49868.99	8.14%	8.14%
2	Small Advertisements	49731.24	8.12%	16.26%
3	Personal/Special Notices	22361.06	3.65%	19.91%
4	Government Depts. (R.O.I)	20896.10	3.41%	23.32%
5	Eircom (Telecom Eireann)	18116.09	2.96%	26.28%
6	Sherry Fitzgerald	8469.84	1.38%	27.67%
7	Esat Digifone	7698.72	1.26%	28.92%

Table 15, continued

8	Guinness Group Sales	6957.29	1.14%	30.06%
9	Proctor & Gamble	5892.76	0.96%	31.02%
10	Showerings	5256.79	0.86%	31.88%
11	Hamilton Osborne King	5150.84	0.84%	32.72%
12	Electricity Supply Board	5076.88	0.83%	33.55%
13	Misc Concerts	4893.01	0.80%	34.35%
14	Mars	4726.38	0.77%	35.12%
15	Lever Brothers	4582.92	0.75%	35.87%
16	Dunnes Stores	4532.45	0.74%	36.61%
17	Kelloggs	4418.15	0.72%	37.33%
18	Van Den Bergh	4000.23	0.65%	37.98%
19	Gunne Auctioneers	3993.19	0.65%	38.63%
20	Cadburys	3822.09	0.62%	39.26%
21	L'Oreal	3472.57	0.57%	39.82%
22	Power City	3294.31	0.54%	40.36%
23	SupeValu	3102.80	0.51%	40.87%
24	Murphy Brewery	3067.33	0.50%	41.37%
25	Bank Of Ireland	3037.49	0.50%	41.87%
26	Beecham (Smith Kline)	2962.33	0.48%	42.35%
27	D.I.D	2791.66	0.46%	42.81%
28	Gilbeys	2706.07	0.44%	43.25%
29	Coca-Cola	2501.13	0.41%	43.66%
30	Ross McParland	2475.36	0.40%	44.06%

Source: IAPI/Adspend 2001

5 Analysis of Advertising Agencies

As the marketing communications and advertising services industry becomes increasingly global, Irish agencies have increasingly sought a variety of relationships with major international agency groupings. These vary from association without ownership through to being wholly or partly owned by multinational agency groups. The relationships of many of the Top 20 advertising agencies to International agency groupings can be observed in the names of the agencies listed in Table 16. This table shows the Top 20 Irish Advertising agencies in terms of their press advertising expenditure with National newspapers of Ireland. Again following international trends the growth of media buying agencies is now a strong feature of the Irish advertising market with major media specialists such as Mindshare, Zenith and Carat all being represented in the Irish market. Agencies in Table 16 are distinguished in terms of whether the agency is a full-service agency (FS) or a media buying agency (media dependent-MD or media independent–MI). Despite the trend towards internationalization, McConnells/MCM Communications, the largest agency in terms of overall billings, continues to be Irish-owned.

Table 16: Top 20 Agencies in Ireland by NNI Expenditure

Position 2000	NNI Agency League Table Top 30	January to December 2000	Agency Type
1	Mindshare (Ogilvy/DDFH&B)	10,952,966	MD
2	Aim/Carat	9,665,741	MI
3	Brindley	9,255,091	FS
4	MCM Communications/McConnells	8,073,724	MD
5	Doherty/Padbury	7,413,378	FS
6	Des O' Meara & Ptns Inc Rubicon	6,891,896	FS
7	Irish International	4,813,338	FS
8	Mediavest (QMP)	4,726,358	MD
9	Media Works (Peter Owens)	3,969,436	MD
10	Eason Advertising	3,713,048	FS
11	Euro RSCG	3,526,334	FS
12	Southern Advertising	3,273,147	FS
13	TMP Worldwide (Eureka)	2,998,111	RA
14	Universal McCann	2,731,875	MD
15	Grey Ireland/Mediacom	2,556,703	FS
16	Zenith	2,407,529	MD
17	Young Advertising	2,265,137	FS
18	AFA Advertising	2,121,766	FS
19	CDP	2,098,528	FS
20	Javelin Young & Rubicam	1,935,562	FS

Note: Amounts quoted are net of VAT in IR £m and refer only to press advertising within NNI Newspapers.
Source: National Newspapers of Ireland – IAPI, 2001

Key:
Agency Type FS = Full-service agencies
MD = Media Dependent
MI = Media Independent
RA = Recruitment Agency

6   Advertising Institutions

6.1   Institute of Advertising Practitioners of Ireland (IAPI)

Web address – http://www.iapi.com

IAPI is the representative body of Irish advertising agencies. Its activities are wide-ranging and include negotiation with the media, trade unions and government nationally while lobbying activity with both the European Union and Parliament is undertaken through its membership of the European Association of Advertising Agencies. IAPI is a non-profit making organization and its broad objective is to represent and further the interests of advertising agencies in Ireland. IAPI's membership consists of 36 companies, including such organizations as Bates Ireland, Young and Rubicam, McConnells, Ogilvy and Mather, and accounts for over 95% of advertising expenditure in Ireland.

The organization also serves a crucial function for the advertising industry in the vital research it jointly carries out with other organizations within advertising. This research includes the Joint National Readership Survey (JNRR) that provides the industry standard database for newspaper and magazine readership in Ireland, and the Joint National Listenership Research (JNLR) that provides the industry standard database for radio. IAPI also runs and supervises a post-graduate course in adverting at one of the colleges in Dublin.

6.2   The AAI

Web address - http:www.aai.ie

The Advertising Association of Ireland (AAI) is a full-time organization that is dedicated to the broad objective of furthering the interests of advertisers (client companies) in Ireland. The AAI is made up of over one hundred member companies, which when combined account for over two-thirds of advertising spend in Ireland. It is co-ordinated by a council of twenty members and honorary officers, all drawn from advertisers, who plan and co-ordinate direction and interests.

The AAI are involved in an array of activities across the advertising industry. It carries out independent research for its members and is also actively involved in a range of joint industry research programs such as the Joint National Readership Survey (JNRR) and the Joint National Listenership Research (JNLR). However, the main function and prime concern of the AAI is to protect and advance the rights of advertisers in the regulatory environment and within the advertising industry. They have been involved in the argument for the right of self-regulation within the advertising industry leading to the establishment of the Advertising Standards Authority of Ireland (ASAI) in which they play an active role. They have also challenged the high production cost levels that exist within Ireland; similarly they have achieved amendments to the 1990 Broadcasting Act capping the national Irish station's (RTE) advertising revenues and time. At present the AAI are addressing problems such as media inflation, the curtailing of advertising of sensitive product categories and fighting an amendment to the Gaming and Lotteries act 1956 that constrains sales promotions.

6.3 Advertising Standards Authority for Ireland (ASAI)

Web address - http://www.asai.ie

The Advertising Standards Authority for Ireland (ASAI) is the independent self-regulatory body for advertising and sales promotion standards in Ireland. Established in 1981, with the full support of the three principle sectors of the advertising industry- advertisers, advertising agencies and the media,-its perceived role is to establish and maintain the highest standards of commercial advertising for the protection of both consumer and industry interests.

The ASAI is funded by the advertising industry itself and relies upon subscriptions from advertisers, agencies, and the media to carry out its role as an independent arbitrator on advertising standards. Its primary duty is to deal with public and intra-industry complaints in an impartial and fair manner with regards to such things as fairness, taste, decency and propriety for advertisements and sales promotions

At present the ASAI deals with about eight hundred complaints per year and this involves up to about five hundred different advertisements and sales promotions. Some three hundred of these complaints go to adjudication by the board. The adjudicating committee of the ASAI then makes decisions whether to uphold or dismiss a complaint by deciding whether the ad or sales promotion breaks the rule of its Code of Advertising Standards or Code of Sales Promotion Standards.

References

Amarach Consumer Trendwatch 2001, Amarach Consulting, Dublin
Campaign – 14 September 2001 (Special feature on Ireland)
Carat, Smart Media Data, Carat International
FIPP/Zenith World Magazine Trends 2001/2002
Irish Internet Association www.iia.ie
Institute of Advertising Practitioners of Ireland (IAPI) – www.iapi.com
MCM Communications, Dublin
Mediaweek – March 16, 2001 (Special supplement – Guide to Targeting Ireland)
www.Medialive.ie (This site provides a comprehensive guide to Irish Advertising data)
National Newspapers of Ireland, (NNI) Dublin
RTE, Sales Department, Dublin
World Advertising Research Centre (WARC). www.warc.com
World Media Trends – NTC Publications, Henley on Thames, UK
Zenithmedia, Western European Market and Mediafact 2000

Advertising in Latvia

Anda Batraga
University of Latvia

1   The Development of Advertising in Latvia

Latvia is one of the three Baltic States, and recovered its independence in 1991. The development of an advertising industry in Latvia started with the decay of the Soviet Union. The recovery of independence and the transition period to the market economy, as in all of the former USSR, required rapid development of the advertising industry. The birth and development of this field was inescapable, and was dictated by the competitive principles of the market economy. As with individual advertisements, the whole advertising market in Latvia is specific, and it is slowly developing its own character. Many foreign companies have entered the Latvian advertising market, each of them bringing its unique contribution. The same is true of local employers and their commercials.

In discussing the development of the advertising market, it is first necessary to state how research into advertising is carried out in Latvia. Many research companies have formed and are functioning. The scope of the research is wide, which attests that experts in Latvia have definite and well-defined views of what they require. The results obtained serve to determine and achieve marketing and communication objectives.

The main participants and development directions in the field of research in Latvia are:

1. SKDS (Social Correlative Data System), a company dealing with social and marketing research and *inter alia* valuation of advertising efficiency.
2. House of The Baltic Data, which deals with marketing research.
3. Baltic Media Facts (BMF), involved in media research.
4. Profindekss, dealing with retail trade research and analysis of different trademarks.
5. Brand sellers DDB, an advertising agency.
6. Latenta, an agency of scientific and technical expertise dealing with audience research and tests of advertising psychology and its effects.

Besides the above-mentioned companies, there are others dealing with marketing and advertising research:

- Baltijas Monitors, a media research company.
- Institute of Philosophy and Sociology, involved in social research.
- Amer Nielsen, an international institute of retail trade research, dealing with research into brand divisions in the Latvian market.

Audience research in the Baltic States themselves has also been undertaken since 1992/93.

The aforementioned research comprises all the traditional mass media, e.g. press, television, radio. The systems available, both in methods and technology, are on a par with those of European countries and international demands.

The purpose of national audience research is to provide standardized and solid frames of reference in the media markets. Such data are used mainly for analysis of the structure of the mass media audience, planning of advertising campaigns for specific target audiences, the achievement of good profits in the current advertising market, and mass media preferences of the target groups, and research into their characteristics.

All the research is based on the following principles:

- The research agencies are independent from their clients.
- The research agencies are supervised and permanently controlled.
- The supervision and control is carried out by the mass media and supervisory organizations – 'joint industry committee'.
- To ensure that all social and demographic groups are represented, all research is based on the principles of representative selection.
- The agencies use standardized and internationally acknowledged methods, thus data comparison, data equity and the stability of the data are guaranteed.

Baltic Media Facts is the most influential and leading company of its kind in Latvia. The company is a member of the international Gallup-Media group. BMF Latvia is a joint-stock venture of Latvia, Estonia and Finland, which was founded by Soumen Gallup Oy in 1993 (the largest research company in Finland, with branches in many other states).

In 2001, the House of the Baltic Data group (BDN) became the partner and representative in Latvia of Taylor Nelson Sofres (TNS), the largest research company in Europe. As the result of consolidation, the global representatives of TNS became companies of the BDN group: House of the Baltic Data (full service agency), BMF Gallup Media (media and advertising research), Profindex Latvia (retail trade research) and Latvijas SOCIĀLO pētījuma Centrs (fieldwork agency). TNS is one of the leading market research companies and the fourth biggest in the world, represented in 80 countries with more than 6000 experts. TNS total turnover exceeds 650 millions USD (http://www.tnsofres.com/).

Baltic Media Facts performs research into the number of readers nationwide, research on target groups, radio and television research and media research related to children. Since 1996, they have published the Advertising Almanac, which comprises the most significant information on the advertising market in Latvia.

Advertising market research is carried out in five media groups, newspapers and magazines, television, radio, outdoor advertising and catalogues. The method used for press and television registration is monitoring. Data for radio, outdoor advertising and catalogues are received from the media. The choice of each media group is determined by the characteristics of the media audience, but is not related entirely to size. The selection structure is designed to include different media, which are represented by a typical target group.

The advertising market is classified according to international standards and is adapted to the peculiarities of the local advertising market structure. If the range of goods and services advertised corresponds to the features of more than one field, it is classified as 'Different Production'.

The volume of advertising is measured in three units:
- Printed area in square centimeters (minutes for TV and radio).
- The advertising expenditures in Latvian currency (lats).
- The total audience reached by advertising (GRP).

The research is performed regularly and independently of orders. The research is done simultaneously in Estonia, Finland and Lithuania.

Historically, the development of BMF can be illustrated as follows:

1992   First media research by the Latvia Social Research Center (printed media, Day-After-Recall for TV and radio).

1993   First presentation of BMF Latvia during the Advertising Exhibition in September, officially established in November.
        Beginning of regular NRS + TGI;
        First introduction visits to clients.

1994   Commencement of TV and Radio Diary survey.
        Programming of TV Facts reporting software.
        Commencement of advertising expenditures survey.
        Programming of ADEX entering and reporting system.
        Start of retail research (DPI, Shops Directory) by the Baltic Market Facts division, programming of calculations and end user software.

Table 1: Media Surveys Offered by BMF (Latvia)

Survey	Periodicity	Methodology	Sample universe	Data collected
National Readership Survey (NRS)	Continuous	Face-to-face interview	6000 persons per year (age 15-74)	Readership of newspapers and magazines, Internet usage, general media consumption
TV Meters Survey	Continuous	People-meter	Nationally representative 250 people-meters	TV ratings, reach, share, net reach and GRP of campaigns
Radio diary Survey	Continuous	Dairy	9000 persons per year (age 12-74)	Latvian radio audience (ratings, reach, share)
Advertising Expenditure Survey (AdEx)	Continuous	Monitoring	Print, media, TV channels, radio, outdoor	Media advertising, expenditures by media type, product group and brand, control of TV spots, print ads, estimation of net advertising market
Target group Index Survey	Continuous	Face-to-face interview	6000 persons per year (age 15-74)	Supplement to NRS enabling analysis of print media audience by target groups consumption habits and opinions

Source: Baltic Media Book 2000

1995   TV and Radio Diary survey adopted on a permanent basis.
        Programming of TV panel control software, TV programs inputting system, ADC Planner for TV. First kids media survey.
1996   First Business to Business media survey.
        Establishing of own TV recording and monitoring system.
        Programming of Press Facts software for the Baltic states.
        Supporting of the Lithuanian TV Diary project.
        First Retail Audit surveys.
        Programming of software systems.
        Start of a regular Household Purchasing Panel.
1997   Start of continuous diary project in Belarus.
        ADC Planner for press.
1998   BMF Latvia with $360,000 research turnover is the second largest research agency after BHD. The BMF rating is media sales currency in the Latvian advertising market.
1999   First Baltic states TV-Meter panel
In the mass media BMF collects and batches different information (cf. Table 1).

2   Advertising Media

2.1   Media Research

Advertising media are communication channels, which transmit the advertising announcement. All the media are divided into two groups, electronic mass media, and the rest (print ads, cinema, environment media).

Media research in Latvia can be divided into five groups: print ads [newspapers (daily, business, advertising, weekly); magazines]; television; radio; catalogues and outdoor advertisements. In 2000 some Internet research was also carried out, but this was done on a pilot basis only, because the Internet is a relatively new medium and research methods are still at a draft stage.

The media in Latvia, as in other Baltic states, is analyzed in different stages. The initial analysis involves the media strategy, which identifies the right advertising commitment in the right mass media at the right time.

Baltic Media Facts functions as a full service media agency in Latvia, Lithuania and Estonia. The partner of the Baltic states agencies is the European media agency 'Carat'. Baltic Media Facts is an independent agency, which provides the following services for 'Carat' clients in the Baltic markets:

- To provide the level of client service, which corresponds to the standards of Carat;
- To provide strategic and tactic planning at high level, by using actual software and methods;
- To provide open co-operation within the framework of the Baltic and the Carat net;
- To provide clients with competitor prices in the media;
- To draw fees for services;
- To be a business partner for the client.

The advantages of the 'Baltic Media Services' are characterized as:
- One administrator and co-ordinator for the client.
- Unification of basic principles of project managing and realization.
- Media strategies and guidelines for the whole region.
- Regional information system.
- Equal strategic and tactic planning methods.
- Utility of experience in practice.
- Powerful national enterprises can each achieve the strategies in their own territory.
- Regional (Baltic) and local co-operation with the media.

Baltic Media Facts works with the following indexes:

- **Rating**: the percentage of a given population, which consumes, i.e. watches, listens, reads, sees, a particular media at a particular time. This is the proportion of individuals reached by media. One rating score corresponds to 1% of the given population group. Most frequently, the index is used in the analysis and assessment of broadcasting and electronic mass media, but it can be used in the reassessment of the financial rewards of any kind of media. Rating plays a significant role in the planning and buying of media. With the assistance of rating, it is possible to assess the success, potential, stability of programs and combination of different programs, all of which are necessary to achieve the purpose of advertising.

- **Audience share**: the share of the potential audience that has turned to a particular TV or radio station or program. This index supplies not only the relative predominance of any media, but also the loyalty of consumer and business quality.

- **GRP** (gross rating points): a rating sum obtained in the media, which is acquired during one campaign, 1 week or 1 month. GRP means the entire audience exposure for the media, not taking into account audience repetition. As different conditions exist in the market, GRP can change to TRP (target rating points). TRP can be defined within the framework of a definite target group. Within the framework of the index is the so-called advertising impression, which is the total number of individuals being subjected to advertising efficiency; it is identical to the GRP and TRP indexes, except that it shows the number of individuals, and not the proportion, who are reached by the advertisement.

- **Audience reached**: the number of individuals to be reached by advertising in a definite period of time. It is a target group, which is expressed proportionally and which is reached by an advertisement at least once.

- **Frequency**: the average number of times an individual is reached within the framework of a particular media plan during 1 year.

- **Indexes:**
  - **Product/brand development index (BDI)**: the potential of product/brand marketing in one particular market segment.
  - **Category development index (CDI)**: the proportion of the population fitting a particular category.
  - **Price per thousand – index**: the price for an audience of 1000, which is reached in the media within the framework of a definite plan.
  - **Price per one rating score.**

The second stage of media analysis is executed after the realization of an advertising campaign. Baltic Media Facts is dealing with those researches. It defines:

- Share of media expenditure.
- Dynamics of the advertising market per media group.
- Share of advertising – press/TV.
- Amount of advertisements in newspapers, magazines and TV.
- Dynamics of advertisement in television channels.
- Number of advertisements in TV channels. Dynamic of advertisement count on TV channels.
- Media satiety with advertisements.

The following indexes can also be defined:

- Dynamic of the advertising market.
- Total amount of the most important spheres per year.
- Total amount of advertisements by spheres.
- Arrangement of spheres by the amount of advertising in media.
- Dynamics of advertising market spheres.
- Top 40 advertisers.
- Largest advertisers – total, press, newspapers, magazines.
- Top 40 brands.
- Largest brand names – total, press, newspapers, magazines, TV.

Before independence in Latvia there was no advertising tradition resembling the Western type. Advertising was perceived as a means of promoting low-grade goods and clearing surpluses. Since independence, the promotion of the advertising market in Latvia has been very rapid and is characterized by the desire to preserve the color of the local character. Translated foreign advertisements were the first to appear; these were suitable for the Eastern European market and especially for TV advertising. Although several multinational agencies that had created local subsidiaries were successfully functioning in the advertising market, national companies owned the largest market share and had the greatest creative influence.

2.2   Main Indexes of the Advertising Market

Research performed in Latvia, Lithuania and Estonia has shown that advertising plays a positive role in the state's economy and contributes to the decision making of consumers in the process of shopping. The results are displayed in Table 2.

Table 2: Attitudes Towards Advertising (percentage of population)

Overall attitude	Latvia		Estonia		Lithuania	
	1995	1999	1995	1999	1995	1999
Positive attitude	51	n.a.	62	38	34	22
Negative attitude	32	n.a.	30	50	63	55

Source: Baltic Media Book 1996, 1999.

Table 3. Baltic Advertising Expenditure Market 1998-1999 (mill USD)

	1998			1999		
	Mill USD	Share%	98 vs 99	mill. USD	Share %	99 vs 98
Latvia						
Newspapers	18.0	42.2		15.8	39.5	-12.0%
Magazines	2.7	6.5		3.0	7.5	9.0%
TV	14.8	34.7		12.8	31.8	-13.0%
Radio	5.4	12.6		6.3	15.6	16.0%
Outdoor	1.7	4.0		2.2	5.6	30.0%
Internet						
Total	42.6	100.0	25%	40.1	100.0	-6.0%
Estonia						
Newspapers	23.7	47.0		20.8	47.8	-12.0%
Magazines	5.8	12.0		5.5	12.7	-6.0%
TV	12.9	26.0		8.9	20.4	-31.0%
Radio	5.0	10.0		5.2	12.0	5.0%
Outdoor	2.8	6.0		2.8	6.5	-1.0%
Internet	0.2	0.0		0.3	0.7	44.0%
Total	50.5	100.0	23%	43.5	100	-14.0%
Lithuania						
Newspapers	21.1			22.8	45.7	8.0%
Magazines	2.9			3.3	6.7	15.0%
TV	22.9			17.5	35.0	-23.0%
Radio	1.5			3.5	7.0	130.0%
Outdoor	1.6			2.8	5.7	79.0%
Internet						
Total	53.6		44%	50.0	100	-7.0%
Baltic market						
Newspapers				59.5	45.0	
Magazines				11.8	9.0	
TV				39.1	29.0	
Radio				15.0	11.0	
Outdoor				7.9	6.0	
Internet				0.3	0.0	
Total				133.6	100.0	

Source: Baltic Media Facts – Unpublished materials

Viewing the results, it can be concluded that the attitude of the population was positive in 1995 in Lithuania, but has become more skeptical since. This can be explained by the fact that more and more information has entered the advertising market, causing customers to be confused about the choices to make, and advertising has therefore become a victim of its own success. It is interesting to note that the fraction of the population who are indifferent to advertising is decreasing. This shows the significance of advertising as an information medium. As the advertising industry continues to develop and grow in Latvia, the state's economy will become more and more oriented to the private sector.

Over a relatively short period of time, the advertising market in Latvia has had a significant influence on Latvia's economy, by generating employment, by stimulating other sectors of the economy, by provision of a taxable quota for the government and through the sharing of information for consumers, thus promoting the process of decision making (cf. Table 3).

A jump in advertising expenses has been evident since 1994, although there this growth is now slowing down. This is probably because the level of new enterprise in Latvia has now stabilized, and the client base is now more or less constant.

2.3 Share of Advertising Market by Spheres

The division of advertising by spheres means the study of homogeneous units of product groups. Sphere analysis shows the engagement of advertisers, which spheres are advertised the most, which ones the least. From the data acquired, it is possible to assess the market satiety of a particular product group and the competition among producers of similar product groups. In Latvia, advertising expenditures are listed in 40 main spheres.

The largest resources in absolute allowance are used for advertising of cars, foodstuffs, consumer services, cosmetics and alcoholic beverages. During the time period from 1996 till 1999, the largest resources were used for spheres as:

- Business and finance
- Transportation means
- Toiletries and cosmetics
- Household chemical goods
- Foodstuffs and soft drinks
- Information and mass media
- Entertainment industry.

These are the seven biggest spheres, which are in the so-called TOP position among the rest of spheres with regard to money invested. The spheres in which the smallest amount of advertising money has been expended are:

- Spheres of agriculture, forestry and fishery
- Sphere of production services
- Sphere of advertising services.

Traditional advertising for those spheres is not effective, because the spheres are very specific. Each has its own special methods to attract clients' attraction. Advertising for these spheres is usually handled by specialist advertising agencies, who also have experience in the wider advertising field. Advertising services, especially advertising agencies, should not advertise themselves at all. The task of the advertising agency is to advertise its clients, not the agency, and to attract clients with interesting presentations and marketing solutions for the sales of the client's goods or to increase the identification of brands.

Data on the largest spheres and their share of the advertising market are displayed in Table 4.

Table 4. Total Amount of Advertising by Spheres (TOP) 1996-1999 (USD)

Sphere	1996	1997	1998	1999
Business, finance	3,582,241.3	5,895,172.4	6,962,068.9	7,656,206.8
Toiletries, cosmetics	5,171,206.8	1,241,068.9	2,075,862.0	1,453,000.0
Foodstuffs, soft drinks	5,836,206.8	9,693,965.5	1,311,896.5	1,276,655.1
Information, mass media	3,019,137.9	4,989,827.5	5,957,068.9	6,525,689.6
Entertainment industry	2,279,655.1	3,413,965.5	5,324,137.9	6,908,275.8
Household chemical goods	9,881,034.4	1,957,068.9	7,430,344.8	8,193,620.6
Transportation means	1,568,620.6	2,211,551.7	3,591,379.3	3,616,551.7

Source: Baltic Media Facts – Unpublished materials

From the data displayed in the table, it can be seen that the largest spheres have increased their advertising spending. Observing the date historically, it is possible to conclude that since 1996, the some of the largest spenders on advertising have been foodstuffs and soft drinks, toiletries and cosmetics and business and finance.

The largest spheres are mainly represented by international companies, which have extended budgets for advertising that allow them to introduce their goods and services to potential customers. Spheres such as information and mass media, and the entertainment industry, rank lower. Resources are less for these areas, because unlike toiletries, which in 1996 were mainly imported and without the support of advertising would not have achieved their current market position, these spheres had a lower profile in Latvia. Also, nowadays these spheres invest fewer resources for advertising than those previously mentioned.

Since 1997, toiletries and cosmetics have topped the market. Several factors are responsible for this changes: market stabilization in the sphere of foodstuffs and soft drinks, the entrance of many cosmetic companies into the market, and the trend to satisfy the highest demands of consumers.

Banks and the financial sector spend a lot of resources to attract clients, because this is the only way to inform large audiences about services offered. Large investments in advertising are therefore justified.

The rank of household chemical goods in the largest spheres can be explained by a decline in Latvia's chemical industry. Foreign producers have therefore been attracted to advertise in this area.

The amount of advertising in the transportation sector results from an increase in purchasing power and the development of leasing and credit services, which makes it easier for consumers to purchase new cars or other means of transportation. The high degree of competition among car dealers has led to significant increases in advertising budgets.

The product groups represented by the largest advertising spheres have different shares in the section of mass media. The TOP five product groups by share in different mass media in the Baltic States are displayed in Tables 5, 6, 7, 8 and 9.

Table 5: TOP 5 Advertised Product Groups in Newspapers by Share of All Newspaper Advertising in 1999

Estonia	%	Latvia	%	Lithuania	%
Communication, electronics, computers	18	Business, financial services, real estate	18	Entertainment, culture, recreation	12
Business, financial services, real estate	16	Communication, electronics, computers	12	Construction, furniture	10
Construction, furniture	11	Construction, furniture	11	Business, financial services, real estate	10
Entertainment, culture, recreation	9	Entertainment, culture, recreation	10	Communications, electronics, computers	9
Transportation means	9	Transportation means	9	Media, publishing	7

Table 6: TOP 5 Advertised Product Groups in Magazines by Share of Total Magazine Advertising in 1999

Estonia	%	Latvia	%	Lithuania	%
Construction, furniture	16	Cosmetics, personal hygiene	26	Cosmetics, personal hygiene	28
Cosmetics, personal hygiene	14	Alcoholic beverages	9	Media, publishing	11
Communication, electronics, computers	10	Household goods	9	Communication, electronics, computers	7
Entertainment, culture, recreation	7	Clothing, footwear	8	Medicine	7
Medicine	6	Media, publishing	8	Clothing, footwear	7

Table 7: TOP 5 Advertised Product Groups in TV by Share of Total TV Advertising in 1999

Estonia	%	Latvia	%	Lithuania	%
Cosmetics, personal hygiene	27	Cosmetics, personal hygiene	22	Cosmetics, personal hygiene	21
Household goods	18	Household goods	15	Entertainment, culture, recreation	17
Food products	13	Food products	15	Household goods	17
Entertainment, culture, recreation	7	Entertainment, culture, recreation	13	Food products	12
Non-alcoholic beverages	6	Medicine	6	Non-alcoholic beverages	8

Table 8: TOP 5 Advertised Product Groups in Radio by Share of All Radio Advertising in 1999

Estonia	%	Latvia	%	Lithuania	%
Entertainment, culture, recreation	24	Entertainment, culture, recreation	32	Entertainment, culture, recreation	41
Communication, electronics, computers	16	Media, publishing	22	Media publishing	11
Transportation means	9	Business, financial services, real estate	15	Communication, electronics, computers	9
Construction, furniture	9	Medicine	6	Food products	8
Food products	5	Food products	5	Transportation means	6

Table 9: TOP 5 Outdoor Advertised Product Groups by Share of Total Outdoor Advertising in 1999

Estonia	%	Latvia	%	Lithuania	%
Communication, electronics, computers	21	Alcoholic beverages	29	Alcoholic beverages	24
Social advertising	16	Communication, electronics, computers	14	Communication, electronics, computers	13
Alcoholic beverages	16	Business, financial services, real estate	14	Construction, furniture	11
Food products	9	Cosmetics, personal hygiene	9	Transportation means	7
Media publishing	5	Non-alcoholic beverages	6	Social advertising	7

Source: Baltic Media Book 2000

2.4 Largest Advertisers and Brands

The advertising market in Latvia is small but still in the development stage. Advertising will develop and expand. Advertising experts consider that Latvia's advertising market has the potential to reach 69-77 million USD during the next 4-5 years.

In Latvia, approximately 70% of the entire advertising investment is made up of resources from foreign companies. The home market for goods and services made in Latvia is comparatively small. It is very hard for local producers to compete with foreign companies, who are better developed technologically. The prime cost of goods and services is also lower than for producers of goods and services in Latvia. Foreign companies can afford considerably more money for the advancement of their goods and services than local companies.

In the time period under consideration, the largest advertisers in Latvia have invested significant sums of money for advertising. From year to year, the leading advertiser in Latvia, as in other Baltic States, is the US company Procter & Gamble. The other leaders tend to change with time. The largest advertisers in the Baltic States during the time period from 1994–1999 are displayed in Table 10, and the investment of these advertisers in Latvia is shown in Table 11.

Table 10: The Biggest Advertisers 1994-1999

Estonia	1.	2.	3.	4.	5.
1994	P & G	Masterfoods	Wrigley's	Unilever	Dandy
1995	P & G	Dandy	Wrigley's	Eesti Loto	Eesti Tubakas
1996	P & G	Dandy	Ferrero	Wrigley's	Philip Morris
1997	P & G	Unilever	Philip Morris	Wrigley's	Dandy
1998	P & G	Unilever	EMT	Wrigley's	Dandy
1999	P & G	Unilever	Tietopuhelin	Ritabell	EMT
Latvia	**1.**	**2.**	**3.**	**4.**	**5.**
1994	Toto-Kurjers	Electrolux	Dandy	Radio 106,2 Rigai	Kellogs Latvia
1995	P & G	Wrigley's	Dandy	Masterfoods	J & J
1996	P & G	Parekss	KJS	J & J	Ferrero
1997	P & G	Unilever	Dandy	Colgate-Palmolive	Wrigley's
1998	P & G	Unilever	KJS	Wrigley's	Dandy
1999	P & G	Unilever	KJS	Avelat Grupa	Benckiser
Lithuania	**1.**	**2.**	**3.**	**4.**	**5.**
1994	..	..	..	..	..
1995	Dandy	KJS	Ferrero	Nestle	Palmolive
1996	P & G	Reemstma	Dandy	KJS	Philip Morris
1997	P & G	Unilever	Dandy	Wrigley's	J & J
1998	P & G	Unilever	Wrigley's	Dandy	Respublika
1999	P & G	Unilever	Omnitel	KJS	Lietuvos rytas

Notes: P & G (Procter&gamble), KJS (Kraft Jacobs Suchard), J&J (Johnson & Johnson), EMT (Eesti Mobiiltelefon).
Source: Baltic Media Book 2000

Table 11: Largest Advertisers (TOP) 1996-1999, USD

Advertiser	1996	Advertiser	1997
Procter&Gamble	1,944,931.0	Procter&Gamble	6,771,637.9
Parekss	1,070,879.3	Unilever	2,526,482.7
Kraft Jacobs Suchard	911,086.2	Dandy	1,293,379.3
Johnsos&Johnson	7,692,068.9	Colgate-Palmolive	1,010,017.2
Ferrero	7,074,655.1	Wrigley's	1,004,793.1
Advertiser	**1998**	**Advertiser**	**1999**
Procter&Gamble	1,758,817.0	Procter&Gamble	1,139,914.1
Unilever	4,787,044.8	Unilever	5,393,850.0
Kraft Jacobs Suchard	1,577,568.9	Kraft Jacobs Suchard	2,156,655.1
Wrigley's	1,430,022.4	Avelat Grupa	1,439,206.8
Dandy	1,427,286.2	Benckiser	1,294,643.1

Source: Baltic Media Facts – Unpublished materials

Observing the largest advertisers from 1996 to 1999, the increase in advertising budgets is striking. The largest advertiser, Procter & Gamble, entered the Latvian market with only three advertised products. When the products were stable in the market and the planned sales were reached, the company increased their advertising spending. The increase in advertising spending is closely connected with the sales of goods achieved.

A little different is the ranking of the main advertisers in separate mass media. The choice of mass media depends upon the sphere of the particular advertiser. Television is used for advertising goods for mass consumption, because it reaches the largest social circle and thus it is possible to achieve the highest GRP. Press advertising is more often used for advertising over a set period of time, for example discounts, lotteries and sales; it is rarely used for advertising product images.

The main advertisers in the Baltic by different mass media and the proportion of the investments are displayed in Tables 12, 13, 14, 15 and 16.

Table 12: TOP 5 Advertisers in Newspapers by Share of Total Newspaper Advertising in 1999

Estonia	%	Latvia	%	Lithuania	%
Tietopuhelin	2.7	Varner Baltija	2.9	Omnitel	4.2
Ritabell	2.2	LNT	2.2	Bite GSM	1.4
Eesti Mobiiltelefon	1.4	Elcor	2.0	Olifeja	0.7
Radiolinja	0.9	Parekss	1.5	Lietuvos Telekomas	0.7
Hansapank	0.9	Lattelekom	1.5	Apranga	0.6

Table 13: TOP 5 Advertisers in Magazines by Share of Total Magazine Advertising in 1999

Estonia	%	Latvia	%	Lithuania	%
L'Oreal	1.8	L'Oreal	4.0	L'Oreal	4.6
Tietopuhelin	1.4	Unilever	3.8	Sarma	3.3
Unilever	1.3	Johnson&Johnson	2.6	Unilever	2.0
Eesti Mobiiltelefon	1.3	Electrolux	2.5	Kristiana	1.8
Procter&Gamble	1.2	Avelat Grupa	2.3	Johnson&Johnson	1.6

Table 14: TOP 5 Advertisers in TV by Share of Total TV Advertising in 1999

Estonia	%	Latvia	%	Lithuania	%
Procter&Gamble	26.8	Procter&Gamble	20.5	Procter&Gamble	30.8
Unilever	10.0	Unilever	9.4	Unilever	10.5
Benckiser	2.4	Kraft Jacobs Suchard	3.8	Benchiser	2.6
Coca-Cola	2.4	Benckiser	2.4	Kraft Jacobs Suchard	2.5
Wrigley's	2.2	Johnson&Johnson	2.0	Wrigley's	2.4

Table 15: TOP 5 Advertisers in Radio by Share of Total Radio Advertising in 1999

Estonia	%	Latvia	%	Lithuania	%
BDG	2.4	LNT	7.1	Olifeja	7.4
Eesti Mobiiltelefon	2.0	Nacionala Teatris	6.3	Omnitel	5.3
Postimees	1.9	Gailītis G	5.7	Interservis	4.8
Riteball	1.8	Linibanka	2.9	Kraft Jacobs Suchard	4.2
Hallo!Telefonipood	1.6	Dailes Teatris	2.8	Bite GSM	3.4

Table 16: TOP 5 Outdoor Advertisers by Share of Total Outdoor Advertising in 1999

Estonia	%	Latvia	%	Lithuania	%
Ritabell	5.8	Avelat Grupa	19.5	House of Prince	10.7
Eesti Mobiiltelefon	5.6	Aldaris	5.8	Philip Morris	6.8
Keskerakond	5.3	Baltcom	3.9	Reemtsma	3.4
Saku Õlletehas	4.1	Hansabank Latvia	3.9	Bite GSM	3.2
Colgate-Palmolive	2.7	Unibanka	3.9	Elektrolux	2.5

Source: Baltic Media Book 2000

2.5   Brand Names

The largest advertisers usually have several brand names, and they do not concentrate the sums invested for advertising on only one brand. Usually each brand has its own separate advertising budget, which varies in relation to turnover, sales, identification and other factors of goods/services.

For example, Procter & Gamble advertises several brands and the largest investments for advertising are made by brands like Tide, Pantene PRO-V, Always, Pampers, Head & Shoulders and others. In total, out of the TOP 40 products advertised in Latvia, 15 belong to Procter & Gamble.

Other advertisers offering several brands of goods and services operate in a similar way. Brand research has been performed in Latvia only since 1997. Every year, the 100 most advertised product brands are evaluated. From year to year, the first places have been taken by brands from the largest advertisers (cf. Table 17).

Table 17: TOP 10 Largest Brand Names 1997-1999 (Latvia), USD

	Brand name	1997 ($)		Brand name	1998 ($)		Brand name	1999 ($)
1	Orbit	1,002,551.7	1	Blend-a-med	1,897,931.1	1	Always	1,296,546.5
2	Dirol	817,258.6	2	Always	1,769,827.5	2	Blend-a-med	1,064,324.1
3	Pantene Pro-V	782,603.4	3	Pampers	1,751,724.1	3	Ariel	1,037,896.5
4	Always	755,103.4	4	Pantene Pro-V	1,667,586.2	4	Omo	908,132.8
5	Pampers	608,827.6	5	Orbit	1,154,482.7	5	LNT	900,798.3
6	Kino-52	567,586.2	6	Ariel	1,152,413.7	6	Ace	882,156.9
7	Veikals 200700	558,189.6	7	Kino-52	1,046,379.3	7	Orbit	776,763.8
8	Blend-a-med	529,310.3	8	Dirol	978,275.9	8	Pantene Pro-V	743,867.2
9	Ariel	492,827.6	9	Head & Shoulders	893,275.9	9	Head & Shoulders	702,622.4
10	Tailenol	482,689.6	10	Renault	885,000.0	10	Wick	676,644.8

Source: Baltic Media Facts – Unpublished materials

2.6   Mass Media

Since 1980, the size of the mass media sector in Latvia has almost doubled. At the end of 1999 in Lithuania, 226 newspapers were registered (109 in Estonia, 415 in Lithuania), 226 magazines (578 in Estonia, 412 in Lithuania), four national and 27 regional/local radio stations (six and 29 in Estonia, eight and 20 in Lithuania), three national, 25 regional/local, 14 closed circuit television channels (four/four and two in Estonia, four, 19 and 48 in Lithuania).

With the increase in mass media, advertising investments also increased. Since 1995, advertising spending for mass media has increased by a factor of 3.5 in Latvia, 2 in Estonia and 3 in Lithuania.

Since 1995, when data collection started, the financial resources invested for advertising have increased, excluding 1999, when they fell slightly, due, to some extent, to the economic crisis in Russia (cf. Table 18).

The indexes displayed are compared to other Baltic States, to see the development. Advertising expenses invested in different mass media show both common and different features in advertising distribution in the mass media of the Baltic States (cf. Table 19).

Table 18: Media Advertising Expenditure 1995-1999 (million)

	Estonia USD	Latvia USD	Lithuania USD
1995	25	12	11
1996	33	19	24
1997	41	34	37
1998	51	48	54
1999	..	42	..

Source: Baltic Media Book 2000

Table 19: Media Advertising Expenditure Distribution by Media 1999 (%)

	Estonia	Latvia	Lithuania
Newspapers	47	43	42
Magazines	12	9	6
Television	26	32	46
Radio	10	12	3
Outdoor	6	4	3

Source: Baltic Media Book 2000

Table 20: Media Satiety with Advertising, %, 1996-1999.

Media group	Satiation %, 1996	Satiation %, 1997	Satiation %, 1998	Satiation %, 1999
Daily newspapers	6	12	12	12
Weekly newspapers	7	17	15	14
Business newspapers	13	26	25	23
Advertisement newspapers	18	21	24	25
Addenda to newspapers	..	..	..	38
Newspapers total	8	15	15	15
Magazines	17	24	29	26
Press (total)	9	16	16	16
TV	4.1	4.6	4.9	3.9
Radio	0.7	..	..	..

Source: Baltic Media Facts – Unpublished materials

A very significant index in the preference of mass media is the media satiety of advertisements. This can be defined as the proportion of advertising, expressed as a percentage. The more advertising a particular media has, the fewer people can remember and memorize it. In Table 20, media satiety with advertisements is shown in the time period from 1996 to 1999 in Latvia. In newspapers, satiety occurs most frequently in business and advertising newspapers. This is related to the high quality of magazines and the frequency of publishing. Television satiety with advertisements is much lower, because the broadcasting time in minutes is much higher than the number of square centimeters in print. Total satiety in press and television increases relatively slowly, and there seems currently to be little danger of advertising taking over the media.

Advertising experts predict that the press satiety with advertisements could remain at its present level or increase by a maximum of 2% in the coming years. The same increase is predicted for television (cf. Table 20).

2.7   Advertising Agencies

Several hundred firms and companies offer advertising services in Latvia. Experts consider that only about ten full service agencies and five media agencies are likely to survive. Although the figures mentioned seem to be small, for the time being they are sufficient for the Latvian advertising market. However, competition in the market continues to increase, and it is likely that the small agencies will gradually be swallowed up by the larger and more professional agencies. The success of new advertising agencies and media agencies is questionable, because the Latvian and the whole Baltic advertising market is too small. Eight years ago, the large international networks began to penetrate the Baltic advertising market, first entering Estonia. Currently, the center of the Baltic advertising market is in Riga, the capital of Latvia. The international networks invest money by buying local agencies, or by becoming the co-partner agency. The same happens to international companies, which employ the services of local agencies. In Riga, companies like Wrigley's, Unilever, Procter & Gamble, Coca-Cola and others have already introduced their representatives.

Forty-six large advertising agencies, 11 media agencies, three media sales companies and public relation companies were operating in Latvia at the end of 1999.

2.8   Organizations and Associations

The first organization in Latvia interested in advertising, was 'Reklāmas klubs' (Advertising club), founded on February 25, 1994. Later, it gained a new status because Latvijas Reklāmas Asociācija (LRA - Advertising Association of Latvia) was founded on the base of it. LRA is Latvia's department of the International Advertising Association. This is the only public organization in Latvia that works in the field of marketing communication and represents the interests of advertisers, advertisement producers, media and other spheres connected with advertising. The purpose of LRA is to control Latvia's advertising environment, to promote its professionalism and fair competition. LRA strives to harmonize the policy of partner organizations in the advertising sphere, the acceptance of common quotas and the implementation of common proceedings. The main tasks are to improve advertising professionalism in Latvia, to facilitate the exchange of experience and ideas among the members, thus adding to their professionalism, and to develop advertising standards. Currently, 46 members are working in this organization, the only one in Latvia which represents the interests of the advertising sphere. LRA has a definite role in the drafting and introduction of different self-governing codes.

The main activities of the LRA are:
- Drafting and acceptance of the code of advertising ethics.
- Amendments of the tobacco self-governing code and prolongation of the action term.
- Organization of the Baltic advertising festival 'Golden Hammer'.

3 Regulating Aspects of the Advertising Sphere

More and more topical becomes the question of Latvia's entrance into the European Union. One of those questions is the harmonization of Latvia's legislation with relevant areas in the legislation of the European Union, in particular with regard to advertising.

Advertising is a sphere that changes with society. A change in the society and its needs leads to a change of production and advertising. In 1934, the first international code of advertising was published; it has been reworked many times since. A peculiarity characteristic of advertising is the regulation of the advertising process by law and the self-governing code of advertising. This is now a generally established practice. Advertising agencies unite in advertising associations, which publish their own codes. This raises the question of the self-government of advertising. In Latvia, the LRA has formed its own code of advertising. Although this question is not related to the sphere of legislation, it plays a significant role in the promotion of the advertising market. Now we can speak about experience gained both in the world and the European Union. Current practice shows that self-government functions best on the basis of the current legislation, which defines principles and is the last refuge, should the advertising industry's own codes of conduct fail. The advantages of self-government are speed, flexibility and cheapness, all of which are impossible to achieve in legislation. Thus self-government and legislation support each other.

The development of advertising is related to regimented laws and regulations. Unfortunately, even up to 2000, in Latvia the law of advertising was not accepted. Therefore the advertising field developed under a variety different laws for many years, and it was impossible to achieve a unified approach. With each new period of time, with every change of government and with changes in business environment in Latvia, new regulating mechanisms were formed, which have influenced the advertising sphere in a direct and indirect manner.

To characterize the judicial sphere of advertising in Latvia, it is necessary to compare Latvian legislation with that of other countries.

Regarding advertising, there are several different directives in the European Union:

- Directive of deceiving advertising, which was accepted in 1994. Its purpose was to protect the interests of consumers against deceiving advertising. The new directive, which corrected the previous one concerning the comparative advertisement, was introduced in 1997.
- Directive of radio and television, also the European convention on foreign television, realized in 1989 with the purpose of forming a market for radio and television media with common regulations in Europe.
- In 1995 the law on radio and television was accepted, and was later supplemented with amendments. Incorporated into the law are separate parts similar to directives of the European Union, but which can be adapted to local circumstances.
- Directive of personal data protection, adapted in 1995. The special tasks for data users and rights of individuals are discussed there. This directive has not been introduced in Latvia, and personal data protection is regulated by national laws.
- Directive of distance sale, adapted in February 1997 with the purpose of harmonizing laws on a member state's obligations among consumers and suppliers negotiating from a distance. In Latvia, that directive is incorporated into the law on consumers right protection.
- Directive related to the marking of foodstuffs, their introduction and advertising, also sale to end consumers. The content of this directive corresponds to the law of the Republic of Latvia on marking of foodstuffs and the law on consumers' protection rights.

Currently in Latvia the law on advertising accepted in January 24, 2000 is in effect. This law incorporates the following directives of the European Union:

- Directive 84/450/EEC of deceiving advertising.
- Directive 97/55/EC, which corrects 84/450/EEC regarding comparative advertising.

The purpose of the law is:
- To regulate the manufacturing and distribution of advertising, also to define rights, duties and responsibilities of people involved in the production and implementation of advertising.
- To protect the interests of the society with regard to advertising.
- To promote a fair competition.

The observance of the law on advertising in Latvia is supervised by:
- The Center of Consumers Right Protection.
- The Competition Board. This is an institution of the state's administration and is supervised by the Ministry of Economy.
- Inspection of state's pharmacy.
- The Board of National Radio and Television. This is an independent institution, which represents public interests in the field of public communication and supervises the observance of assembly, laws, and provides the freedom of speech and information.

With regard to legal cases which have arisen in the field of advertising, supervisory institutions have the right to demand and receive explanations, documents and other proof about the accuracy of advertised announcements and correspondence to the law and other regulations on normative acts from the adviser, producer or performer of the advertisement.

Besides the law on advertising, a succession of other legislative and normative acts have been introduced in Latvia. The main ones are:
- Law on competition.
- Law on radio and television.
- Law on 'Realization of Tobacco Products'.
- Law on distribution of alcohol.
- Law on pharmacy.
- Law on consumers protection rights.
- Law on state language.

Likewise, a succession of specially drafted regulations applies:
- Regulations on medicine advertising.
- Regulations on consumers protection center.
- Regulations on distribution of tobacco products.
- Regulations on medicine registration.

- Regulations concerned with Rīgas Dome on municipal duties for the disposal of advertisements and other informative materials in the public places in Riga.

The regulatory role of the state is very significant in the advertising sphere, but meanwhile in none of the legislative acts are the aspects of ethics and aesthetics discussed. Until 2001, there was no regulatory mechanism in Latvia that provided control over advertising ethics. However, the Advertising Association of Latvia, in cooperation with the Board of Competition and the largest advertising agencies, are already working on the drafting of 'Reklāmas Ētikas Kodekss' (Code of Advertising Ethics), and it is hoped that effective regulation will soon be implemented.

Advertising has had a significant effect on the economy of Latvia, providing:
- Availability of information for consumers.
- Assistance in creating an effective market.
- Financial assistance for mass media.
- Incomes artists and graphic designers employed by advertising agencies.
- A link between society and the government.

Likewise, advertising has led to new areas of employment, both directly and indirectly. It is an industry which has a very sensitive reaction on changes in economical circumstances, regulations on taxes and legislation. The attitude of the government and legislative restrictions has a significant influence to the market development.

Multinational companies, which see the Baltic market as a united common market, could possibly concentrate on countries where self-regulation of the advertising market is promoted. Latvia's advertising industry has a significant potential for development, if the general expansion of the market and the current sophistication of advertising continues. Undeniable is the fact that in this case a significant role is played by preparations for entrance into the European Union, which could promote significant internal investments.

Advertising and marketing are becoming more and more significant as a strategic part of a company's development in Latvia. This is also understood by local companies, which use advertising as a key part of their marketing strategy.

References

Baltic Media Book 2000, ISBN 9985-9080-3-1,ISSN 1406-0671, BMF
 Gallup Media
Latvian Association of Advertising, unpublished materials
Advertising Yearbook, Latvia 1996, 1997, 1998 1999, BMF Gallup Media
 - Unpublished materials
http://pro.nais.dati.lv
http:// www.bmf.lv
http:// www.iaa.lv
http:// www.emor.ee/omnibus
http:// www.emor.ee/adbrand
www.media-house.com

Advertising in Malaysia

Prof. Dr. Iskandar Abdullah, Ph.D.
University Putra Malaysia

1   Brief History of Malaysian Advertising

Advertising started in Malaysia and Singapore in the 19th century, when the foreign traders were coming come to Malaysia (at that time it was called Malaya). The medium used for advertising then was very limited and techniques used for producing the advertisement were not very attractive. The basic function of advertising at that time was to inform and to sell the products or services to the local and to the other traders. Most of the media used for advertising were posters, brochures, newspapers and pieces of woods.

The first newspaper advertisement appeared in the Prince of Wales Island's Gazette. It was published in Penang in 1805. During those days, the newspapers and magazines were first introduced in the trading centers such as Singapore, Penang and Malacca. It was reported that the first edition of The Straits Times, published in Singapore on 15 July 1845 was filled with various types of advertisements, from shipping to medicinal products. The advertisement is very straightforward and copy-oriented. To get the full support from the advertisers, the publisher inserted a special notice to the advertisers,

The scale of charges for advertisements in The Straits Times *is made on liberal terms. Contracts may be entered into with the printer. Advertisement intended for insertion in* The Straits Times *must be sent before 12 o'clock on the day previous to the publication of the paper.*
The Straits Times, Singapore, 15 July 1845.

The same principles are still being used today especially for newspapers and magazine publishers (Ishak and Badaruddin, 1993).

The first advertising agency in Malaya belongs to Mr. J. R. Flynn Anderson, addressed at No. 18, Change Alley, Singapore. He had advertised his services in The Straits Times on 4 January 1919, with the message "Picture Your Advertising, Let Me Help You".

The advertising industry soon developed into a vast industry where many international advertising agencies began to set up their branches in Malaysia and Singapore. The first international advertising agency that set up an office in Malaysia was Grant International Incorporated, from Chicago.

In 1945, the Associate of Accredited Advertising Agents (4As) was established in Singapore, which was then under Malaya. Soon, in 1952, Malayan Advertiser's Association (2As) was also formed. The formation of these two entities was aimed at looking after the professional interests of the advertisers.

Despite the formation of the 4As and 2As, real professionalism in advertising practices started only after experienced advertising personnel from outside the country began setting up their bases in Singapore in the mid 1950s.

During that time, the print media, radio and rediffusion were the main advertising media. Soon, the agencies in Singapore began opening their offices in Kuala Lumpur to service clients on mainland Malaya. Among the other early agencies were Cathay, Grant, Master, Benson and Young.

When Malaya gained independence from the British in 1957, the Malaysian Government formulated programs to attract foreign investors in the manufacturing and industrial activities of the country. Marketing activities were carried out which in turn led to an increase in advertising activities. More agencies were then set up in Kuala Lumpur and advertisements in the available media became more prominent. While newspapers and magazines were the most popular media among advertisers, the cinema too became a strong medium with still slides of 30 and 60 seconds commercials. Radio and rediffusion too started using jingles as a popular form of advertising.

In 1964, with the introduction of commercial television into the country, multinational advertisers and agencies, which set up their bases in Malaysia increased in numbers. The agencies then, which are now among the top ten agencies in the country, include Ogilvy and Mather, Ted Bates, Lintas and Mc Cann-Erickson. When Singapore and Malaysia split to become two separate countries, the agencies that were formerly operating as one entity, worked independently.

In the early 1970s, the 4As and 2As Joint Media Committee was formed to deal with the government concerning advertising rules and policies. It was also set up to verify and recommend advertising rate increases and other conditions imposed by the media organizations. Following this, in 1977, the advertising Standards Authority of Malaysia or ASAM was launched by the 4As, 2As, media owners and later on the consumer association formulated the Malaysian Code of Advertising Practice as a regulatory guide for advertisement s that appear on Malaysian media. Before this, the representatives from advertising agencies, advertisers and media publishers formed the Audit Bureau of Circulation or ABC to secure uniform methods of audit in print media circulation.

Since the beginning of the 1980s up to the present moment, the Malaysian advertising industry is no longer a small industry. The multinationals and the local agencies are now growing with multi-million-dollars in billings. Malaysia's good infrastructure, regional production and post-production facilities, coupled with the emergence of a quite affluent middle-class society, make it possible for Kuala Lumpur to be a key center of advertising in Asia.

2 The Malaysian Market

Complementing the impressive economic growth is the rise in per capita income of Malaysians. Thus, the Malaysian market has become more sophisticated since consumers have a wider choice in the purchase of goods. However, the 22 million odd Malaysians do not yet add up to a market of 22 million since much of the wealth and buying power of Malaysians are concentrated among the 2.0 million population in the capital city of Kuala Lumpur and its vicinity. But it must also be noted that Malaysians living in other market centers, particularly Johore Bahru in the south are also showing signs of experiencing a higher standard of living. Nevertheless, looking at the proliferation of shopping centers, office buildings and housing projects in Kuala Lumpur and its vicinity, it is safe to say that about 60 percent of the purchasing power in Malaysia is in Kuala Lumpur and the Klang Valley. It represents Malaysia's prosperity and growth. However, about 50 percent of the Malaysian population is still located in the rural areas. In terms of expenditure patterns, about 60 percent of urban and up to 80 percent of rural household expenditures go towards basics such as food, rent and taxes. All other products are competing for the remaining 40 and 20 percent of the disposable income respectively. The many new goods available in the Malaysian market are actually targeted at the rising middle-class Malaysians who are high-income earners. These consumers go for luxury goods like video disc recorders, karaoke sets or expensive cars. Furthermore, because of the multiracial nature of the Malaysian market, consumers who are of different individual backgrounds have different needs. With higher purchasing power and standard of living, Malaysian consumers are demanding increased convenience, sophistication and variety – what with the migration of younger consumers from the rural areas to towns and cities.

The 1990 findings from Survey Research Malaysia on the segments of Malaysian adults would provide a clearer picture of the Malaysian adult market. They are segmented into seven different demographics and psychographics, namely The Kampong Trendsetters, The Not Quite Theres, The Upper Echelons, The Inconspicuous, The Sleepwalkers, The Rebel Hangouts and the Rural Traditionists.

The "Rural Traditionist" comprises the biggest segment, that is, 32 percent of Malaysian adults. They are Malays living in rural areas, conservative and traditional in outlook.

The "Kampung Trendsetters" come from a young age group and more than 60 percent of them are Malays. They comprise 16 percent of the population, are ambitious, outgoing, brand and fashion conscious but are also family and community-oriented.

The "Rebel Hangouts", who comprise 16 percent of the population, are mainly young urban Chinese who have high personal incomes. They are non-conformists and the least religious and moralistic.

The next largest group, which accounts for 12 percent of the market are "Sleepwalkers" who are mainly Chinese females above forty years of age. They are a pessimistic lot who are the least house-proud and the least family- and community-oriented.

The "Not Quite Theres" comprise about 10 percent of the market. They are young Malays with good personal incomes. However, they are lack of confidence, are introvert but moralistic.

The "Inconspicuous" comprise about 10 percent of the population. The majority are urban female Malays who are average income earners. Similar to the "Not Quite Theres", they have high optimism.

Finally, the 5 percent "Upper Echelons" are generally urban Malays in the upper income bracket. They perceive themselves as leaders, are socially active, ambitious and confident. However, like most Malays they are also family-oriented, moralistic and nationalistic.

It must be noted that the seven clusters of Malaysians mentioned above represent the Malaysian way of thinking, and not their culture or way of life.

3   Advertising Industry in Malaysia

The advertising industry in Malaysia showed a marvelous increase, when the expenditure for advertising rose to about 23 percent since 1988 after showing a flat trend during the world recession in 1986 and 1987. In 1991, the total advertising expenditure on monitored media surpassed billion-ringgit, which is quite impressive for a small country like Malaysia (Table 1). Nevertheless, despite the high increase in media expenditure and the proliferation of new advertising media, the power of newspaper and television as a major advertising media is still intact (Table 3). This occurred because 80 percent of the adult population in Malaysia is able to read and write, and almost 90 percent of household in Peninsular Malaysia owns one television set (Hashim, 1994).

Table 1: Advertising Expenditure in Malaysia

Year	RM Million	Year	RM Million
1980	226	1991	1,016.0
1981	271	1992	1,128.0
1982	290	1993	1,415.0
1983	349	1994	1,641.8
1984	401	1995	2,021.7
1985	418	1996	2,419.5
1986	382	1997	2,630.0
1987	409	1998	2,180.0
1988	507	1999	2,525.0
1989	645	2000	2,870.0
1990	818		

Source: SRM Adex Report, 1980 – 1996; AC Nielsen, Malaysia, 1997 – 1999;
Zenith Media Worldwide, 2000
Note: 1USD = RM 3.80

According to Zenith Media Worldwide, Malaysia ad expenditures expected to reach RM3 billion for the first time in year 2001. The ad expenditures for year 2000 are expected to achieve the highest level of RM2.87 billion, increased about 12.7 percent compared to RM2.25 billion for the year 1999 (Berita Harian, Sept. 12, 2000). (Note: 1USD = RM 3.80)

The total ad expenditure will be expected to increase about 9.8 percent to RM3.15 billion for year 2001 and further reach approximately 8.6 percent to RM3.43 billion for the year 2002 (Berita Harian, Sept. 12, 2000).

Table 2: Top Ten Advertisers in Malaysia

Advertising Agencies (according to total media)	Jan-Dec 1999	Rank
British American Tobacco	109,121	1
JT International Trading Sdn. Bhd.	59,981	2
Nestle	56,850	3
Unilever Malaysia	37,317	4
Telekom Malaysia Berhad	35,663	5
Procter & Gamble	28,989	6
Petronas	26,578	7
Measat Broadcast Network Sdn. Bhd.	23,672	8
National Panasonic	23,487	9
Celcom	23,415	10

Source: Media Guide 2001, Whiteknight Communications Sdn. Bhd.

3.1   Advertising Spending by Media

Advertising expenditures in Malaysia were spent more in year 2000 compared to the corresponding period last year. It is about RM 164,374 higher to the advertisers to buy space in the media (The Star, Aug 28, 1999). Table 3, shows the media spending in Malaysia being complied by Media Guide 2001 by Whiteknight Communication Sdn. Bhd.

The data shows television, newspaper, magazine, radio, video, POS (point of sales) but cinema's adverts are apparently under utilized. The cinema shows zero improvement in the Advertising Spending Comparison 1999 vs 2000.

On the TV scene, the launching of NTV7 in April 1998 indicated that the medium has the most significant growth. It was reported that from just 4 percent share of the TV advertising market initially, the TV market expanded their market share up to 21.3 percent increased. In 1999, there were only four local TV broadcasts in this country, which are TV1, TV2, TV3 and NTV7. Metro Vision terminated its broadcast from November 1, 1999 and in December 1999, TV3 starts to increase their transmission times by 12.5 hours a week.

Table 3: Advertising Spending Comparison 1999 vs 2000

Media '000	1999 (RM)	2000 (RM)	% Change
TV	771,351	935,725	+21.3
Newspaper	1,471,006	1,866,177	+26.9
Magazine	104,108	131,171	+26
Radio	85,077	101,961	+19.8
Cinema	9,665	9,673	-
Video	10,918	9,377	-14.1
POS	22,138	24,184	+9.2
TOTAL	2,474,262	3,078,267	+24.4

Source: Media Guide 2001, Whiteknight Communications Sdn. Bhd.

From Table 3, the major increase in comparison of year 1999 and 2000 is in newspaper and TV media. The high growth is shown by newspaper media with 26.9 percent followed by TV media with 21.3 percent. In comparing both years, all media show increase excepts cinema, which show no progress.

3.2 Spending by Product Category

In terms of product category spending in 1998, Classified/Appointment held on firmly number one spot for the first six months. This was despite a slight drop, which is less than 2 percent to 159 million. Entertainment/ Franchise advertisement (i.e. tobacco companies program promotions) tumbled from second spot in Jan – June 1998 period to RM 52.5 million for the same time period in 1997. The second spot was filled by Telecommunication Advertisements, which increased their spending up to 2.6 percent or RM 56.9 million compared to the previous year.

In the year 1998, Real Estate was the biggest newcomer in the advertising industry in terms of their spending pattern. It posted RM 31.2 million in their spending for advertising activities. The second newcomer was radio, hi-fi and recorders advertisements with RM 23.1 million spending. Besides the emergence of these two categories, on the other hand, two categories tumbled out of the top ten chart; Sport/Sporting Goods and Department Stores/Emporiums (The Star, Aug 28, 1999).

However, in 1999, the trends of top ten advertisers regarding the product category, the classified/appointment topped the list, which shows an increase by 13 percent to RM 366.9 million. It was followed by telecommunications in the second place with RM 144.8 million in advertising expenditures, corporation, government agencies and utilities with RM 137.3 million expenditure in third place. Table 5 shows the top ten advertisers based on product category in 1999.

Table 4: Spending by Product Category

No.	Category	Spending (RM million)
1	Classified/Appointment	366.9
2	Telecommunications	144.8
3	Corporation, Government Agencies and Utilities	137.3
4	Entertainment/franchise	120.3
5	Real Estate	83.2
6	Banks, Credit cards and Securities companies	82.8
7	Educational, Bookstores	82.4
8	Communication, Publishing, Media and Exhibition	67.4
9	Entertainment, Leisure activities	64.9
10	Radio, Hi-fi systems and recorders	57.4

Source: ACNielsen Malaysia extracted from The Star, Feb 12, 2000

3.3 Media Trends in Malaysia Advertising

The trend in advertising always changes over time due to the economic factors or the changes in market itself. In Malaysia, television and newspapers had enjoyed a large number of audiences in 1998 due to interesting news events, free-copy and subscription-drive promotions and the launch of NTV7 (The Star, Sept 18, 1999).

The trend of media audience is shown in Figure 1. TV audience and newspaper readership dipped between 1998's second quarter and 1999's second quarter. The coverage for TV fell from 88.5 percent for Peninsular Malaysia adults to 86.5 percent, while newspaper readership declined from 59.7 percent to 53.4 percent for the same period.

The drop for newspaper readership percentage was mainly due to a sharp drop in Bahasa Malaysia daily reader, from 31 percent of adult in Peninsular Malaysia to just 25 percent. It was also caused by the increased readership of Harakah newspaper, which may have an effect on leading Bahasa Malaysia newspapers or dailies.

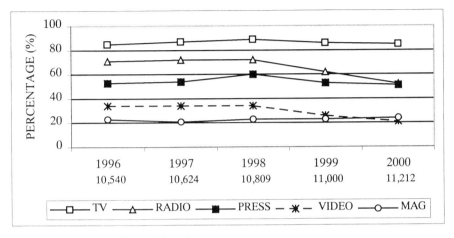

Figure 1: Media Audience Trends
Source: Media Guide 2001, Whiteknight Communications Sdn. Bhd.

For television, the main events over the last 18 months were reduction of transmission time and the launching of NTV7 in April 1998. The causalities of reduced broadcast hours were Bahasa Malaysia and English programs and the increase in Chinese and Tamil programs. Besides the shorter transmission time, there was an increases in average daily viewing hours for individuals aged 6 years and above during the year ended June 1999. As for subscription of cable TV, there was a 1.7 percent viewership growth up for June 1999.

Video rental viewership had fallen from 34.5 percent of Peninsular Malaysia adults in 1998's second quarter to 26.1 percent in 1999's second quarter. This is probably due to because of the emergence of video compact discs. For Cinema/Cineplex audience also slipped from 6.8 percent to 4.7 percent (The Star, Sept 18, 1999).

With the advent of Information Technology (IT), the Internet has become the latest medium for advertising. The internet users soared by 52 percent to 657,000 adults during past 12 months ended June 1999, while LRT (high rapid transport) and commuter train users rose by 2.7 percent and 11 percent respectively.

From the graph, Christina Low, a media measurement services executive of ACNielsen Sdn. Bhd. mentioned that TV and Internet would continue to grow but they are unlikely to affect the audience of the traditional media.

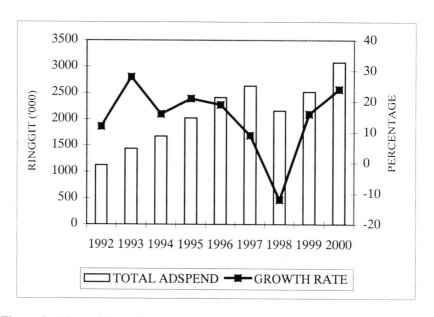

Figure 2: Adspend Trend (1992 – 2000)
Source: Media Guide 2001, Whiteknight Communications Sdn. Bhd.

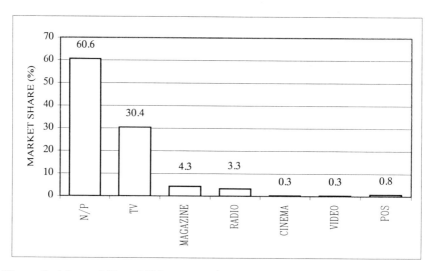

Figure 3: Adspend Year 2000
Source: Media Guide 2001, Whiteknight Communications Sdn. Bhd.

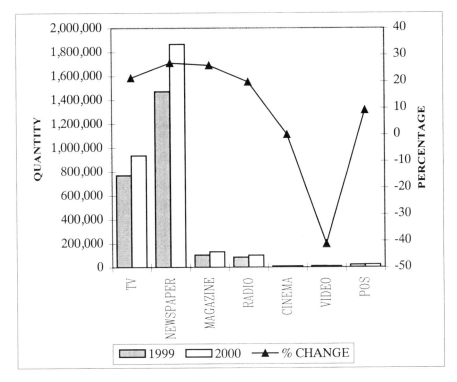

Figure 4: Adspend Comparison 1999 vs 2000
Source: Media Guide 2001, Whiteknight Communications Sdn. Bhd.

4   Media in Malaysia

4.1   Newspaper

The newspaper gained the lion's share of industry ad spend, holding a market share of 60.6% or RM 1.86 billion an increase of 26.9% over 1999 period against the year ending 2000.

The spending by the IT industry saw rapid growth last year, particularly from IT services which registered a 473% increase in 2000. The service industry continues to dominate and within this, major growth last year can be seen for communication/publishing (+103%) which seems to be largely from in-house ads, travel + tour agencies (+100%) and sports/sporting goods (+95%). Classified ads continue to make up 38% of the service industry and saw an increase of 30% in the year 2000. The year also saw classified ads went to English newspapers, 26% to Chinese and 11% to Bahasa newspapers.

Another major spender in the service industry is telcos, which grew by 47%. Indeed the top four advertisers in newspapers are Telekom Malaysia (+46%), Maxis (+45%), Measat (+48%) and Celcom (+81%) respectively.

Figure 5 shows the newspaper readership trend of varies languages in Malaysia from 1996 to year 2000.

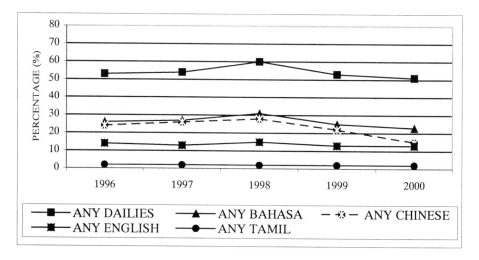

Figure 5: Newspaper Readership (1996 – 2000)
Source: Media Guide 2001, Whiteknight Communications Sdn. Bhd.

4.2   Magazines

In the year 2000, magazine adex revenue clocked at RM 131.1 million for the year, an increased of 26.9% over 1999. However, the market share situation does not show improvement at 4.3 %.

Many local magazines, particularly Bahasa magazine – benefited from this growth. From a mere 3 Bahasa magazines in the "top 25" list for ad revenue in 1996, there were 7 for the year 2000, most of which registered double – digit growths.

Popular categories in Bahasa magazine, with a disproportionate amount of ad revenue in comparison of English and Chinese magazines are categories such as Corporation/Government agencies (+73%), Communication/ Publishing (+49%), Hair Dressing (+54%) and Classified (+156%). However, English magazine continue to gain the majority of ads in high spending categories such as Face/Hand Care, Cosmetics and Clothing.

Table 5 shows the comparison for the years 2000 and 1999 on the magazine adex share by title and language.

Table 5: Magazine Adex Share by Title/Language (2000 vs 1999)

Magazine Adex Share By Title / Language		
RM (Million)	1999	2000
Regional English	44.2	49.2
Local English	26.1	36.7
Bahasa	14.6	20.7
Local Chinese	14	19.2
Regional Chinese	4.3	4.7
Tamil	0.8	0.7

Source: Media Guide 2001, Whiteknight Communications Sdn. Bhd.

4.3   Television

Approximately about 85% of Malaysia population can be reached by television medium. Station reached and racial coverage is as stated in the table below.

Interestingly, the Malay viewers tend to watch more TV1 in comparison with other TV Stations. Chinese viewers are concentrated in TV2 and TV3. Among the Indian viewers, NTV7 top them against the other station with 12% reach. This is due to strong Indian programming strategy on Sundays for almost 5 hours. Figure 6 shows the television viewship trend between the years 1996 to 2000.

Table 6 : Station Reached and Racial Coverage (Percentage)

STATIONS	MALAYS (%)	CHINESE (%)	INDIAN (%)
TV1	73	18	9
TV2	61	29	10
TV3	61	29	10
NTV7	53	35	12

Source: Media Guide 2001, Whiteknight Communications Sdn. Bhd.

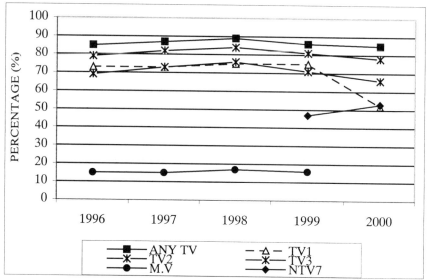

Figure 6: TV Viewship (1996 – 2000)
Source: Media Guide 2001, Whiteknight Communications Sdn. Bhd.

Table 7: Age Coverage by Station (in million)

Age Coverage by Stations	
15 - 19 years old	1,700
20 - 24 years old	1,500
25 - 29 years old	1,300
30 - 34 years old	1,200
35 - 39 years old	1,100
40 - 49 years old	1,800
Over 49 years old	2,000

Source: Media Guide 2001, Whiteknight Communications Sdn. Bhd.

4.4   Radio

Radio sees a growth of 20%, most of this is for the AMP stations. From holding only 38% of market share in 1999, AMP stations now lead the show with 52% market share. ERA radio station is fast-catching up with the leading AMP station Hits FM, seeing a hefty growth of 120%. Following this is the Chinese channel MY FM, which sees a growth of 97%. This is hardly surprising as confirmed by the ACNielsen Radio Diary Survey 2000, which lists ERA radio station and MY radio station as the most listened-to radio stations in Malaysia, gaining the most attention from the Malay and Chinese population respectively.

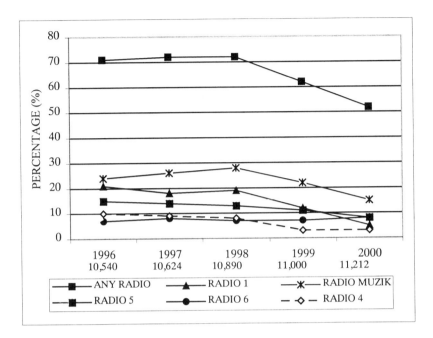

Figure 7: Radio Listenership (1996 – 2000)
Source: Media Guide 2001, Whiteknight Communications Sdn. Bhd.

4.5   Out-Of-Home Advertising

The demand for outdoor advertising seen in 1999 has not been taped yet in 2000 and thus has put the medium in a very enviable position vis-à-vis the other key supportive mediums.

The high demand for outdoor sites in high traffic, especially in the Klang Valley region, has in fact led to a situation that heavily favors the major outdoor contractors, who control perhaps close to 90% of the total outdoor business. The high demand for space has also led to a pricing structure that is often pegged at rate card rate, unless the Advertisers' commitment is substantial.

Demand remains very high, especially in prime locations that are of strategic values. Whilst demand for space and cheaper cost options has been on the increase, the more expensive ones such as the *Unipoles* are readily available. Prohibitive advertising cost has led to advertisers with

small budgets staying away from them. Understanding the market sentiments, many of the media contractors offering *Unipoles* have lowered their
advertising cost quite substantially to lure advertisers, and this has to some
extent helped to fill up some of the available space.

At the same time, existing traditional billboard advertising too has gone
through a face of change with better quality visual presentation through the
availability of state-of-the-art printing facilities with MMT technology locally.

Other newer outdoor opportunities such as transit advertising on LRT
station panels and city buses have also grown in popularity in 2000. The
Outdoor Medium was given a further boast with the arrival of Out-door
Media Specialists from U.K. For the first time, advertisers are able to
measure the Outdoor Traffic with the assistance from this Outdoor Specialists where prices can be fixed accordingly to its audience level for each
signpost.

5   Advertising Controls and Constraints[1]

5.1   Government's Code of Advertising Practice

The main government organization that monitors and regulates advertising
practices in Malaysia is the Ministry of Information. It has an advertising
code that provides guidelines for advertising agencies and advertisers to
abide by, particularly concerning broadcast commercials. Among other
thing, the code stipulates that:
> Advertisements must project the Malaysian culture, identity, reflect the
> multiracial character of the population and advocate the philosophy of
> "Rukun Negara".

The other guidelines in the code specify details that require all advertisement to be "legal, decent, honest and truthful". For instance, scene of
an amorous, intimate or suggestive nature are forbidden on Malaysian
television. Also not permitted are commercials for pork and pork products,
liquor and alcoholic beverages since they are forbidden in Islam. In addition, provocative scenes that show naked or scantily clad models are also
not allowed to be shown. There are also sections of the code that protect
children and women against exploitation.

As recent as 1991, the Ministry of Information, in response to the industry's and public's complaints against the vagueness of some aspects of its

---

[1] Taken from Hashim A. and Frith K.T. 1994, Advertising in Malaysia

advertising code, has made some changes to the code. They include forbidding certain advertisements such as those that highlight western values and project and promote inspirational lifestyles as well as advertisements on feminine napkins.

However, the new code did not ban the advertisement of non-tobacco products like belts, camping gear, perfume, ties and shirts using cigarette brands names and logos. In fact, cigarette logo advertisers dominate more than 30 percent of the total advertising expenditure ever since tobacco advertisements were banned on television in 1982.

Because of the increasing awareness against the danger of smoking and rise in the number of young Malaysian who smoke, the government is now seriously considering a total ban on direct and indirect cigarette advertising in all media.

5.2   Government Regulation on Television Commercials

An advertiser who wishes to air a television commercial on any of the three Malaysian networks must first submit the script and the storyboard for approval to the Ministry of Information at RTM or Radio Television Malaysia. Once the script and the storyboard have been reviewed by the Advertising Division, they will be returned with comments and changes to the advertiser or its advertising agency. If the client and the agency agree to the changes, then the script and storyboard would receive a "Station Approval" from RTM and the agency can then proceed to production (cf. Figure 8).

The ministry of Information has certain requirements that have an impact on the television commercial production process. For example, the commercial's footage and music must be produced locally and must use local talents. This means that all the people involved in the production of the commercial must be Malaysians, including actors and actresses, technical people, voice or music. Hiring of foreign experts to produce local commercials is allowed only if no Malaysian can perform the job.

The government requires a Made-in-Malaysia (MIM) certificate issued by RTM's Advertising Division to be submitted with the final checkprint, that is, the finished, edited footage.

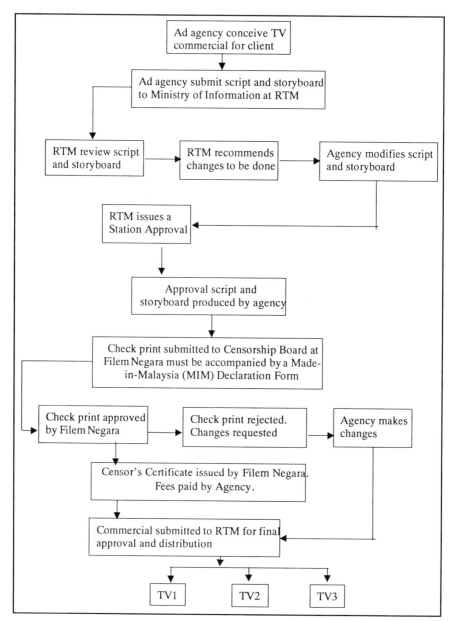

Figure 8: Television Commercial Approval Process
Source: Hashim A. and Frith K.T. (1994), Advertising in Malaysia

In certain cases, the Ministry will allow up to 20 percent of the footage to be shot outside Malaysia. However, this is only allowed under special circumstances and the Ministry must give prior approval. One television-commercial for Salem High Country featured a snow-covered mountaintop filmed in a foreign country. The Ministry approved this foot age because there are no snow-covered mountains in Malaysia, but only 20 Percent of the commercial could this foreign-shot footage.

In addition, if the advertiser wants to run his commercial on the government-run Television Malaysia, TV1, the commercial must be produced in Bahasa Malaysia, the national language. It has been estimate that almost two-thirds of all television commercials are now produced in Bahasa Malaysia. TV2, also government-run, concepts commercials in other languages but requires that they carry Bahasa Malaysia supers. TV3, the private network, accepts commercials in any language. All television commercials must end with a super title that explains the product in Bahasa Malaysia.

Once the commercial has been shot, copies of the check prints and the soundtrack must be submitted to the Filem Negara Censorship Board. The check prints must be accompanied with a "Made-in-Malaysia" (MIM) declaration form. After being reviewed by the Censorship Board, a Censor's Certificate will be issued for the particular check print that has been approved. The advertiser must pay a fee for this certificate based on the length of the commercial and the amount of time the advertisement will run in the media.

The check print with the approval and the Censor's Certificate will then be sent to RTM for final approval. An important point to note is that the Ministry has the right to sub edit, reasonably, any advertising material without prior reference to the advertisers or their agent.

5.3 Government Regulation on Print Advertisements

RTM Advertising Code, enforced by the Advertising Division of the Ministry of Information, also applies to print advertisements. Of particular concern are advertisements for "medicine, treatments and appliances for the prevention and alleviation of any ailments, illness or diseases". The Medical Advertising Board must approve all advertisements containing health claims as in aspirin commercials, which is part of the Ministry of Health. When the advertisement has been reviewed and the claims approved, a Kementerian Kesihatan Lembaga Iklan Ubat (KKLIU) approval will be issued. All advertisements of health care products, which appear in the print media, must have the KKLIU approval displayed on them, or the print media may not run them.

In addition to the Ministry of Information, which acts as a gatekeeper for the media in Malaysia, the Ministry of Domestic Trade and Industry, has a Consumer Affair Division, which deals directly with consumer complaints against advertising. Another one of its tasks is to regulate the packaging and labeling of food products. All important food products must have a label translated into English and Bahasa Malaysia.

5.4   ASAM: Advertising Standards Authority of Malaysia

The ASAM committee comprising representatives from the advertising agencies, advertisers and Malaysian newspaper and magazine publishers was sent up in 1975 as a voluntary self-regulatory body to oversee advertisements. In 1977, the consumer associations also represented an advertising code, known as the Malaysian Code of Advertising Practice was launched by ASAM, which at all time. However, in 1978, representatives from the Federation of Malaysia Consumer Associations or FOMCA withdrew its membership due to disagreements on the term "offending advertisements". Nevertheless, the advertising code is a comprehensive document that, among other things, state that the 'advertiser should not exploit consumers' lack of knowledge and expertise", "advertisements shall not unfairly attack or discredit other products, advertisers or advertisements directly or by implication".

The code also spells out factors like advertisements must project a Malaysian identity, no typecasting of racial groups and must be legal, decent, honest and truthful.

The committee, which meets monthly works closely with government departments and deals with complaints on advertisements that go against the code. Complaints that ASAM receive every year come mostly from within the industry and consumer movements. When a complaint is filed, ASAM will attempt to rectify the situation by asking the advertiser and the agency to modify or change the advertisement. When a compromise cannot be reached, the advertiser is then asked to withdraw the advertisement from the media. Out of an average of about forty complaints received yearly, only about 10 to 15 percent of the advertisements are withdrawn while some are either amended or allowed to appear in the media due to invalid complaints.

5.5 The Consumer Movement

Malaysia is a multiracial country with Islam as the national religion, the practice of advertising should consider the sentiments of Muslims because the public is very sensitive to advertisements that they consider an insult to their culture or religion. Any products that are considered forbidden by Islam are banned from being advertised on television and radio, but they are not restricted to other media.

Beside the religious constraints, advertisements that are related with social and cultural insensitivity are also banned or not allowed to be shown to the consumers to avoid unsatisfied feelings among races when they believe the advertisement is insulting their culture or way of life.

5.6 Adherence of Religious and Social Constraints

Television came to Malaysia 30 years ago and become the most dominant advertising medium in Malaysia. Although, it is still behind newspaper in terms of advertising revenue collected, the gap is very close. Television medium is the fastest growing medium with about 100 percent increase in advertising money within a span of 4 years.

On the three available channels at that time, which are TV1, TV2 and TV3, TV3 has been the leading station for both viewers and advertising revenue collected. According to SRM, Advertising Expenditure Report in 1991, TV3 took up 45 percent of the total revenue expenditure of RM 400 million spent on television.

The advertisement rates during the prime-time shows are between RM 6,500 and RM 8,000 for a 30 second commercial. Eventhough, the rate for ad on TV is relatively high, it has not affected demand for TV commercials. One of the most popular way used by big advertisers to ensure that their advertisement will be available at all times was done by sponsoring one series of television slot on their favorite channel like Dunhill Double sponsored by Dunhill and Salem Cool Planet sponsored by Salem. These advertisers would monopolize the entire program lasting a minimum of about 2 hours daily to advertise their sponsored program as well as their line of products or services.

The massive amount of commercials on television at late 80s has created a clutter at alarming levels. In 1991, there was an average of 435 commercials per day on all three stations, which represents an increase of about 65 percent from the 1989 figures at 264 commercials (The Star, Dec 14, 1991).

Today, with the addition of other television channels like NTV7, Astro and Mega TV, the already intense competition among channels to get big advertiser becomes very difficult. This situation will be an opportunity to the advertisers because they have a wider choice on where to advertise their products, but it is difficult for the viewers who have to consume many types of advertisements from existing channels today.

References

The Straits Times, Singapore, 15 July, 1845
Berita Harian, Sept. 12 2000
The Star, Aug 28, 1999
The Star, Feb 12, 2000
The Star, Sept 18, 2000
Media Guide 2001, Whiteknight Communications Sdn. Bhd.
Hashim A. and Frith K.T. Advertising in Malaysia, 1994
SRM Adex Report, 1980 – 1996 AC Nielsen, Malaysia, 1997 – 1999 Zenith Media Worldwide, 2000

Advertising in Singapore

Prof. Dr. May O. Lwin[1]
Faculty of Business Administration, National University of Singapore
Mr. Martin Lee, Regional Creative Director
Dentsu Young & Rubicam

1 Introduction

Situated at the southern tip of Peninsular Malaysia, Singapore is a newly industrialized country and is fast developing into an international center for finance, transport and communication. The general trend for the Singapore advertising industry is towards globalization and liberalization, resulting in a small number of large agencies, some specialized local agencies, and a growing number of independent media buying houses.

2 Advertising Environment

2.1 Economic

Singapore produces a gross domestic product (GDP) of S$143,981 million.[2] The unemployment rate has been constantly stable and low at 2%.[3] Consumers in Singapore are becoming more affluent. Both household income and personal income have risen from 1990 to 2000 (cf. Figures 1 and 2). The median household income rose from S$893 in 1980 to S$3,529 in 2000, while the median personal income increased from S$641 in 1984 to S$1,824 in 2000.

Consumer durables ownership, which indicates the level of wealth, can be considered high for many products including television and washing machines. The ownership of mobile phones has increased by more than

---

[1] The authors wish to thank Mr Wei Hong Sim for his research assistance.
[2] US$1.00 = S$1.7315. Source: Monetary Authority of Singapore (2000)
[3] Source: Census of Population/Yearbook of Statistics 2000 (Singapore)

threetimes within a short period of 3 years, from about 0.4 million in 1997 to 1.2 million in 2000. The popularity of personal computers and laser/video/compact disc players has also increased.

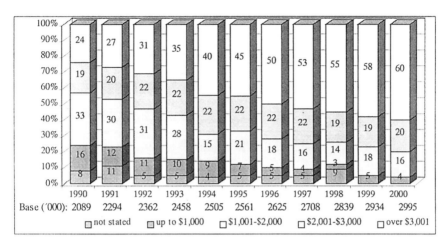

Figure 1: Household Income in Singapore
Source: ACNielsen Media Index 2000

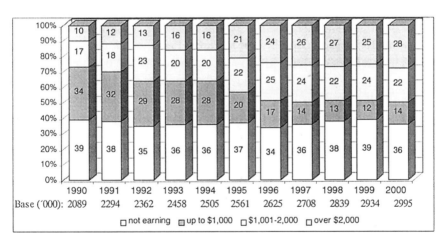

Figure 2: Personal Income in Singapore
Source: ACNielsen Media Index 2000

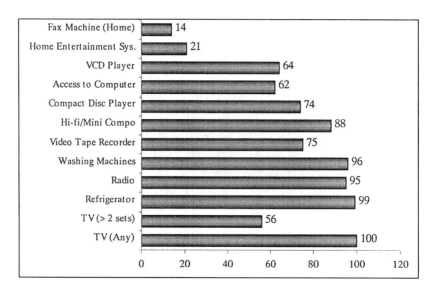

Figure 3: Consumer Durables Ownership
Source: ACNielsen Media Index 2000

2.2   Political

The leadership of Singapore has remained stable for the last 36 years. Since May 1959, the People's Action Party (PAP) has dominated all elections. The number of opposition members elected in parliament remains small. Lee Kuan Yew, who led the PAP, remained the Prime Minister of Singapore for over 30 years. He gave way to his deputy, Goh Cheok Tong, who took over as Prime Minister in 1991.

2.3   Demographic

Singapore has a population base of 4.02 million, comprising 3.26 million citizens/permanent residents and 0.75 million expatriates. Singapore's annual population growth rate of 1.4% (2000) is expected to remain the same for the next few years. The average household size has been found to be shrinking (cf. Figure 4).

The 0 to 19-year-old age group makes up 27.9% of the total population. The 20 to 24 age group accounted for 6.5% of the population; those 25 to 29 year-old accounted for 8.1%; those 30 to 34 accounted for 8.9%; those

35 to 39 accounted for 9.9%; those 40 to 49 accounted for 17.6%; and the aged 50 and above make up 20.8% of the population. There is a shift in population structure towards the older age groups. While the age group 0-19 years expanded, there is a decline in the number of citizens aged 20-29 years (cf. Figure 5).

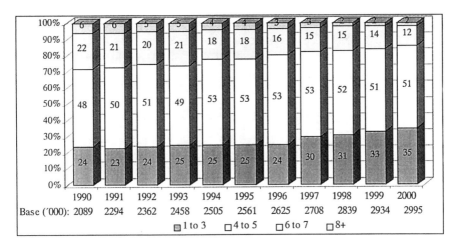

Figure 4: Household Size
Source: ACNielsen Media Index 2000

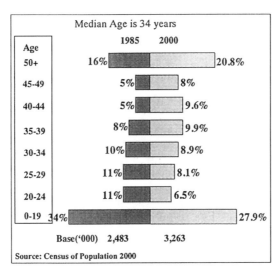

Figure 5: Age Distribution
Population base: 4.02 million, comprising 3.26 million citizens/PR and 0.75 million expatriates. Annual population growth rate: 1.4% (2000)

The largest ethnic grouping of Singapore's population consists of the Chinese, making up 77% as of 2000. The Malays form the next largest group, accounting for 14%, followed by the Indians with 8%. Others make up the remaining 1%. The existence of the three main races in Singapore makes it a challenge for advertising to have national appeal.

There is a shift in occupational categories as compared to 20 years ago. In 1980, 40% of the working population was blue-collared workers and 24% was white-collared workers. In 2000, 40% of the workforce was white-collared and 22% was blue-collared (cf. Figure 6).

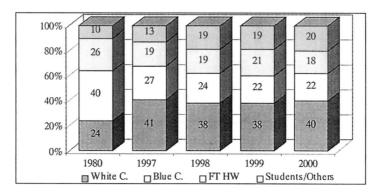

Figure 6: Breakdown of Occupation
Source: ACNielsen Media Index 2000

The educational profile of Singapore's residents has shown marked improvement over the last 15 years. The number of people who received secondary education and above increased from about 55% in 1984 to 75% in 2000. The literacy rate in Singapore is high at 94%. As English continues to be adopted as a medium of education, English (80%) is the language most understood by the population, followed by Mandarin (75%) and Malay (55%).

82% of Singaporeans live in public housing (HDB) while the remaining 18% live in private housing (bungalows, terraces and condominiums).

2.4 Technological

The government has emphasized growth in higher-technology industries for both products and services through channels such as the Economic Development Board and involvement in technology exchanges with US and other developed countries. The role of the government is to provide guidelines, incentives and infrastructure for businesses to exploit the benefits of IT.

In Singapore, people are considered the most valuable asset. There is also emphasis on constant acquisition of knowledge and upgrading of skills to maintain competitive advantage. This accounts for the keen interest in information technology training courses and further education among the people.

Advertising agencies appear to be looking to create an individual perspective or process, to offer a strategic point of difference. There is rapid adoption of sophisticated software optimization and planning systems in the industry, enabling agencies to offer a unique positioning in the marketplace to attract new business.

3   Advertising Trends

3.1   Advertising Expenditures

The Singapore advertising industry recorded 23% growth in total advertising expenditures in 2000. Annual total advertising volume increased from US$718 million in 1999 to US$883 million in 2000 (cf. Figure 7). Accordingly, Singapore takes the eighth position in terms of advertising expenditure in the Asia Pacific region, being in advance of Malaysia and Vietnam.

The print media remains the dominant medium for advertising, with a 50% share of the total advertising volume, or about S$750 million in expenditure. Daily newspapers take up the biggest part of print advertising. These are mainly a local medium for advertisements from the retail business and the rubric markets (estate, car or job offers) (cf. Figure 8). Singapore Press Holdings' flagship newspaper The Straits Time topped the list, having attracted S$514 million worth of advertising.

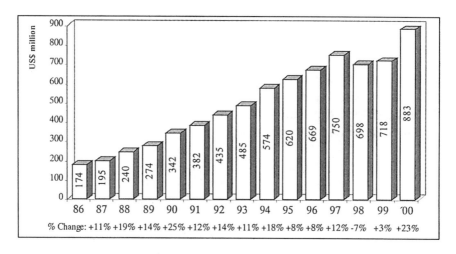

Figure 7: Annual Total Advertising Volume
Source: ACNielsen ADEX Reports, Rate of exchange: US$ 1.00 = S$ 1.70

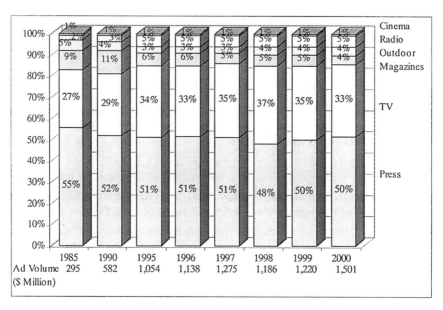

Figure 8: Advertising Expenditure by Medium
Source: ACNielsen ADEX Reports

TV advertising expenditures take a second place, with a share of 33% or S$495.3 million of the total advertising volume. TCS' Channel 8 was the hottest TV channel, commanding S$241.3 million. Radio, outdoor and cinema advertising is of minor importance, used either for special target groups (cinema: 14- to 29-year-olds), special products (outdoor: beer, spirits, mass media, cars) or for local advertisements (radio).

The growth in advertising volume and expenditures has largely been driven by the intensive marketing war following the deregulation of the telecommunications industry in Singapore, according to ACNielsen Media International (source: www.acnielsen.com.sg). Advertising by the major players in the telecommunications industry has provided a strong impetus which brought the Singaporean advertising industry out of the doldrums since 1997.

Since the government liberalized the telecommunications industry in April 2000, the industry has experienced a sudden surge in advertising. AC Nielsen's AdEx recorded 99.4% growth over 1999 to S$151.186 million (cf. Table 1). In the face of rigorous competition from new entrants, Singtel, the government-owned carrier, aggressively promoted the Singapore Telecom, Singtel Mobile and Singtel IDD brands under its umbrella, in an attempt to maintain their leadership in the market. Started in April 2000, Starhub - Singapore's second fixed line operator also actively featured its range of services such as Starhub IDD 008 and Starhub Mobile, as well as the corporate brand. The third player, M1 has launched strong campaigns to beat competition from both Singtel and Starhub in the mobile communications segment. Accordingly, Singtel, Starhub and M1 were the top 3 advertisers in 2000 under the product category (cf. Table 2). Singtel invested S$68 million, way ahead of new players Starhub and M1 who posted S$28.2 million and S$24 millions respectively.

Table 1: Advertising Expenditure of Top 10 Product Categories in 2000

Product Category	Expenditure $ '000	% Increase over 1999
1. Telecommunication	151,186	99.4
2. Retail	98,933	9.8
3. Entertainment	92,822	8.4
4. Real Estate	76,738	24.4
5. Banking / Investment	65,323	41.9
6. Govt./ Social Organizations	61,543	14.8
7. Computer	54,681	18.4
8. Media	49,745	24.3
9. Travel Agency/Tourist Comm.	46,054	21.5
10. Automotive	45,896	39.0

Source: ACNielsen

There was 42% growth to S$65.3 million in advertising expenditures in the banking and investment sector. Two of the top banks, United Overseas Bank (UOB) and Overseas Chinese Banking Corporation (OCBC), devoted much of their advertising to promoting their online banking services, namely www.uobgroup.com and www.finatiq.com, respectively.

Among individual brands, McDonald's restaurant was the most advertised brand for the third consecutive year, with total advertising expenditure amounting to S$16.6 million. Its closest competitor, Kentucky Fried Chicken followed behind with S$7.4 million.

Table 2: Advertising expenditure of top 10 brands in 2000

Brand	Amount Spent , S$ (M)
1. McDonald's Restaurants	16.6
2. Courts	13.8
3. Starhubidd 008	9.3
4. S'pore Telecom	9.0
5. Singtel Mobile	7.9
6. Ntuc Fairprice	7.7
7. Kentucky Fried Chicken	7.4
8. M 1 (Mobileone)	6.3
9. Tiger Beer	5.7
10. Best	5.6

Source: ACNielsen

3.2 Media Inflation

From 1998 to 2001, the media inflation index for TV and newspapers have increased more rapidly relative to other audio-visual and print media.

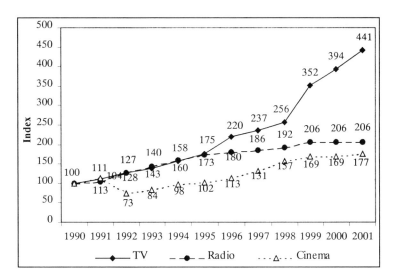

Figure 9: Media Inflation for Audio-Visual Media
Source: Media Owner Rate Cards/Agency Estimations

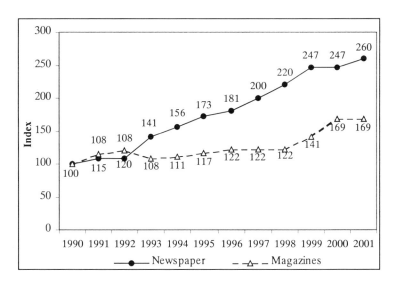

Figure 10: Media Inflation for Print Media
Source: Media Owner Rate Cards/Agency Estimations

4   Advertising Media in Singapore

Within the new millennium, Singapore's government has been loosening its reins on the media industry. In 2000, the sole newspaper publisher in Singapore was allowed to venture into broadcasting business and radio services, and the sole broadcaster was permitted to apply for a newspaper license. The local cable company is also poised to enter into cable telephony and Internet TV. Although this media liberalization is seen as modest, the move has resulted in three new newspapers being launched in 2000 and two more free-to-air channels going on air in 2001. Following these may be a possible review of the existing ban on satellite dishes.

Table 3: Media at a Glance

Media	Number	In-Home Penetration %	Coverage
Television	1 MCSN 3 TCS 2 TV 12 3 Malaysian channels	99	90.3
Video	---	82	4.0
Cinema	122 Halls	---	10.0
Electronic Media			
In TV	2 channels	71	n.a.
Cablevision	3 channels	17,000 household subscribers 12,000 commercial subscribers	12.0
SCV	36 channels	161,000 household subscribers	19.4
Radio	16 Singapore 2 Batam 6 Malaysia plus int. Network channels	92	62.0
Rediffusion	2 channels	6	2.0
Newspapers	8 Dailies 6 Sundays	1,008,406 (Daily circulation) 904,170 (Sunday circulation)	85.0 86.0
Magazines	150+ titles	130 million (annual circulation)	56.0
Outdoor			
Posters	317 posters	---	n.a.
Bus panels	2,700 buses	---	n.a.
MRT	42 stations	---	n.a.
Taxi roof top	5,500 taxis	---	23.0

The advertising pie is also set to expand with these changes. TV mobiles are already introduced inside buses. This is in addition to existing outdoor advertising media such as restrooms, and exteriors of buses and taxis.

4.1 Newspapers

Newspaper readership has shown steady increases from 1991 to 2000 (cf. Figure 11). The newspaper medium in Singapore is monopolized by Singapore Press Holdings (SPH), a listed blue-chip company. SPH controls a total of 19 titles in the market.

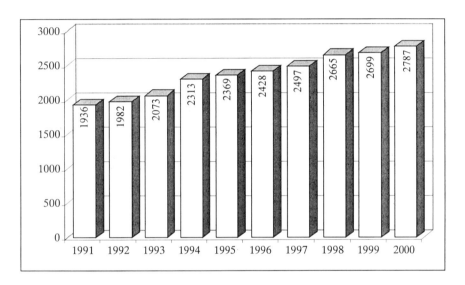

Figure 11: Newspaper Readership in Singapore
Source: Nielsen Media Index 2000

Five newspapers are available every morning. They are The Straits Times and The Business Times (English), Lianhe Zaobao (Chinese), Berita Harian (Malay) and Tamil Murasu (Tamil). In the afternoon, there is The New Paper (English). Lianhe Wanbao and Shin Min Daily News (Chinese) are available in the evenings. With the exception of The Business Times, there are Sunday editions for all the dailies.

Four of the papers are available on the internet, The Straits Times, Business Times, The New Paper and Lianhe Zaobao. From July 2000, Lianhe Wanbao and Shin Min Daily News publish afternoon editions as well.

Since its launch on 15 July, 1845, The Straits Times has grown to become the English flagship daily of SPH and one of the most respected newspapers in the region. The Straits Times and its Sunday issue, The Sunday Times, are the largest circulating newspapers in Singapore (cf. Table 4).

Table 4: Newspaper Circulation

Newspaper	Circulation in Feb. 2001
The Straits Times	391,216
The Sunday Times	392,133
The Business Times	33,312
The New Paper (TNP)	118,380
TNP (Sunday edition)	140,626
Berita Harian	64,261
Berita Minggu (Sunday)	73,269
Lianhe Zaobao	195,209 (Weekday)
	206,758 (Weekend)
Lianhe Wanbao	127,656 (Weekday)
	123,283 (Weekend)
Shin Min Daily News	117,520 (Weekday)
	115,087 (Weekend)
Friday Weekly	51,714
Tamil Muraso	9,003
	15,306 (Sunday)
Streats	200,000 (Free daily)

Source: Singapore Press Holdings

The Business Times is a key source of information for investors and businessmen in Singapore and in the Asia region, since its launch on 1 October 1976. On 26 July 1988, SPH launched The New Paper, which is targeted at younger Singaporeans and presents complex issues in an easy-to-read manner.

The leading Chinese newspaper is Lianhe Zaobao, started in 1983. Lianhe Wanbao and Shin Min Daily News provide leisure reading in bold and creative writing style. Tamil Murasu and Berita Harian cater to the Indian and Malay segments of the population respectively.

According to a survey conducted by Optimum Media Direction (OMD) in December 2000, the average readership is 45% for The Straits Times and 23% for Lianhe Zaobao (cf. Figure 12). The price per copy of The Straits Times/The New Paper is S$0.60 and S$0.65 for Lianhe Zaobao.

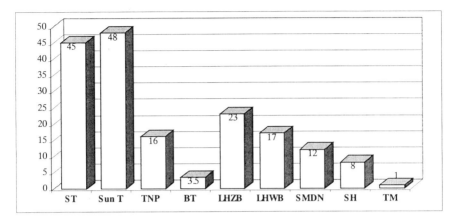

Figure 12: Singapore Press Holdings' Newspaper Readership
Source: Nielsen Media Index 2000

The government issued a newspaper license to MediaCorp group in the interest of injecting more direct competition in the local newspaper industry. MediaCorp, together with their partners, Singapore Mass Rapid Transit (SMRT), Delgro and SingTel Yellow Pages, launched Today, a free morning tabloid on 4 November 2000 (cf. Table 5). Today operates within the conditions of the Newspaper and Printing Presses Act (NPPA), which includes a 3% ownership rule and a management share framework, similar to newspapers under SPH.

The Singapore Gazette, a free bi-monthly regional newspaper publishes 17 local papers covering 80% of Singapore households with a circulation of 688,110. It offers customized sampling or promotions as it can be localized down to the private apartments, 4-room HDB or in selected parts of the island.

In 2000, SPH launched 3 newspapers, Thumbs-up, Streats and Project Eyeball.

Thumbs-up is a weekly Mandarin newspaper launched on 17 Jan 2000. It targets students from Primary Three to Six. This new offering features fun articles, tips and guides in mastering Mandarin. Subscriptions are available through schools and it is used as part of the school curriculum in some cases. The circulation is 35,000 to 40,000 and estimated readership is from 70,000 to 80,000.

Streats is a morning tabloid that fashions a lifestyle paper with news presented in a quick nugget-style. Launched on 4 September 2000, it targets at heartlanders between 15 to 39-years old. The paper is distributed free at MRT, bus interchanges and petrol kiosks. Its targeted circulation is 200,000.

Project Eyeball targets at net-savvy executives in their 20s and 30s. This morning paper which focuses on interaction with readers, has a target circulation of 30,000 to 50,000, mostly through subscriptions.

Table 5: Comparison Between the Tabloids

	Streats	Today		The New Paper	
	Mon-Fri	Mon-Wed	Thu-Sat	Mon-Sat	Sun
Circulation	200,000	200,000	350,000	112,000	130,000
FPFC (ROP)	$4,062.50	$350.00	$10,850.00	$4,038.00	$4,038.00
Cost Per Thousand	$20.31	$31.75	$31.00	$36.05	$31.06
Distribution	Free MRT, Bus Interchange Offices	Free MRT, Bus Interchange Offices, Selected Homes		Paid Available at News Stand	
Targeted Audience	Mass	Mass		Mass	
Targeted Profile	Students/Working Adults	Students/Working Adults		Relatively greater skew towards PMEB, working lunchtime crowd and male sports/EPL followers	
Editorial Slant	2 Main Sections: 1) Streatsmart (local/regional news) 2) Easystreats (Ent./Movie/Sports/Daily Horoscope	3 Main Sections: Today, Relax, Sports			
Remarks	Aim at capture readers attention while they are on the move. Crisp, bite sized news for quick leisure read	Relatively more lengthy news coverage, stronger in Ent. News (due to its MCS heritage)		The only lunch time tabloid to provide updated and quick summary of major newsbreaker	
Premium Position	Back Page (S$7,898)	Front Page (S$7,100)	Front Page (S$11,600)	Front Page (S$4,038)	

According to the similar survey by OMD, 46% of those reading Streats and Today are reading less of The New Paper. 16% of adults and those above 15 years old, or 479,000 people read Streats, 10% read Today and

1% read Project Eyeball. The survey was conducted while Today was only 2 weeks old.

Credibility is higher for Today at 62%, whereas 57% of Streats readers agree that they believe what they read in it. There is high duplication amongst Streats and Today, as 76% of Today readers claimed to have read Streats.

In 2000, SPH announced major changes in the price structures of their major press. These included revisions in master contract entitlements, increase in rates for The Straits Times, Lianhe Wanbao, Shin Min Daily News and differing rates for weekday and weekend editions of the Straits Times.

SPH has also offered more creative use of newspapers, for instance fancy shapes, sampling exercises, joint promotions, free standing inserts and couponing (cut deal that appears every Thursday until November 2000) (cf. Figure 13).

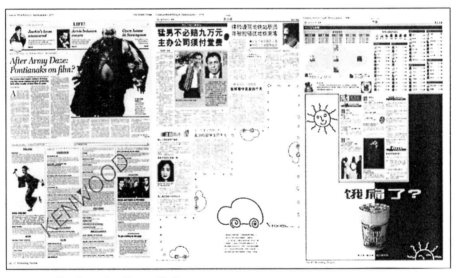

Figure 13: Creative Press Units

4.2   Consumer Magazines

There are more than 200 magazines circulating in Singapore targeting at the different population segments. Currently, 41 titles are monitored by AC Nielsen Singapore.

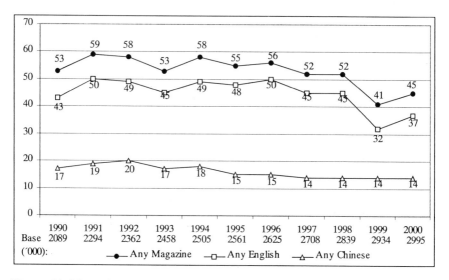

Figure 14: Magazine Readership
Source: Nielsen Media Index 2000

Although consumer magazines principally address the total population, a classification is made with regard to the textual focus:

1. **General interest magazines** address the total population with a range of topics of general interest.
    ▪   Radio and TV program magazines (*8 days, bi-weekly*).
    ▪   General interest magazines are characterized by high circulation figures and high reaches, so that the readership is structured similarly to the population.

2. **Target group magazines** address distinct sections of the population, such as women, men or teenagers, with a specific range of topics:
    ▪   Women's magazines (*Female, Her World, Cleo, Women's Weekly*)
    ▪   Men's magazines (*FHM, NSMen*)
    ▪   Family magazines (*Kids Central/Family*)

- Youth magazines (*Teens, Teenage*).

Although target group magazines have a comparably low circulation, they do have a high reach within the respective target groups.

3. **Special interest magazines** are characterized by a single editorial focus:
   - Housing and living (*Home & Décor, Posh*)
   - Lifestyle magazines (*Prestige, Wine & Dine*)
   - Motor press (*Motoring, Torque*)
   - Sport magazines (*Sportsworld, Tiger Football*)
   - Magazines on Internet (*Upload, Planet e, i-life*).
   - Magazines on science, nature subjects (*Asian Geographic*)

Special interest magazines are normally characterized by low circulation figures and low reach, but distinct focuses within their own readership.

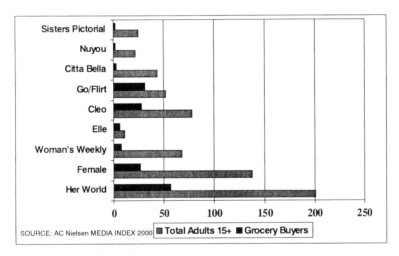

Figure 15: Female Magazine Readership

4.3   Television

In 2000, the percentage of TV ownership in Singapore had reached 100%. The penetration of television in Singapore increased gradually from 82% in 1990 to 89% in 2000. However, the percentage of Malaysian TV viewers has dipped from 49% in 1990 to 16% in 2000 (cf. Figure 16).

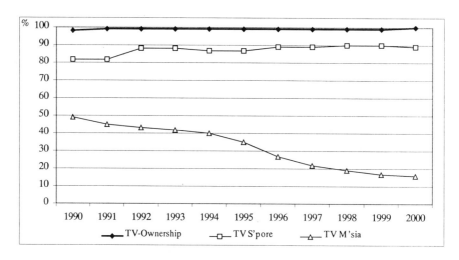

Figure 16: Television Penetration
Source: ACNielsen Media Index 2000

4.3.1 Terrestrial TV

Terrestrial broadcasting in Singapore is incorporated into Media Corporation of Singapore (MCS). Under MCS, Television Corporation of Singapore (TCS), MediaCorp News and Singapore Television Twelve manage the respective channels.

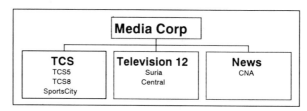

Figure 17: Television Channels Under MCS

TCS operates TCS5 (English), TCS8 (Chinese) and City TV (bilingual, formerly known as Sportscity). MediaCorp News broadcasts Channel News Asia. Singapore Television Twelve operates a new all Malay channel, Suria and another channel, Central, running three distinct belts of Kids programs, Arts programs and Tamil programs (cf. Table 6).

Table 6: Basic Characteristics of MCS' Channels

Details	TCS 5	TCS 8	City TV	C.N.A
Transmission Hours	24	24	M-F 5pm – 12mn Sat 3pm – 12mn Sun 10am – 12 mn	20 6am – 2 am
Coverage	National Johore (M'sia)	National Johore (M'sia)	National Johore (M'sia)	National Johore (M'sia)
Language of Program	English	Chinese	English and Chinese	English
Content	General Enter-tainment	General Enter-tainment	Sports and Enter-tainment	News, Financial, Lifestyle

Details	Kids Central	Vasantham Central	Arts Central	Suria
Transmission Hours	M-F 9am –11am M-F 3pm – 7pm SaSu 8am-1pm	M-F 7pm – 9.30pm Sat 4pm – 12mn Sun 3.30pm – 930pm	M-F 9.30pm – 1am Sat 1pm – 3pm Sun 1pm – 3.30pm Sun 9.30pm- 12.30mn (Sun = Earthvisions)	M-F 5pm – 12mn Sat 3pm – 12mn Sun 10am – 12mn
Language of Program	English	Tamil/Hindi	English/Foreign Language	Malay 100%
Content	Kids Pro-gramming	General Enter-tainment	Arts, Drama, Documentaries, Music	General Enter-tainment, Cur-rent Affairs, Kids, Arts

Television viewership is the highest for TCS Channel 5 and 8 (cf. Figure 17). Monday and Friday night movies and local dramas (*Growing Up*) enjoy the highest TV ratings on Ch 5, while foreign dramas (*My Fair Princess*) and local lifestyle and entertainment shows (*Travel Hunt and City Beat*) receive the highest ratings on Ch 8.

There is also a growing audience for Channel NewsAsia and cable (SCV), but a decline in the number of Malaysian TV (RTM 1 & 2) and SportsCity viewers. Consequently in May 2001, TCS revamped and re-named Sportscity as City TV, a bilingual channel that features lifestyle and entertainment programs in the day and sports highlights at night.

In June 2000, the Singapore government granted a television license to SPH. SPH has set up SPH MediaWorks and launched two television channels in May 2001, one English and the other Mandarin. The new channels focus on local entertainment and are in direct competition with TCS5 and TCS8. MediaWorks provides free-to-air service, which is accessible to all

homes and offers eight to ten hours of daily transmission. It plans to capture 30% of television advertising revenue, worth S$495 million, by the
first year.

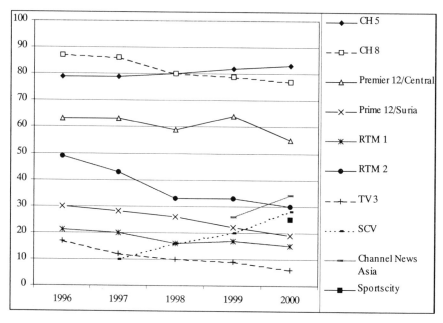

Figure 18: Television Viewership by Channel
Source: ACNielsen Media Index 2000

There are a number of implications for terrestrial TV. First, it encroaches
on cable TV's unique niche programming offering. As such, cable TV
only has dedicated movies and documentaries channels left. Secondly,
terrestrial TV provides many free-to-air opportunities, as compared to
cable TV, and this attracts viewers who do not have to pay. Thirdly, terrestrial TV has stronger local offering to cement relationships and prevents
erosion of viewership. Lastly, there is audience fragmentation for terrestrial TV and advertisers need to spend more to secure the audience. As a
result, more contract negotiations are undertaken to secure advertising
time slots (cf. Table 7).

Table 7: Prime vs. Fringe Time Spot Advertising

Channel 5	Ave. Cost/Spot (30")	Ave. Tarp	Ave.Cost/Tarp
Prime Time Spot (19.00 – 23.59)	$ 4,000	3	$ 1,333
Fringe Time Spot (07.00 – 18.59)	$ 1,300	1.2	$ 1,038
Channel 8			
Prime Time Spot (19.00 – 23.59)	$ 5,000	15	$ 333
Fringe Time Spot (07.00 – 18.59)	$ 1,511	4	$ 378

Source: ACNielsen (Jan-Jun 2000) Macrozone Report

4.3.2 Cable TV

The operator of cable television in Singapore is Singapore Cable Vision (SCV), which provides a spectrum of 39 channels.

- News: CNBC, CNN, CTN, Bloomberg TV, BCC World
- Music: MTV Asia & Mandarin
- Sports: ESPN, Super Sports, Football Channel, Star Sports
- Education: Discovery, Eureka Learning Channel, Nat Geo
- Entertainment: CM & Cartoon Network, Variety Vision, TVBS, AXN, Hallmark, CETV, Phoenix, Star World, SunTV, TVRI, Disney, HBO, Cinemax, Star Movies
- International: Deutsche Welle, Worldnet, Australian TV, TV5, TV3, CCTV-4, NHK, Zee TV

There are 4 tiers of subscription rates. Basic subscription is S$33.94 for 23 channels; Basic Plus includes the basic 23 channels, plus S$1.50 for an additional channel; International is S$20.60 for 8 international channels; International Plus includes the 8 channels, plus S$12.36 for an additional international channel; Premium charges S$12.36 for 4 channels.

SCV subscribers generally have a higher purchasing power than terrestrial TV viewers and are more discerning in taste. 76% of the total SCV subscribers gave an average household income of S$2,500. 80% of them live in private residentials or HDB 4 rooms and above. The audience is skewed towards the non-Chinese.

Table 8: Cable TV (SCV) Overview

	Adults 15+	Adults 15-24	Grocery Buyers	PMEB
Discovery	527	91	51	191
National Geographic	282	37	141	117
HBO	266	63	124	94
CNNI	255	27	135	131
Football Channel	254	51	81	99

Source: ACNielsen Cabsat 2000

Ad rates are pegged on ad spend committed, ranging from S$14 to S$80 per spot. The base rates for prime and fringe time slots are S$250 and S$100 respectively. Key channels carry loadings. For instance, Discovery, CNNI and Football channel carry (2x) loadings and ESPN, CNBC, AXN and TVBS carry (1.5x) loadings. All channels have regional commercial pass-through but only 19 channels accept local advertising.

The effect of cable on terrestrial TV is the reduction of viewing for local TV by 1.8 hours daily.

4.4 Internet

Singapore has one of the highest Internet penetration rates (45% of total population) in the world, behind the United States and Hong Kong. There is a steady growth of Internet usage among adults 15-34 years of age and a faster rate of growth with the younger age groups (cf. Figure 19).

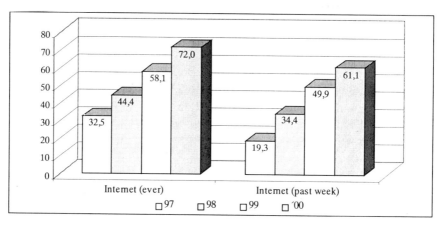

Figure 19: Internet Growth among Adults
Source: Nielsen Printscope 1997-2000, Adults 15-34 years

The internet is used mainly at home and at work. The trend is towards more regular usage of the Internet and longer sessions (cf. Table 9). The majority of users have access to e-mails. Other popular usages among adults include downloading software, gathering online information, reading electronic newspapers. The younger users chat and play online games.

Table 9: Internet Usage

	15-24 506,000	15+ 2,995,000
Usage		
▪ Ever Use	72.0%	41.0%
▪ Past Week	61.2%	36.7%
▪ Past Month	65.7%	38.3%
▪ Longer Ago	2.9%	1.3%
Place of Using Internet		
▪ At Home	56.7%	29.6%
▪ At Work	9.4%	21.5%
▪ At School	28.3%	5.1%
Frequency of Using Internet		
▪ Daily	31.5%	21.9%
▪ Several Times a Week	19.6%	10.6%
▪ Once a Week	10.4%	3.8%
▪ Less than Once a Week	7.0%	3.5%
Internet Time per Ave. Session		
▪ 30 mins or Less	10.8%	8.8%
▪ 31 – 60 mins	23.2%	14.3%
▪ 1 - > 2 hrs	24.4%	10.4%
▪ 2 hrs +	10.2%	6.1%

4.5　Radio

There are 3 main radio stations in Singapore (all in the FM bands), Radio Corporation of Singapore (12 channels), National Trade Union Congress (2 channels) and SAFRA (2 channels). Listeners can also tune into 9 Malaysian channels, 2 Indonesian channels and the BBC World service. Digitized transmission is possible for 4 RCS channels since November 1999. Owners of digital radio sets can tune into CD quality sounds as well as view information on the display.

The most popular radio stations are FM 93.3 & Capital 95.8 (Chinese), and Class 95 & Perfect 10 (English) (cf. Figure 20).

Table 10: Radio Channels/Stations

Channel/ Station	Content	Frequ.	Lang.	Broadcast Hours	Owned by
Gold 90.5 FM	Music from the 60s to 80s and special music programs during week-ends (Country, Jazz, Latin/Disco)	90.5	Engl.	24 hrs	RCS
News Radio 93.8	Local, regional and world news, current affairs programs, traffic, weather, Biz/Finance and local talk-shows	93.8	Engl.	18 hrs (6am-12am)	RCS
Symphony 92.4	Western Classical Music	92.4	Engl.	18 hrs (6am-12am)	RCS
Perfect 10 98.7	Contemporary music from America top 40s, Billboard hits & top local hits	98.7	Engl.	24 hrs	RCS
Class 95	Contemporary music/hits from 70s and 80s	95.0	Engl.	24 hrs	RCS
Coast	Contemporary hits of the 70s and 80s	100.0	Engl.	6am-12mn Sun-Thu	PT Pama-ko Batam
Zoo	Contemporary hits, Jazz and Rock&Roll	101.6	Engl.	6am-12mn Sun-Thu	PT Pama-ko Batam
Power 98 FM	Contemporary music from 80s and 90s, news & information, defence-related news	98.0	Engl.	21 hrs 5am-2am	SAFRA
Capital Radio 95.8 FM	Chat station, news, music & magazine style programs	95.8	Chi.	20 hrs 6am-2am	RCS
Y.ES 93.3	Contemporary hits from late 80s to 90s	93.3	Chi.	24 hrs	RCS
Love 97.2	Familiar favorites from 70s to 90s, recreational & lifestyle features and regular news updates	97.2	Chi.	24 hrs	RCS
Dongli 88.3	Hot hits from 80s & 90s, news, information & defence related news	88.3	Chi.	21 hrs 5am-2am	SAFRA
Warna	Chat station, news, music & magazine-style programs	94.2	Malay	19.5 hrs 4.45am-2am	RCS
Ria	Contemporary Malay & English pop hits	89.7	Malay	20 hrs 6am-2am	RCS
Olikkalanjiam	Chat station, information and music	96.8	Tamil	21 hrs 5am-2am	RCS
Heart	Chat station, music & magazine style programs	91.2	Engl. Malay	2am-11pm (Engl.) 11pm-2am (Malay)	NTUC Voice
Heart	Chat station, music & magazine style programs	100.3	Chi. Tamil	2am-11pm (Chi.), 11pm-2am (Tamil)	NTUC Voice
Hello Singapore	Music, news & business programs	96.3	Jap. Fr Ger.	6am-12mn	RCS
Passion	World music, classical, traditional & Jazz	99.5	Engl.	11am-11pm	Nat. Arts Council

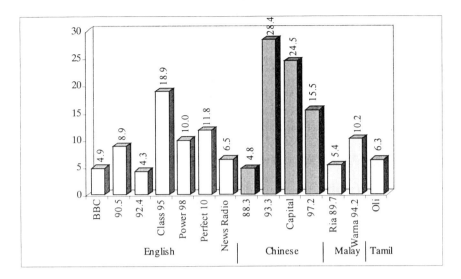

Figure 20: Radio Listenership–Reach
Source: ACNielsen Radio Survey 2000 – Wave 2

The number of transmission hours per week for radio has increased from 653 hours in 1988 to 2843 hours in 1999, almost 4.4 times (cf. Figure 21).

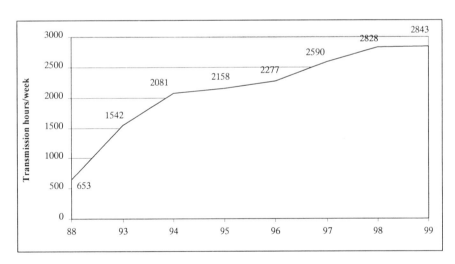

Figure 21: Radio Airtime
Source: Yearbook of Statistics

4.6   Cinema

There is a proliferation of cineplexes in Singapore, offering multiple screens in a single location. Cineplexes are moving into the housing estates in-line with the development of satellite towns. Currently, there are 162 cinema halls, as compared to only 47 in 1985.

72% of cinema goers are between 15-29 years. Students make up 30% of total cinema goers (cinema goers - visited a cinema in past 7 days). Cinema viewership is low for older adult groups. Most of the cinemas screen action films (34%), comedies (33%), love and romance (20%) and horror (19%).

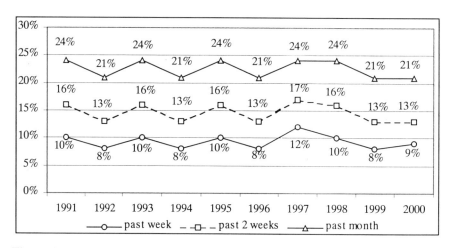

Figure 22: Cinema Viewership
Source: Nielsen Media Index 2000

4.7   Outdoor

Outdoor advertising opportunities have expanded rapidly over the past 5 years to include transit locations, such as buses, taxis, bus shelters, Mass Rapid Transit (MRT) and Light Rail Transit (LRT) trains. Advertising is accepted on all public buses in Singapore – on the back, the sides and the interior of the buses. Taxis accept advertising inside the taxi and on the taxi-top.

The MRT has become a popular mode of transport for many Singaporeans. Thus, advertising on MRT has exposure to a large proportion of the population. About 60% of those aged between 15 and 34 years commute on the MRT (cf. Figure 23).

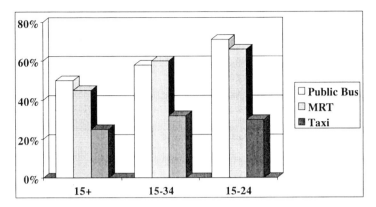

Figure 23: Mode of Transport
Source: ACNielsen Media Index 2000

Posters, billboards and videowalls can be found at shopping malls, underpasses and hotels. Most poster advertising is available in different sizes and comes in rear-illuminated light-boxes. Banners and neon advertising signs are also common on shopping centers and hotels, but they must be non-movable. Advertisers with large outdoor posters and banners usually negotiate with the management of the sites privately with regard to long-term contracts for limited outdoor advertising space.

Other forms of outdoor advertising include e-posters, postcards, washroom media, Suntec media wireless broadcast, TV mobile, i-One and advertising at the airport, Singapore Cruise Center and on Bintan ferries (cf. Table 11).

Although any language is permitted in outdoor advertising, outdoor advertising of all forms require a license fee and must be approved by the government. The government draws strict regulations for outdoor advertising so as to preserve the beauty of the country.

Magic billboards are the latest outdoor advertising media in Singapore. Invented in France, this patented poster scrolling display system on 14-foot high trucks costs $3,500 per month per panel. Advertisers can book poster ad panels on the sides and rear of the truck. Each panel displays up to 7 posters. Printed in vinyl, the computerized images create an impact and attract attention when the trucks roam high traffic routes in the morning and evening rush hours. All panels are backlit during the night. Although their mobility extends coverage, the small number of trucks (5-6) lowers frequency of exposure and several advertisements on a single truck (up to 21) might distract the audience away from the message.

Table 11: Outdoor Advertising Rates

	Cost (S$)
CCP Bus Shelters (until mid Feb 2001)	
• Prime Network (16 sites)	$6,800/week
• Financial District (10 sites)	$3,800/week
• Downtown Shopper (10 sites)	$2,800/week
• Youth Network 1 (10 sites)	$2,688/week
JC Decaux Free Standing Panels	
• Islandwide (165 panels)	$98,835/fortnight
• Islandwide (82 panels)	$49,118/fortnight
• Shleter Light Islandwide (250 panels)	$99,750/month
Comfort Taxi Tops	$80/taxi/month
City Cab Taxi Tops	$90/taxi/month
Washroom Media (Ngee Ann City)	$9,220/month
MRT	
• Wholly-painted train	$2,400/week
• Handgrip	$700/week
LED Displays	
• Shaw-House	$20,000/month
• Orchard Emerald	$12,000/month
• Liat Towers	$3,375/month
• Comcentre	$8,000/month
• Suntec City	$27,000/month
i-One Kiosks	$18,000/month
Neon	$17,000/month
Cineleisure Pillar Wrap-around	$5,500/month
Backlit Billboard	$20,000/month

5   Advertising Regulation and Control

The Singapore advertising scene is governed by two forms of controls - regulatory processes and voluntary controls. The Ministry of Environment, Ministry of Health and the Department of Customs and Excise regulate advertising laws in Singapore.

Although laws and regulations exist to moderate advertising practice, advertisers and agencies do practice voluntary control. Most media houses and owners also control their advertising by establishing their own guidelines for advertising and advertising agencies. SPH, TCS and RCS have their own code of advertising that has been effective and acceptable to the advertising industry.

Legislative and voluntary controls need to be in equilibrium to advance the interest of advertising in Singapore. Too much control discourages the growth of advertising and technology and the lack of control may promote unethical practices among advertisers and agencies, who may find ways to get around existing codes.

6   Institutions of the Singapore Advertising Industry

6.1   The Advertising Standards Authority of Singapore (ASAS)

The Consumers' Association of Singapore (CASE) established the ASAS in 1976 to act as an advisory council to the former. ASAS comprises representatives from the following organizations:

- Singapore Advertisers Association (SAA)
- Association of Accredited Advertising Agencies (4As)
- Advertising Media Owners Association of Singapore (AMOAS)
- Broadcast Association of Singapore
- Representative from CASE
- Singapore Medical Association (SMA)
- Pharmaceutical Society of Singapore
- Singapore Broadcasting Authority (SBA)
- Ministry of Health (MOH)
- Ministry of the Environment (ENV)
- Singapore Confederation of Industries (formerly Singapore Manufacturers Association)

ASAS is a wholly voluntary organization and is the most successful instance of industry self-regulation in Singapore. The main objective of the ASAS is to protect consumers from misleading, misrepresenting or offending advertisements in the various media channels.

It adheres to the principle that advertising must be honest, truthful, legal and decent. It draws specific guidelines on the use of research, testimonial, prices, discount, and compares and identifies advertisers and promoters. The powers of ASAS enable it to immediately suspend an ad pending investigation, invite the party to provide the details about the ad, invite the party to amend or withdraw any ad, and to ban the advertisement.

The authority promotes fair competition in business including non-denigration, non-exploitation of goodwill and non-imitation. It also abides by the core values and family values of Singapore. It is funded from member associations paying the bills and there are plans to have half a percent from ads. The scope of its code includes all advertisements of any goods and services in any form on any media. Advertisements are "any form of commercial communication for any form of goods or services, regardless of medium used, including advertising claims on packs, labels and point of sale material."

6.2   Advertising and Research Agencies

The number of Singapore agencies has increased over the years to serve the needs of multinational brands as well as local firms with small advertising and promotional budgets. There is keen competition between foreign subsidiaries and their local counterparts in terms of creativity, technology and advertising concepts. The top agencies account for a large proportion of the total advertising expenditure.

There are also a number of research houses in Singapore providing qualitative and quantitative research studies. Their services also include syndicated studies and providing media and product indices.

7   Conclusion

The increasing trend towards globalization and international alignments has prompted Singapore to deregulate and liberalize its markets. Under similar circumstances, the Singapore advertising industry is also attempting to develop its own culture and technologies. The challenge facing Singapore advertisers, agencies and media owners is to tap on the sophisticated infrastructure and propel the industry to the level of developed countries within an improved regulatory framework.

References

Frith, Katherine T., Felix, *Advertising in Asia*, Iowa University State Press (1996)

Ministry of Information and The Arts, *Arts & Media in Singapore*, MITA (2000)

Lan, LL. and May Oo Lwin, (forthcoming 2001) *An overview of the advertising laws and regulations in Singapore*. The Journal of Business Law

A Pecotich and C Shultz, *The Rise of Marketing and Consumer Behavior in East and Southeast Asia*, edited by A Pecotich and C Shultz, Sydney: McGraw-Hill Book Co Pty Ltd, November 1998

AC Nielson Reports 2000 Singapore

Singapore Press Holdings, http://www.sph.com.sg

Census of Population/ Yearbook of Statistics 2000 (Singapore)

Useful Addresses

ACNielsen Research (Singapore) Pte Ltd
51 Newton Road, Goldhill Plaza #09-01/12
Singapore 308900
Tel: (65) 252 8595   Fax: (65) 253 4287
Website: *http://www.acnielsen.com*

**Advertising Standards Authority of Singapore (ASAS)/ Consumers'
Association of Singapore**
170 Ghim Moh Road, Ulu Pandan Community Building #05-01
Singapore 279621
Tel: (65) 463 1811   Fax: (65) 467 9055

Association of Accredited Advertising Agents Singapore (4As)
333 Orchard Road #05-00
Singapore 238867
Tel: (65) 837 9973   Fax: (65) 836 0700

Customs and Excise Department, Singapore
55 Newton Road, Revenue House #10-01
Singapore 307987
Tel: (65) 272 8222   Fax: (65) 250 8663
Website: *http://www.gov.sg/customs*

MediaCorp Singapore Pte Ltd
Andrew Road, Caldecott Broadcast Centre
Singapore 299939
Tel: (65) 256 0401   Fax: (65) 253 8119
Website: *http://www.mediacorp.com.sg*

Ministry of Environment, Singapore
40 Scotts Road, Environment Building
Singapore 228231
Tel: (65) 732 7733   Fax: (65) 731 9456
Website: *http://www.env.gov.sg*

Ministry of Health, Singapore
16 College Road, College of Medicine Building
Singapore 169854
Tel: (65) 325 9220   Fax: (65) 224 1677
Website: *http://www.gov.sg/moh*

Pharmaceutical Society Of Singapore
2 College Road
Singapore 169850
Tel: (65) 221 1136   Fax: (65) 223 0969

Singapore Advertisers Association
111 North Bridge Road, Peninsula Plaza #03-42
Singapore 179098
Tel: (65) 339 8468   Fax: (65) 339 8478

Singapore Broadcasting Authority
140 Hill Street, MITA Building #04-01
Singapore 179369
Tel: (65) 837 9973   Fax: (65) 336 8023

Singapore Confederation Of Industries
20 Orchard Road, SMA House #01-00
Singapore 238830
Tel: (65) 338 8787   Fax: (65) 336 8837

Singapore Medical Association
2 College Road #02-00
Singapore 169850
Tel: (65) 223 1264   Fax: (65) 224 7827

Singapore Press Holdings Ltd
82 Genting Lane
Singapore 349567
Tel: (65) 743 8800   Fax: (65) 748 0747
Website: *http://www.sph.com.sg*

Advertising in South Korea

Prof. Dr. Dae Ryun Chang
Yonsei University, Seoul

1   Overview of the Korean Advertising Industry

The 1988 Seoul Olympics was a watershed event for the Korean Economy as it marked the opening up of the country to foreign capital and competition. The Korean advertising industry was no exception and with double-digit growth since 1988 the industry comprised 1.35% of the gross national product in 1996 and 5.6 trillion won in billings making it the 7th largest market in the world. However, another no less dramatic event was the IMF crisis in 1997 that put a screeching halt to the once unabated growth and in 1998 the industry shrunk to less than 3.5 trillion won. In 1999 with consumer spending and confidence restored and with the introduction of new products, advertising spending increased about 32% from the previous year. Another factor adding to the increased spending was the emergence of ventures and among them internet companies (dotcom) needing to increase awareness of their sites.

Table 1: Advertising Spending by Major Media (units: million won)

	TV		Radio		Newspaper		Magazine		Total	
1997	1,555	-2.9%	189	10.9%	2,873	2.2%	241	1.7%	4,858	0.8%
1998	1,050	-32.5%	110	-41.7%	2,298	-20.0%	168	-30.5%	3,626	-25.4%
1999	1,533	46.0%	146	32.3%	2,908	26.5%	219	30.7%	4,805	32.5%
2000	2,070	35.0%	211	44.9%	3,392	16.7%	277	26.5%	5,950	23.8%

Source: KAAA, Advertising Year Book 2000

The Korean advertising industry in the 90s can be summarized in the following table.

Table 2: Korean Advertising Industry in the 1990s and Key Trends

	Steady growth				Structural growth			IMF aftermath era		
Year	90	91	92	93	94	95	96	97	98	99
Growth	27.8	19.8	17.5	14.7	24.8	22.9	13.4	-4.2	-35.2	32.6
Real GDP growth	0.0	9.2	5.4	5.5	8.3	8.9	6.8	5.0	-5.8	10.2
Media Changes	• 1990 KBS 1 eliminates block advertising, religion channels emerge • 1991 SBS goes on air • 1992 cable TV begins • print media liberalized				• KBS 1 goes to no ad policy • 1995 private provincial broadcasting begins • satellite and internet broadcasting, internet newspapers and magazines emerge • peak of newspapers and magazines			• 2nd round of provincials broadcasting allowed • boom of internet, portal sites, and E-media • correction of print media • multi-media emerges • correction of media industry		
Economic Changes	• the boom and bust of construction • increased consumer spending • consumer spending recession after construction decline				• boom of semiconductors • export and manufacturing recovery • currency crisis in 1997 and widespread bankruptcy of conglomerates • after Nov. 1997, the IMF bailout			• restructuring – increase in demand for information technology		

Source: Cheil Communications, Advertising Year Book 2000

2   Advertising Spending

The total advertising spending in 1999 was 4.6 trillion won that represented an increase of about 32% from the previous year. This is about 86% of the amount recorded during the height of the Korean advertising industry in 1996 that was the year right before the IMF crisis. Even though the industry has not fully recovered to the level of its glory days nonetheless it demonstrates its resiliency.

As we can see in Table 3, the largest share of the advertising spending is represented by newspapers with about 39%, and is followed by television with about 32%. Thus the two media dominate the Korean advertising industry and the other media are relatively minor with radio only capturing less than 4% of the total spending, and magazines taking up about 3%. While the share of online media is very low, given the high growth as compared to the previous year, this market holds great promise in Korea.

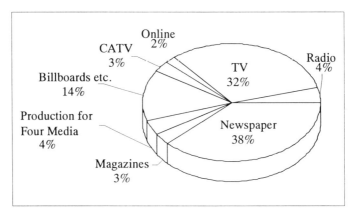

Figure 1: Advertising Spending

Table 3: Advertising Expenditure in Million Won, %

Media		Ad Expenditures		Growth Rate		Proportion	
		1999	1998	1999	1998	1999	1998
Four Media	TV	1,492,122	1,026,098	45.4	-33.7	32.3	29.4
	Radio	175,121	137,227	27.6	-40.7	3.8	3.9
	Newspaper	1,805,462	1,343,722	34.4	-36.8	39.1	38.6
	Magazine	130,028	102,431	26.9	-51.9	2.8	2.9
	Subtotal	3,602,733	2,609,478	38.1	-36.6	78.0	74.9
Production for Four Media		181,449	135,339	34.1	-35.8	3.9	3.9
Billboards, SP, etc		627,091	569,476	10.1	-35.4	13.6	16.3
New Media	CATV	128,100	116,588	9.9	-9.1	2.8	3.3
	Online	81,200	53,700	51.2	41.3	1.8	1.5
	Subtotal	209,300	170,288	22.9	2.5	4.5	4.9
Total		4,620,573	3,484,581	32.6	-35.2	100.0	100.0

Source: Cheil Communications, Advertising Year Book 2000

1999 marked the transformation of the Korean advertising industry from a strictly offline business to one that can accommodate both online and offline communication. About 78% of an overall total of about 462 billion won was represented by offline advertising. After the IMF crisis, the sponsors shifted to proven media such as television and newspapers at the expense of more uncertain media such as magazines and radio. Also the promise of new media such as the internet has sparked interest in their use as well. In Table 4, we can see the results of a study done by Cheil Communication where between 1998 and 1999 the exposure to online media has not only increased but their reliability and likability have increased as well. Not shown here are the data for those respondents in their 20s and teens, and their affinity to online media and radio is much higher as compared to the other age brackets.

Table 4: Exposure, Reliability and Likability of Various Media (unit: %)

type	Main exposure		Reliable media		Likable media	
	98	99	98	99	98	99
TV	82.0	80.5	44.6	44.1	46.2	46.0
Newspaper	10.6	9.7	40.9	37.5	19.5	18.1
Radio	4.1	5.3	5.2	5.1	6.9	6.5
Online	2.4	3.4	8.5	9.1	20.8	24.6
Magazine	0.6	0.5	1.3	1.3	4.5	3.4
CATV	0.8	0.6	0.4	0.5	2.1	1.4

Source: Cheil Communications, ACR data

Table 5 shows the advertising expenditures across different industries for the four major media. Total expenditures in 1999 were about 2.6 trillion won and this marked an increase of about 38% as compared to the previous year. Among the 22 industries examined 11 reported increases of over 30%, and 8 reported increases between 10 and 30%, and only 3 industries reported actually negative growth.

Table 5: Ad Expenditure by Major Media and Industry (unit: million won)

Industry	TV	Radio	News	Mag	Total	+/- %	Share	98
Energy	7,812	2,247	16,704	619	27,382	12.5	0.8	24,331
Food	228,492	15,509	71,708	7,341	323,050	33.3	9.0	242,258
Drinks	136,294	10,074	60,929	6,006	213,303	22.3	5.9	174,478
Drugs	88,889	8,150	54,457	3,626	155,122	27.3	4.3	121,817
Cosmetics	173,612	5,992	20,604	19,088	219,296	32.5	6.1	165,539
Publishing	43,796	20,198	146,420	3,599	214,013	39.9	5.9	152,983
Fashion	33,750	6,657	57,919	26,044	124,370	31.2	3.5	94,800
Machinery	192	290	6,050	2,078	8,610	-13.7	0.2	9,975
Instruments	6,430	2,010	20,186	2,380	31,006	51.4	0.9	20,481
Electronics	59,588	3,161	37,641	3,052	103,442	31.0	2.9	78,960
Computers & telecom.	256,824	18,462	231,773	13,658	520,717	40.0	14.5	372,066
Delivery equipment	82,710	16,282	58,247	3,452	160,691	10.6	4.5	145,303
Household goods	66,591	7,387	40,352	6,623	120,953	28.5	3.4	94,161
Chemicals	13,771	1,158	4,471	397	19,797	-10.4	0.5	22,086
Construction	28,271	11,012	188,356	2,051	229,690	104.9	6.4	112,084
Distribution	21,700	3,658	114,877	3,880	144,115	22.8	4.0	117,322
Finance	133,584	20,565	135,949	2,941	293,039	202.7	8.1	96,800
Travel	63,022	14,303	267,328	11,825	356,478	32.5	9.9	268,968

Table 5, continued

Sports	12,086	1,003	49,940	7,276	70,305	-1.1	2.0	71,065
Religion	6,511	1,396	95,177	1,030	104,114	32.4	2.9	78,635
Medicine	5,674	4,675	84,398	2,528	97,275	9.0	2.7	89,263
Company PR	22,523	932	41,976	534	65,965	17.6	1.8	56,104
Total	1,492,122	175,121	1,805,462	130,028	3,602,733	38.1	100.0	2,609,479

Source: Cheil Communications, Advertising Year Book 2000

The industry reporting the highest growth was financial products that included securities, insurance, and banking with growth of over 202 percent as compared to 1998. Also showing a high growth was construction and real estate with an increase of about 105%. The recovery of these two industries spearheaded the recovery of the Korean economy in the aftermath of the IMF crisis. The finance sector was primarily blamed for the onset of the financial crisis and the resulting bankruptcies, mergers and acquisitions, and overall restructuring of finance companies necessitated the increased communication of new identities, new positioning, and overall new marketing strategies of Korean finance-related companies. And with the recovery of the Korean economy, new housing construction and demand increased the need for advertising of this industry as well. In terms of leaders in share of advertising expenditure, the high demand for information technology and communication products, in particular, desktop/notebook personal computers and digital cell phones, spurred on this industry to maintain its number one position from 1998 to 1999.

Table 6: Ad Expenditure by Top 10 Companies (unit: million won)

	1999			1998		
	company	Ad. Exp.	growth	company	Ad. Exp.	growth
1	Samsung Electronics	107,132	59.4	Samsung Electronics	67,201	-34.2
2	SK Telecom	83,036	18.2	SK Telecom	59,940	18.2
3	Kia Motors	57,923	95.5	Daewoo Motors	55,886	-1.5
4	Nam Yang Milk	55,433	33.5	Hyundai Motors	51,343	-5.9
5	Hyundai Motors	54,616	6.4	Pacific Corp.	41,512	1.8
6	LG Chemical	50,933	43.2	Nam Yang Milk	37,170	2.8
7	Daewoo Motors	50,888	-8.9	LG Chemical	35,380	-24.0
8	Pacific Corp.	49,667	19.6	Nhong Shim	33,192	28.7
9	Maeil Milk	46,088	114.1	Korea Tel. Freetel	31,895	84.4
10	Hyundai Securities	46,047	-10.3	Shinsegi Telecom	29,784	51.8

Source: Korea Advanced Digital Data Inc., www.adchannel.co.kr

In Table 6 we can see the top ten ad spending companies in Korea. As was true in 1998, the top one and two spenders were Samsung Electronics and SK Telecom. The former recorded a spending increase of over 59% and the latter increased its spending by over 38%. Even though Kia filed for bankruptcy, after its acquisition by Hyundai its business performance improved dramatically and increased its ad spending over 95% to about 58 billion won. As noted above finance-related companies were a major factor in the advertising recovery and in particular Hyundai Securities was a prominent player spending about 46 billion won centered around its "Buy Korea" campaign.

3 Advertising Industry Structure and Characteristics

The Korean advertising industry, as can be seen in Figure 2, is characterized by the presence of six types of players. With the exception of the consumer and ad production houses these players are described below.

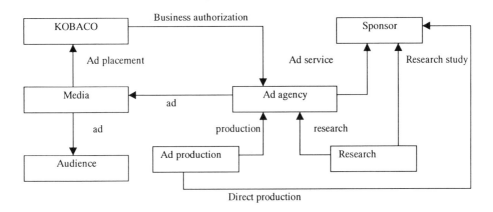

Figure 2: Korean Advertising Structure
Source: Chang, Dae Ryun and Minhi Hahn (2000), *Integrated Advertising Management*, Hakhyunsa

3.1 The Korean Advertising Broadcasting Company

Almost a uniquely Korean characteristic is the presence of The Korean Advertising Broadcasting Company (KOBACO) that was founded in 1981 by the Korean government. The official role of KOBACO is fivefold. First, it holds the authority to permit advertising agencies to operate in business.

Second, its perhaps most controversial role is that it acts as an exclusive agent for the sale and placement of broadcast advertising space. For this role it receives a commission that varies depending on the type of agency (in-house versus independent agency) that buys media placement from KOBACO. Third, it invests the money generated from its commission in a special fund that has the purpose of advancing Korean broadcasting and improving society. Fourth, KOBACO funds internal and independent research devoted to measuring the effectiveness of broadcast advertising. Fifth, it operates education and publishing branches that aim to develop advertising specialists in Korea.

3.2   Advertising Agencies

As of November, 1999, there were a total of 162 KOBACO authorized advertising agencies in Korea. The biggest agency in Korea for the last few decades has been Cheil Communication, formerly part of Samsung but now a publicly listed company.

Table 7: Top 10 Agencies and Billings (unit: million won and %)

99 rank	98 rank	Agency	99 billings	98 billings	Change 99/98
1	1	Cheil	703,953	576,157	22.2
2	2	LG Ad	541,030	391,882	38.1
3	3	Diamond	540,177	311,072	73.7
4	4	Dae Hong	238,214	169,337	40.7
5	6	Korad	157,983	85,035	85.8
6	5	Oricom	140,539	91,531	53.5
7	-	TBWA Korea	126,892	-	-
8	13	Pheonix	121,892	45,321	168.7
9	7	Wellcomm	105,830	81,148	30.4
10	14	Adventure Worldwide	82,567	42,680	93.5

Source: ADIC, Advertising Trend, March, 2000

Cheil reported an increase of over 22% as compared to 1998 and this resulted in billings of about 700 billion won. Cheil has been followed by LGAd and Diamond Communication for the last several years. A new member in the top ten agencies in Korea for 1998 was TBWA Korea and falling out of the top ten were Dongbang Communication and MBC Adcom. The entry of TBWA and Dentsu joint venture Pheonix into the top ten is notable in terms of the increased presence of foreign-based agencies in Korea. Moreover, many agencies such as Diamond and Dongbang are now selling partial or full equity to foreign agencies, thus changing the agency landscape of Korea.

3.3 Market Research Companies

The financial crisis of 1998 demonstrated the sensitivity of the market research industry to the state of the Korean economy. In the period prior to the IMF bailout, market research generated from such activities as corporate and academic studies was about 850 billion won in 1997. After the economic collapse, this market decreased about 30% in 1998 and with the recovery in 1999, it surpassed the previous high of 1997 to record billings of about 900 billion won.

The tracking of television viewership began in 1991 with the research being provided by Media Service Korea (MSK) and until 1999 it was the sole outfit performing this function. In the fall of 1999, however, Taylor Nelson Sofres also began a rival program.

3.4 Advertising Related Associations

There are many different advertising related associations in Korea with the most prominent ones being the Korean Advertising Sponsors Association, Korea Association of Advertising Agencies (KAAA), Korean Commercial Film Producers Association, Korean Newspapers Advertising Association, Korean Advertising Business Association, and the biggest one is the Korean Confederation of Advertising Organizations. Also there are a number of academic associations such as the Korean Advertising Studies Association, and the Korean Consumer Psychology Advertising Studies Association. There is also the Audit Bureau of Circulation Korea that has the purpose of accounting for newspaper circulation and the Advertising Regulatory Commission that regulates broadcast advertising before they are put on air.

4 Media Situation

4.1 Print Media

As in other countries the primary print media in Korea are newspapers and magazines. The two types accounted for about 1.9 trillion won in 1999 as

can be seen in Table 1 earlier. As compared to the previous year print media spending increased about 34%. Magazines also grew about 27% to
billings of about 130 billion won.

Table 8: Ad Expenditure by Media (unit: million won)

media	Ad expenditure		growth		Share	
	1999	1998	1999	1998	1999	1998
Newspapers	1,805,462	1,343,722	34.4	-36.8	39.1	38.6
Magazines	130,028	102,431	26.9	-51.9	2.8	2.9
Total	1,935,480	1,163,325	30.7	-44.4	21.0	20.6

Source: KAAA, Advertising Year Book 2000

4.1.1   Newspapers

In the year 2000 there were 10 national dailies, 45 provincial dailies, 5
economic dailies, 4 sports dailies, 106 special newspapers, 4 children
newspapers and 3 English dailies. About 51% of all Korean households
subscribe to at least one newspaper and the average length of subscription
is about 39 months.

   The standard advertising rate is based on the size of the ad as measured
in "dan" units (3.4 centimeter x 1 centimeter). Newspaper advertising,
especially the national dailies, is usually considered the most expensive
media in Korea on a monetary basis. A large national audience can be
reached with high frequency. As is the case in other countries, newspapers
have the limitation of having low selectivity. Despite this drawback newspapers enjoyed double-digit growth until 1995 but even before the 1997
financial crisis, the slowdown in newspapers growth emerged in 1996
partly due to rate hikes, and of course in the wake of the economic melt-
down, 1998 showed a drop of over 38% as compared to 1997. But in 1999
newspapers again demonstrated its resiliency by showing high growth. The
recovery in newspaper advertising was fueled by the advertising of investment trusts and mutual funds products as well as that of other new
financial products such as securities and insurance. The advertising of new
housing, educational print, food, travel services, and heavy competition in
the mobile communication service industry contributed to heavy advertising spending in the period after 1998. Newspaper advertising by the construction industry grew over 72% whereas that of financial products grew
over 115%. Strengthened by the growth of newspaper advertising across
most industries, the national dailies, economic dailies, and sports dailies

witnessed advertising increases of over 25% as compared to the previous year. Contributing to this growth were the increases of newspaper pages and the division of newspapers into sections in these types of newspapers. In contrast, the provincial dailies saw a continued drop in advertising demand as sponsors, in particular, the large conglomerates reduced their corporate image advertising whereas the financial and housing sponsors concentrated on the national outlets.

On closer inspection of the newspaper advertising spending patterns of 1999, many sponsors elected to use expensive full-page ads and color ads in order to increase brand attention vis-à-vis competition. According to a research conducted by the Korean Advertising Sponsors Association, the highest attention in newspapers was reported by ads for movies and video (48.7%), followed by books (40.4%), personal computers (39.6%), housing and real estate (39.4%), telecommunication (38.8%). As for newspaper advertising that directly lead to sales, the most successful products were electronics (16.2%), apparel (12.7%), books (12.3%), and household items (8.2%). Also, the highest attention in terms of location were the front page lower side with over 52.7%, followed by the back page ad of the main section, two-sided full page ad in the main section, and back page ad of a supplement section. Some key characteristics of newspaper advertising in 1999 were contents focused on corporate competencies that enabled Korean companies to overcome the economic crisis, expectations about the coming New Millennium, and the digital transformation of the economy such as the widespread adoption of the internet.

4.1.2 Magazines

With the recovery of advertising spending in 1999, spending on magazines increased as well, but not to the extent of other media. New publications began decreasing in 1996 and finally hit bottom in 1998 only to recover modestly in 1999. As of 1999, Korean Magazines are sorted usually in the following manner (cf. Table 9).

The peak for magazines in Korean advertising was in 1995 and 1996 when it recorded growth of 13.1% and 18% respectively. Then in 1997 it dropped to just 2.5% growth and like other media in wake of the financial crisis experienced the highest drop in sales with -51.9% growth. In 1999 it rebounded with the first double-digit growth since 1995 with increases of 26%. Even though the total number of subscriptions has decreased, women's magazines, PC magazines, and weekly news and economic

magazines have spearheaded an increase in advertising sales between 30 to
40%. This increase in demand for magazine advertising can be seen across
the board in different industries, but in particular the key drivers appear to
be fashion and cosmetics sponsors that decreased spending in the economic downturn period but came back strong with growth of about 31%
and 33% respectively.

Table 9: Classification of Korean Magazines

Current news	19
Economics	10
Women/men/housekeeping	26
Entertainment	7
Hobbies/Leisure	18
Special Interest	56
Daily Living	11
Educational Print	13
Children/Student	6

Source: KAAA, Advertising Year Book 2000

4.2   Broadcast Advertising

In part due to the economic recovery of 1999 broadcast advertising was
estimated to be about 1.7 trillion won that year. This represented a much
larger growth than that of the general economy and about an increase of
43% as compared to the previous year. During the same period the overall
economy increased by 11%, meaning broadcast advertising growth was
nearly four times as large. Advertising spending on television was about
1.5 trillion won, and this meant an increase of over 45% making it the
highest recovery among the four major media. In fact television's share of
overall advertising increased from 29% to about 32%. As for radio, its
spending increased to about 175 billion won and this marked an increase
of about 28% over the previous year. Radio's overall share of advertising
remained at slightly under 4% making it along with magazines a less used
media among the 4 major media types. Nonetheless, radio's growth in the
previous year was about minus 41% thus making the modest growth more
notable. The share between television and radio was 88% to 128% in 1998
and remained at a similar level 90% to 10% indicating a slight increase for
the former media. Ironically the emergence of new media such as the
internet is actually promoting demand of television advertising since new
sites need to use the time-proven television medium to obtain wide exposure of their sites in a short period of time.

Table 10: Ad Expenditure by Media (unit: million won)

Media	Ad expenditure		growth		share	
	1999	1998	1999	1998	1999	1998
TV	1,492,122	1,026,098	45.4	-33.7	32.3	29.4
Radio	175,121	137,227	27.6	-40.7	3.8	3.9
total	1,667,243	1,163,325	36.5	-37.2	18.1	16.7

Source: KAAA, Advertising Year Book 2000

A key trend emerging in Korean advertising is the decreasing dependency of agencies on large sponsors. In contrast to 1998 when the top 100 sponsors captured over 70% of advertising spending, in 1999 the top 100s share dropped to about 67%. Moreover, sponsors advertising at least once increased from 6,254 in 1998 to 6,614 in 1999 implying the expanded user base of broadcast advertising in Korea. In terms of the concentration of demand by the top sponsors, the top ten captured 21%, the top 20 obtained about a 33% share and the top 50 comprised about 52% of the spending share. This indicates the spreading out of advertising spending in Korea.

Table 11: Top 10 Advertising Sponsors (unit: million won and %)

rank	99			98		
	sponsor	amount	share	sponsor	amount	share
1	Samsung Electronics	62,271	3.7	Samsung Electronics	37,180	3.2
2	SK telecom	46,673	2.8	SK telecom	31,030	2.7
3	LG Chemical	43,579	2.6	LG Chemical	29,983	2.6
4	Pacific	34,033	2.0	Nhong Shim	29,426	2.5
5	Daewoo Motors	30,850	1.9	Pacific	28,470	2.4
6	Namyang Milk	29,014	1.7	Daewoo Motors	25,598	2.2
7	Maeil Milk	27,962	1.7	Lotte Confectionay	25,337	2.2
8	Nhong Shim,	27,623	1.7	Hyundai Motors	25,296	2.2
9	Lotte Confectionary	25,917	1.6	LG telecom	21,840	1.9
10	Cheiljedang	25,083	1.5	Namyang Milk	20,132	1.7
	Total	353,005	21.2	Total	274,292	23.6

Source: Cheil Communications, Advertising Year Book 2000

As mentioned above the sale and placement of Korean broadcasting advertising space has been traditionally handled by KOBACO. But since 1999 there are some changes taking place in this arena as well. First, beginning in October of 1999, as opposed to the inflexible method of advertising sales in the past, a new global standard sales system has been adopted. The new system aims to increase preemption, sale of fixed ad order and also to offer temporary discounts (ROC) on the sale of broadcast ads. Second, there has been a significant improvement in the sale and efficiency of spot TV advertising. Third, the new system will target key vehicles for different types of discounts and bonuses intended to increase the sale of broadcast advertising. Fourth, in order to nurture venture companies in Korea, starting in July of 1998, KOBACO has extended the period for special broadcast advertising support of these companies. Fifth, sponsors must now show that payment will be guaranteed by financial institutions and KOBACO will help finance the commissions related to these guarantees.

4.3   Television

In Korea, the advertising rates for television vary according to the four time types of SA, A, B, and C and by region.

Broadcast television consists of 5 channels and radio consists of 9 channels. In terms of audience share, the three major channels of KBS, MBC, and SBS enjoy over 90% with a religion channel (2.3%) and private provincial channel (6.8%) taking up the rest. Among the major channels, SBS had sales of about 35 billion won which was an increase of about 54% over the previous year. The highest growth could be claimed by private provincial advertisers with a growth of about 72% which was higher than the industry average of 45%.

Cable television consists of 31 channels that include DCN, HBO, and CJ Shopping. In 1999 the number of subscribers to cable television was about 1.6 million households, and this marked an increase of over 55% from the previous year. However, in terms of those subscribers actually paying for the service the number of households was 1.4 million, meaning about 10% did not pay. The percentage of subscribers paying in 1998 was under 83% and thus the channel tiering system is having a positive impact on converting free subscribers to paid ones. The following table shows the number of paid subscribers.

Table 12: Cable Subscribers (paid) (unit: 10,000 households)

95	96	97	98	99 Oct.
20.7	50.4	82.5	82.9	139.8

Source: New Media Journal

In 1999 the total national cable advertising sales accounted for by Program Providers amounted to about 1.1 trillion won. This is about a 27% increase over the previous year, and with the increase demand of cable advertising, this media is finally becoming a viable outlet for Korean advertising. Looking at the advertising sales by cable Program Providers, we can see that the leader is the cable news channel YTN with sales of 270 million won which is an increase of 88% over the previous year, followed by another economic news channel MBN with sales of 110 million won (growth of 21%).

4.4   Radio

In Korea, the advertising rates for radio are standardized according to the three time types of A, B, and C. In terms of radio advertising spending share, MBC captured the lion's share of over 60%. MBC-AM had sales of 69 billion won, which was an increase of about 20% over the previous year, and MBC-FM had sales of about 37 billion won, an increase of 24% over 1998. KBS-2 radio had sales of 14 billion won, a growth of a modest 2 percent over the previous year.

5   Online Advertising

In 1999 Korea's total online advertising spending amounted to about 65 billion won. Compared to 1998's sales of about 38 billion won, the growth was an impressive 70% between the two periods. In this mix, internet advertising captured about 35 billion won, and PC communications about 30 billion won. Because internet advertising was a late comer to the Korean market, the latter continued to capture a sizable share of the Korean online market, but the functionality and efficiency and overall effectiveness of the internet advertising platform will make this market the key online advertising market for the future.

Beginning with the paid IBM banner ad, the internet advertising expenditure has grown significantly with Yahoo Korea, Daum Communication as examples of sites recording positive profits from just advertising sales alone. The potential advantages of internet advertising as compared to other media with the exception of television are the higher entertainment, interest, ease of use, definition, and likability of the online medium. As we can see in Table 13, as of year 2000 the estimated size of the Korean online

market is about 900 billion won , and international online media representatives such as Doubleclick, 24/7 and similar domestic agencies are obtaining an increasingly stronger foothold in the Korean advertising marketplace. The Korean online market consists of PC telecommunication and
internet with the former recording 44 billion won in sales and the latter
about 37 billion won but showing much higher growth. The number internet users has increased with a multitude of domestic portal, hub and electronic commerce sites popping up in the last two years.

Table 13: Online Advertising Sales

1996	1997	1998	1999	2000
25	65	110	350	900

Source: LG Economic Research Institute

In Korea the most noted market research organization that tabulates the
size of the Korean internet market is KRNIC which tracks the size in terms
of the number of hosts, domains and users. In Table 14 we can see that the
number of users of the internet in Korea has increased twofold and three-
fold in the last few years. If this trend continues the number of internet
users is projected to be about 20 million in the year 2001. According to
research conducted by the Korean Advertising Sponsor Association, over
53% of the people between the ages of seven and fifty-nine are regular
internet users. Also looking at a study conducted by KNP (Korean Netizen
Profile) in April of year 2000, the share of women (about 47%), including
housewives, and users below 20 have risen significantly. As for weekly
time of usage, a surprisingly high 47% reported that they used the internet
for more than 10 hours. Also interest in banner advertising increased from
38% to about 46% from 1999 to 2000.

Table 14: Domestic Internet Users (unit : 10 million and %)

Period	94. 12	95. 12	96. 12	97. 12	98. 12	99. 12	2000. 5
Users	139	366	732	1,635	3,103	10,860	15,340
growth	-	165	100	123	90	249	41

Source: Cheil Communications, Advertising Year Book 2000

6   Integrated Marketing Communication

6.1   Sports Marketing

The recent success of Korean athletes such as Se Ri Pak and Chan Ho Park in foreign markets has spurred significant interest in sports marketing on the domestic scene. The field of sports marketing in Korea includes "marketing of sports" which includes the marketing of various sports such as professional baseball, soccer, and basketball and the individual teams and facilities. The other categories are the marketing of individual athletes, and also "marketing through sports," i.e. the marketing of other products using sports as a medium[1]. In Korea, the major advertising agencies have created specialized sports marketing divisions where the marketing of sports teams and special events and sponsorships are planned and implemented.

In Table 15, we can see that in 1999 in Korea, the total sales promotion expenditure was about 6.5 billion won of which sports sponsorship accounted for about 25%. However in the last three years the share captured by sports sponsorship is increasing continually and this trend is expected to become more significant in light of the 2002 World Cup hosted by Korea and Japan.

Table 15: Spending on Ads, Sales Promotion, and Sports Sponsorship (unit: 100 million won)

Type	1997		1998		1999	
	amount	share	amount	share	amount	share
Total ad	53,767	100%	34,846	100%	47,531	100%
4 major media	43,290	81%	27,448	79%	38,876	82%
Sales promotion	8,817	16%	5,695	16%	6,549	14%
Sports sponsorship	450	0.8%	593	1.7%	1,621	3.4%

Source: KAAA, Advertising Year Book 2000

In preparation for the 2002 World Cup, Hyundai motors has been selected as an official partner in the automotive sponsorship category. The sponsorship amount is estimated to be about 38 million dollars and the marketing is being organized by Diamond agency with the purpose of changing the positioning and image of Hyundai cars from "value for money" to that of "high quality" in markets outside of Korea. In addition

---

[1] KAAA, Advertising Year Book 2000

to sponsoring the 2002 World Cup, Hyundai automatically becomes an official sponsor of the 1999 Junior World Soccer Championship, the 2000 Women's World Cup in the U.S., the Intercontinental Cup held in Mexico, the under 17 World Soccer Championship and the Euro 2000 Championship co-hosted by the Netherlands and Belgium.

6.2 Product Placement

A recent popular trend in Korea has been the placement of products and brands in television programs and films. Moreover, a modified version of product placement has been the placement of movies in advertising as tie-up promotions. For example the movie "Godzilla" was placed in ads for KFC and Daewoo Motors in Korea. These type of product placements can be effective in integrating conventional media with on site media and thus increase the overall effectiveness of marketing campaigns.

7 Brief History of Korean Advertising and Basic Characteristics

7.1 Brief History of Korean Advertising

7.1.1 Emergence of Mass Advertising (1886-1969)

The introduction of mass media in Korea is generally believed to be around early 1886 with the publication of an ad in the Han Sung Weekly. This practice became a regular fixture in this weekly and in other newspapers around 1896. In 1920 the first ads with photographs were introduced. In 1956 television was first broadcast in Korea and along with it television advertising.

7.1.2 Modernization of Advertising

In 1968 and 1969, two multinational companies Coca-Cola and Pepsi Cola entered the Korean market thereby introducing Korea not only to foreign competition but also to modern advertising practices. Concurrently in 1969, competition in television advertising began with the addition of MBC-TV, and in 1970 the first color ads appeared in Korean newspapers. Another significant event was the broadcasting of color television in 1980. All of these factors combined to lay the groundwork for the modernization of advertising organization, advertising personnel management, copy writing, and media placement in Korea.

In 1980, following the recent assassination of President Park and the subsequent turmoil the way led to the reorganization and control of Korean media. Part of the new structure was the creation of the Korean Broadcast Advertising Company (KOBACO) which remains in existence to this day. In spite of KOBACO, the heated growth of the Korean economy pulled an even higher growth for Korean advertising. In 1989, the Audit Bureau of Circulation was founded to account for circulation of newspapers. However, because of the lack of cooperation by the major newspapers in Korea in accounting for paid circulation, ABC has not lived up to its intended role. In 1991 the Korean advertising industry, for all practical purposes, was open to foreign competition. In 1999 the Revised Broadcasting Rules was legislated and with that the almost twenty years of monopolization of broadcast media placement by KOBACO was altered with the authorization of private media representatives. Also regulation of broadcast advertising, unlike in the past, is being allowed to be self-regulated. Therefore in the next few years the key matter of interest is the impact of these changes on the commission structure and operation of agencies in Korea.

7.1.3 Recent Characteristics of Korean Advertising

Some of the creative appeals used in Korean advertising in recent years are as follows:

Affection Appeal
In June 1999, the multinational research company Taylor Nelson Sofres conducted a study for Ogilvy & Mather Korea with supervision by Prof. Dae Ryun Chang. They interviewed about 200 people working in the marketing departments and advertising agencies about the key success factors for advertising. The highest response given was having a long term strategic perspective. What was interesting was that the second highest response was for creativity that leads to high emotion. Korean advertising is traditionally well known for having emotional appeals and in this regard some famous campaigns have been Choco Pie, Dashida, Kyung Dong Boiler and Sejin Computers.

Appeal to the N Generation (cf. Figure 3)
With the widespread adoption and use of the internet and wireless communication, the young population that are familiar and almost dependent on

these technologies have been branded the N (network) generation. The marketing and advertising industries in Korea have targeted the N generation as a key market. The marketing and advertising campaigns have been characterized not only by the familiar digital-oriented content but also by the so-called "dotcom" type of creativity; simple, funny and almost kitsch-oriented advertising that was popular in other countries as well.

Table 16: Success Factors for Advertising (1, 2 or 3 ranked responses)

Long term perspectives/good strategies	56%
"Moving" creativity	42%
Sufficient budget	38%
Focused targets and their understanding	28%
Good products and reasonable price	23%
Effective marketing research	20%
Break-through creativity	16%
Tie-up with other promotions	13%
total	300%

Figure 3: Example of N Generation Ad

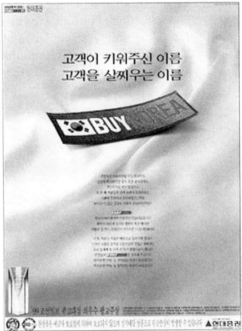

Figure 4: Examples of Patriotic Appeal Ads

Patriotism Appeal (cf. Figure 4)

As a direct outgrowth of the financial crisis in 1997, a common creative theme found in Korea in its aftermath was an appeal for Koreans to bond together. This patriotism appeal was exemplified by the "Buy Korean" campaign of Hyundai Securities but could also be found in other categories such as automobiles and was leading up to the economic recovery of 1999.

8   Korean Advertising Regulation

Simply put, the regulation infrastructure of the Korean advertising industry is very complex. Broadcast advertising is regulated by the Broadcasting Commission of Korea and the Cable Broadcasting Commission of Korea. In turn print advertising is self-regulated after insertion of advertising by the print industry such as by the Korean Newspapers Ethics Commission and Korean Print Ethics Commission. Moreover, there are differences across industries such as the self-regulation before insertion by the Korean Cosmetics Industry Association, and the before insertion regulation of the pharmaceutical and food industry advertising as dictated by laws from the Korean Health and Welfare Ministry.

Some notable aspects of Korean advertising regulation are rules against restraint of trade and monopolization, consumer protection, copyrights, brand regulation, food safety, drug safety, medicine, and rules for advertising movies and records. Among them the most important regulations are those concerning fair trade and monopolization and are supervised by the Ministry of Finance.

References

ADIC, Advertising Trend, March 2000

Advertising Annual Report year 2000

Cheil Communications, Advertising Year Book 2000

Cheil Communications, ACR data

Chang, Dae Ryun and Minhi Hahn (2000), Integrated Advertising Management, Hakhyunsa

Chang, Dae Ryun (1999), Branding and Advertising in Korea: In Search of the Missing Link

Chosun daily, February 28, 2001

KAAA, Advertising Year Book 2000

KAA journal, Jan, 2000

Korea Advanced Digital Data Inc., www.adchannel.co.kr

New Media Journal, 2000

Advertising in Spain

Prof. Dr. Cristina Etayo
University of Navarra

1   The Advertising Industry in the Spanish Economy

Advertising is beginning to take its place as a very important industry in the Spanish economy. Advertising contributes to the GNP by generating value for the goods and services advertised as well as the means and media used by the industry. In order to analyze the evolution of this industry within the Spanish economy, let us first analyze the behavior of this industry within the last few years.

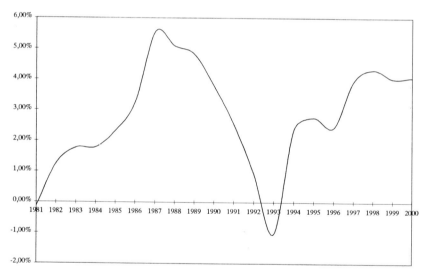

Figure 1: Real Growth of the GNP in Spain 1981-2000
Source: Boletín Mensual de Estadística

The GNP real growth chart in Spain shows us how the Spanish economy has been behaving during these last 20 years. From the Petroleum crisis of

1973, which had a very negative effect on the Spanish economy, followed by a stage of economic growth that extended until the 80s. In the first part of the decade, the Spanish economy reached levels of impressive growth. From 1984 these levels increased considerably, however they did not repeat the spectacular growth seen in the 70s. The second half of the decade also saw growth in the GNP levels although from 1989 other indicators of the Spanish economy began to show that the period of expansion was nearing its end. Unfortunately, these indicators did not predict that a crisis was about to arrive until 1992. The crisis of 1993 was a short crisis, but it had a lot of serious consequences. The GNP fell to its lowest levels and this considerably increased the unemployment levels in Spain. The succeeding recovery was slower but it was resting on more solid foundations. From 1996 the economy was growing at a good pace and other necessary structural reforms that were late in coming, were finally done.

To determine the participation of advertising in conjunction with the goods and services produced by the Spanish economy, we present in this paper the evolution of the amount of investment that advertising infused in the total GNP during the last years.

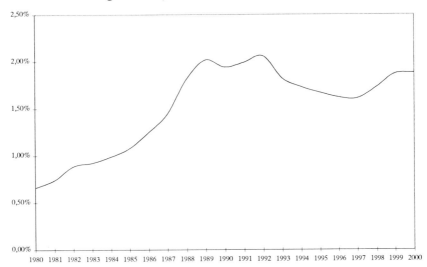

Figure 2: Advertising Spending (% of GNP) 1980-2000
Source: INFOADEX and Boletín Mensual de Estadística

As one can observe in the chart, advertising investment in the GNP of the Spanish economy has grown in an extraordinary way in the last few years.

This fact allows us to affirm that advertising is a fast rising sector within the Spanish economy. This growth was occurred in a more noticeable way during the 80s, starting from 1980, the year when the investments in advertising were at 0.66% of the Gross National Product. This lasted until 1989 when it was 2.02% of the GNP. In one decade, advertising contribution to the GNP tripled. Years of special growth were 1982 and 1983 and the years of the second part of the decade, from 1986 to 1989. In the 90s, it has maintained the levels of the 80s, although with other ups and downs. In the first part of the decade and as a probable consequence of the slow down of expansion of the 80s following the economic crisis at the beginning of the 90s, it produced a considerable decrease of advertising contributions to the GNP. The shrinking continued from 1993 to 1997. From 1998, its participation began to improve. Because of these developments, it can be said that the 80s were a very important decade in determining the development of advertising in Spain. At least insofar as the number of dedicated resources to this endeavor is concerned. It can also be deduced from the analysis of the data that it was good that advertising experienced impressive growth during the decade. The crisis of the 90s affected advertising negatively. The consolidation of the Spanish economic sector probably in the next stage of economic growth is predicted to improve advertising's participation in the Spanish economy.

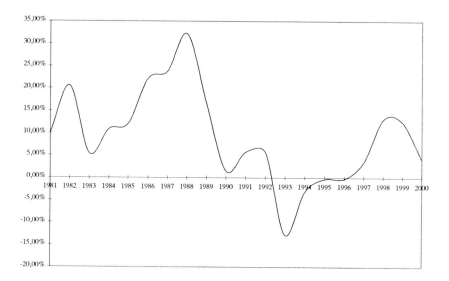

Figure 3: Real Growth of the Advertising Investment in Spain 1981-2000
Source: INFOADEX

Figure 3 shows the real growth of the advertising investment that has been produced each year from 1981 to 2000. As can be seen, 1989 showed a quick growth of advertising investment. This was seen especially in the years 1986, 1987, and 1988. In 1990 the growth was smooth but it slowed down from 1993-1997. Growth began again on 1998, although only in modest levels.

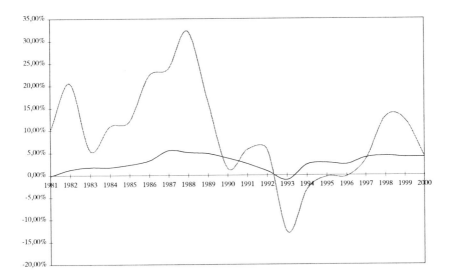

Figure 4: Growth of Advertising Investment in Spain and Growth of the GNP 1981-2000
Source: INFOADEX and Boletín Mensual de Estadística

The analysis of the charts that shows the real growth of the advertising investment and the GNP allows us to make other conclusions besides that of the relationships that can exist among this sector of activity and the economic cycles. As is well known, the economy has a circular character that makes an epoch of expansion follow one of a recession. The majority of the economic indicators reflect this characteristic in its evolutions. However, sometimes trade determines, with its magnitudes either antici-pating or backstopping changes in the global behavior of the economy. This translates into more or less those same problems that can be seen in the date of each country. In the same way, there exist some industrial sec-tors that effectively anticipate the cycle and delay their growth whenever they see that the economy is entering a recession. These in turn show their maximum levels. The previous chart tries to get closer to a very basic form of determining the cyclical, procyclical and countercyclical character of this activity. However, the fundamental problem is that a relatively short time period of 20 years is insufficient to obtain viable conclusions. At best conclusions can be made when this period coincides with the consolidation of Spanish economic activity and a notable increase of its contributions to the GNP. Nevertheless, an analysis of the previous graphic shows in a very clear way the behavior of advertising investments and more specially, that of the GNP. It is said that the fluctuations are stronger in the case of investments in advertising. In the 20 years considered, we encountered growth that was going from 32.2% in 1988 (an atypical year for those living in Spain with the cultural and sporting events of the Olympics of Barcelona and the Expo in Seville) until its slowdown to 12.79% the economic crisis. With regards to the GNP, its limits of fluctuation in this period were from a growth of 5.55% in 1987 and to a loss of 1.03% in 1993.

Another conclusion that can be made with the detailed observation of the graph is that when the GNP was growing, the growth of investment in advertising was always at the top. It is said that during the peaks of economic growth the investments in advertising increased in a very considerable way at highest levels to this growth. In the same way, when the economy enters a recession and the levels of development decrease, the investments respond with the same impetus and likewise decreases. This way, advertising can be seen as a sector that highly affected by economic situations. For example, the advertising expenses of companies are intimately related with the situation of the economy, from where it can be deduced that the politics of company advertising investment are done in a very short period. There is no strategic planning for a long period. It therefore seems that advertising is not considered as a fixed expense, but as an expense, which varies depending on the economic climate it finds itself in. To determine if advertising will be growing or not in the next years we to have to take into account the economic situation, the importance that it has in the GNP (analyzed earlier) and the expenses of advertising per capita.

As can be observed in Figure 5, the level of advertising expenses per capita has grown in a very important way, much higher than the rest in the period concerned. This growth has been very large in the 80s, as was seen in the decade of sector consolidation, especially in the second half and during the beginning of the nineties. The crisis of 1993 slowed down this growth, but from 1997 it had a tendency to recover its rhythm. All the data that has been offered in this sector comes from the same direction and allows us to affirm that advertising, as a sector consolidated within the Spanish economy, has promising expectations to offer.

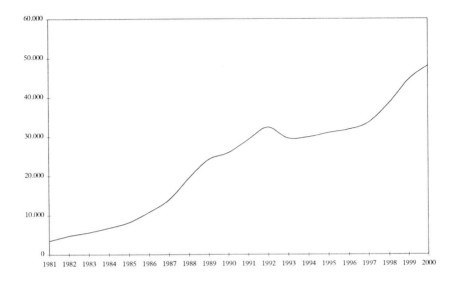

Figure 5: Advertising Investment per Capita in Spain, 1981-2000
Source: INFOADEX and Boletín Mensual de Estadística

2   Structure of the Industry in Spain

2.1   Advertising Media

2.1.1 Types of Media

Each advertising medium has one particular property that makes them different from the others but for a complete study, the media will be classified into two: conventional and non-conventional.

The dominant conventional media are newspapers, supplements and Sunday magazines, monthly magazines, radio, movie, television, outdoor advertising and the Internet, which has recently been converted to conventional media given its spectacular growth.

Among non-conventional media we have: direct mail, mailbox leaflets and catalogues, telephone marketing, advertising gifts, the PLV, signs and stickers, fairs and expositions, sponsorships, merchandizing and social marketing, sports sponsorship, corporate advertising, internal magazines, bulletins and memoirs, annual reports, guides and directories, promotional games, loyalty cards and the point of sale animations.

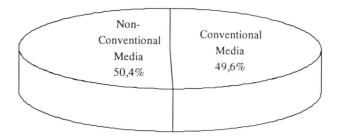

Figure 6: **Advertising Investment in Conventional and Non-Conventional Media**
Source: INFOADEX

In the year 2000, the real investment estimated in conventional media was 941,062 millions of pesetas with a total of 1,897,534 millions of pesetas. This figure was higher than the investment in non-conventional media which only grew to 956,472 millions of pesetas. Of the total real investment estimated conventional media spending was pegged at 49.59%.

It has been observed that during this period produced a convergence between the investments in conventional and non-conventional media, and although in the year 2000 the investment in non-conventional media slightly surpassed the investment in conventional media the differences were insignificant and they leveled out it over time.

During the start of the 80s, wherein non-conventional media spending was at its lowest, investments started to increase with growth accelerating in 1987 and equalizing in 1991. This tells us that we did not find before a sector that can modify its essence in a very short period of time, much attention must be paid to all the changes that are felt to be introduced through the market.

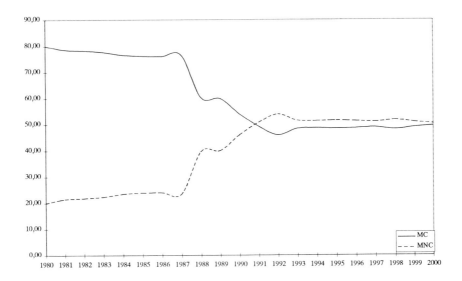

Figure 7:   **Development of Advertising Spending in Conventional and Non-Conventional Media**

Source: INFOADEX

2.1.2 Conventional Media

Spending in conventional media has grown in considerable forms although much slower than the growth of spending in non-conventional media. It can be said that the growth of an investment is not produced uniquely in any type of media without sharing this growth among the others.

The investments conventional media was considerable during the decade of the 80s. However, spending in this media slackened in 1990 owing to the growth of non-conventional media spending. This caused the valuation of growth to be negative up until 1996.

As can be observed in Figure 9 conventional media much of the invest-ments were concentrated on television receiving 40.84% of the investment. Newspapers likewise received 29.91%. These two forms of media jointly make up 70% of the total investment in conventional media. Next are the magazines and the radio. A similar albeit lesser percentage is given to outdoor advertising, the supplements and Sunday magazines, movie ad-vertising and the Internet.

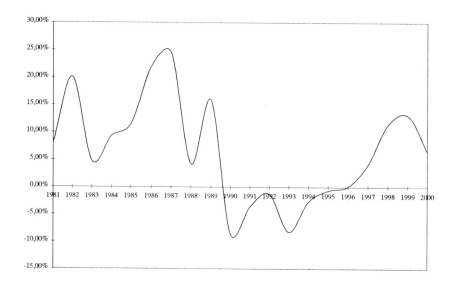

Figure 8: Growth Rate of Investment in Conventional Media
Source: INFOADEX

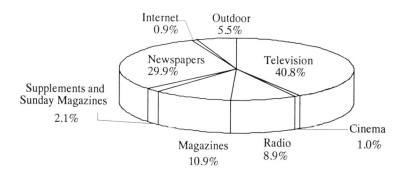

Figure 9: Media Split of Conventional Media
Source: INFOADEX

2.1.2.1 Television

The behavior of the advertising investment in television is of great interest due to the magnitude of the investments in this medium in comparison to the rest of conventional media. We see that the investments are maintained constantly during the first years of the study and increased considerably from 1997.

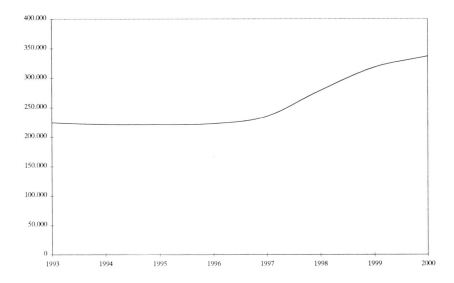

**Figure 10: Development of the Advertising Investment in Television
                 (in Real Terms, Prices of 1995)**
Source: INFOADEX

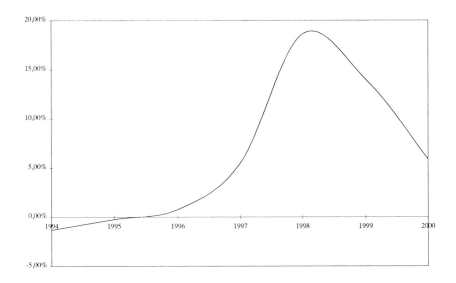

Figure 11: Valuation of Real Growth of the Investment in Television
Source: INFOADEX

As can be seen in Figure 11, the investment in television did not decrease
much in the first years of the 90s. Still heavy with the impact of the crisis

of 1993 television belonged to the majority of the media. In 1996 television began a spectacular growth followed a similar trend during the last 2 years. The television is the media more chosen in advertising for its high level of affectivity. Naturally television spending decreases when advertising spending in general decreases such as in the case of an economic crisis. During these times advertisers are likely to resort to other forms of media. Television spending increases again during times of fair economic weather.

2.1.2.2 Newspapers

The advertising investment in newspapers did not experience any great decline. It is an investment that has maintained its levels from the beginning and from 1996 has grown considerably in a sustainable way.

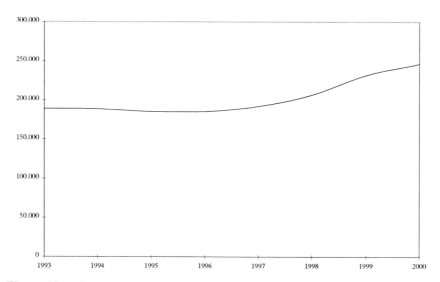

**Figure 12:   Development of the Advertising Investment in Newspapers
             (in Real Terms, Prices of 1995)**
Source: INFOADEX

As we have seen before the advertising investment in newspapers happens in a scale that is normally stable. It seems minimally affected by the crisis of the sector, but from 1996 its growth valuation grew progressively, although minor growth is detected in the same way in the year 2000.

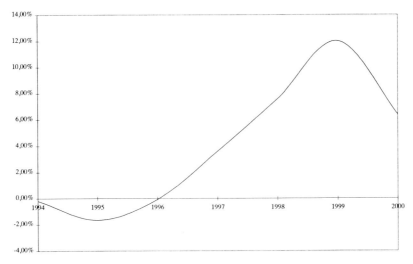

Figure 13: Valuation of Real Growth of the Investment in Newspapers
Source: INFOADEX

2.1.2.3 Magazines

The advertising investment in magazines is more stable than that of the previous case, although lately, this is a medium that has been affected by the crisis.

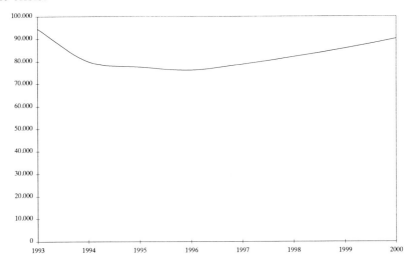

**Figure 14: Development of the Advertising Investment
                (in Real Terms, Prices of 1995)**
Source: INFOADEX

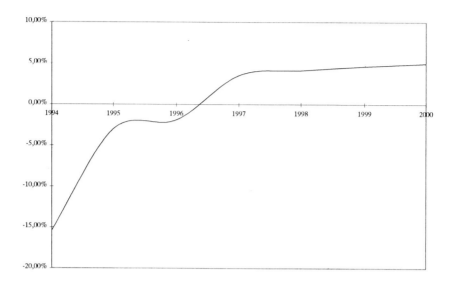

Figure 15: Valuation of Real Growth of Investment in Magazines
Source: INFOADEX

The evolution of the valuation of growth in this media repeated the same behavior that was observed in the case of supplements and Sunday magazines although in this case, recovery started and maintained its stability.

2.1.2.4 Radio

The advertising investment in radio has increased progressively during the years in the period analyzed. It is one medium wherein investments did not decrease as a consequence of the crisis.

The growth of investments in radio seems to have been minimally affected by the crisis, recovering rapidly. Despite having fluctuations, it retains its important levels all throughout the years.

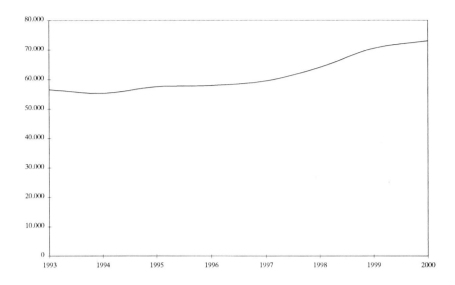

**Figure 16: Development of Advertising Investment
            (in Real Terms, Prices of 1995)**
Source: INFOADEX

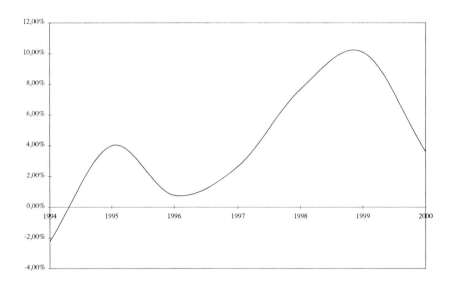

Figure 17: Valuation of the Real Growth of the Investments in Radio
Source: INFOADEX

2.1.2.5 Supplements and Sunday Magazines

Supplements and Sunday magazines were observed to have an important decrease from 1994 to 1997. The plunging values stopped at 1997 and its started growing again although not to the levels of growth reported in 1993.

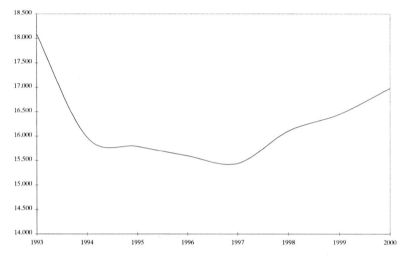

Figure 18: Development of the Advertising Investments in Supplements and Sunday Magazines (in Real Terms, Prices of 1995)
Source: INFOADEX

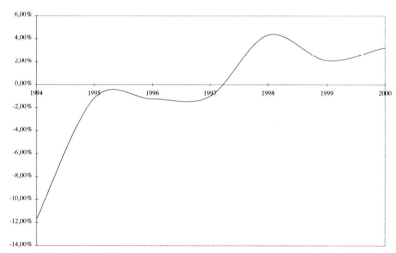

Figure 19: Valuation of Real Growth of the Investments in Supplements and Sunday Magazines
Source: INFOADEX

The great fall of the advertising of supplements and Sunday magazines was seen in the year 1994 as a direct consequence of the crisis that affected this medium with special strength. It took a lot time to return to a growth stage. Something it has not experienced since 1998

2.1.2.6 Outdoor Advertising

The investment in outdoor advertising has been at progressive increments, especially in the last years with the addition of investments in transport and mobile urban advertising.

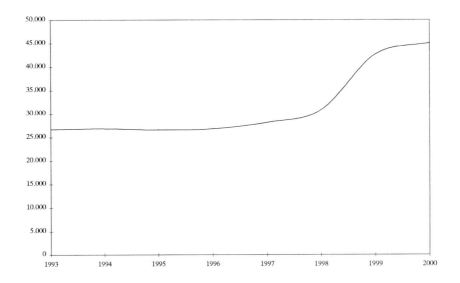

**Figure 20: Development of Advertising Growth in Outdoor Advertising
(in Real Terms, Prices of 1995)**
Source: INFOADEX

These investments in outdoor advertising do not seem to be very affected by the crisis and from 1998 increased considerably.

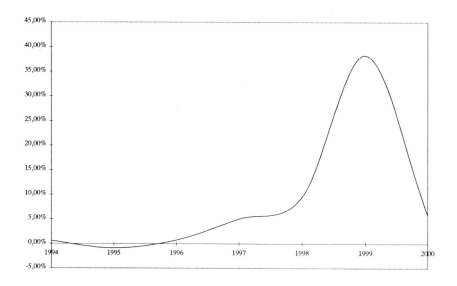

Figure 21: Valuation of Real Growth of the Investments in Outdoor
Advertising
Source: INFOADEX

2.1.2.7 Movie Advertising

The advertising investment in movies has remained relatively stable during the first years of the analyzed period, experiencing a considerable growth from 1996. It is a medium in which the magnitude of advertising investment is still rising in comparison to the other media.

It can be observed clearly in Figure 23 that from 1996 a period of rapid growth began in the investments in this medium.

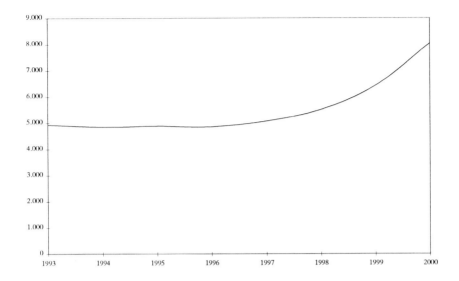

**Figure 22: Development of the Advertising Investments in Movies
(in Real Terms, Prices of 1995)**
Source: INFOADEX

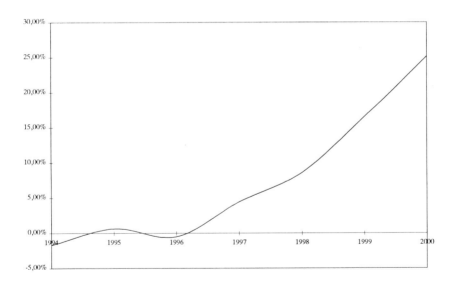

**Figure 23: Valuation of the Real Growth of the Investments in Movie
Advertising**
Source: INFOADEX

2.1.2.8 Internet

A complete series of data is not available in order to evaluate the evolution of this Internet spending. Nevertheless, the data of 1999 and 2000 allows us to forecast that advertising investment in this media is going to see a very considerable increase.

One can infer from the data presented that the evolution of each one of the media in the general investment is realized in conventional media. The newspapers, supplements and Sunday magazines, magazines and radio have seen reductions in their total participation in the investments in conventional media. Television has stabilized at the same time with an increase of an important form of outdoor advertising (especially Transport and Urban Transport advertising).

2.1.3　Non-Conventional Media

Table 1 presents the investment in non-conventional media broken down according to the media that has been utilized in the last years.

Table 1: Investments in Non-Conventional Media

NON CONVENTIONAL MEDIA	1998	1999	2000
Direct mail	230,984	241,379	271,310
Mailbox leaflets and catalogues	110,720	126,553	134,652
Telephone marketing	31,646	60,420	64,287
Advertising gifts	51,998	56,158	60,875
P.L.V, signs and stickers	150,836	154,432	166,478
Fairs and expositions	18,050	20,360	20,767
Sponsorships, merchandizing and social marketing	44,952	47,964	51,705
Sport sponsorship	65,701	70,957	73,866
Corporate advertising	8,173	8,903	9,037
Annual reports, guides and directories	46,882	49,091	49,778
Catalogues	24,808	29,710	32,919
Promotional games		6,089	6,597
Loyalty cards		4,385	4,944
Point of sale animations		8,646	9,257
TOTAL	784,750	885,047	956,472

Source: INFOADEX

On account of the participation of each one of the non-conventional media in the total investments made, one cannot observe significant changes during the last 3 years, except with the apparition of new forms of media, were not contemplated before. These new forms of media will logically be absorbing little by little a part of this investment.

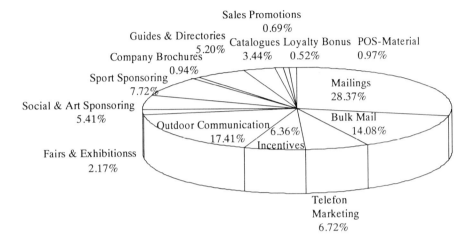

Figure 24: Media Split: Non-Conventional Media
Source: INFOADEX

2.2 Agents of Advertising in Spain

2.2.1 Advertising Agencies

2.2.1.1 General Overview

The Advertising Agencies are companies that offer their services to the advertisers. Generally within these companies there are persons dedicated to take care of the accounts of the agencies. The marketing and advertising directors are those who do this task. This assignment is done, following certain criteria, which depend on the company involved. Other criteria that influence the decision to choose one agency over another are creativity, service costs and the capacity to execute an image campaign. Other factors that also play a role are the experience of the agency, the personal relations, the negotiations with media, the size of the agency and recommendations from the mother company.

The advertisers usually favor creativity and service as the more valuable criteria in deciding for an agency. They also value strategic planning, return on investment, good research, proactivity, media management and planning, transparency, global vision of communications, below the line services, and the existence of an international network. The tools used by the advertisers when they have to select a new agency are the order, the work done by the agency, personal experience, examination of the credentials, the recommendation of friends and colleagues, personal relations with agency professionals, contests, brochures and creative reels. They also consider other instruments such as the annual reports of the agencies, selection consultants, the ranking of the agencies and articles in specialized presses although these are not so important in the decision making process.

The methods that are used by Spanish advertisers to choose an advertising agency to entrust their campaigns are creative contests, strategic contests, and direct selection. The creative contests are not paid for most of the time although there are arguments that favor or are against getting remuneration for these pitches. The arguments in favor claim that since its is a job, one ought to pay for the service, that one ought to charge for the costs that have been incurred and that this can be a factor for motivation. The arguments against point out that these are risks that the agency has to bear and that these practices are normal in the market and that it should be part of any agency budget. With regard to the size of the agency, the majority of advertisers prefer to work with medium sized agencies, while multinational companies and public administration are more inclined towards large sized agencies.

The normal duration of work between an advertiser and its respective advertising agency is 3.4 years and about 40% of advertisers work with more than just one agency.

With regard to the compensation system, the basic forms of compensation of agencies are commission, honoraria and a mixed system. In Spain, approximately 35% of accounts are studying about paying its agency by commission (while 10% of the media compensation is by commission) and 43% by honoraria. There also exist mixed systems, which combine honoraria and commissions. Some 5% work with a system of compensation based on marketing results.

2.2.1.2 Number, Size and Importance of the Agencies

To measure the importance of the agencies in the sector one can use diverse criteria, such as billings, prizes obtained for campaigns done or the good reputations of the agencies. These can be spontaneous or suggested. The Council of Advertising Consultants made a survey among people of the sector to determine which agencies were the most famous and they offered a ranking.

Table 2: Agency Ranking According to the Council of Advertising Consultants 1998

Rank	Agency
1	Bassat, Ogilvy &Mather
2	Tiempo BBDO
3	Delvico Bates
4	McCann Erickson
5	Young & Rubicam
6	Tandem DDB
7	J.W. Thompson
8	FCB Tapsa
9	TBWA
10	Casadevall, Pedreño & PRG
11	Lorente Grupo de Comunicación
12	DMB&B
13	Contrapunto
14	Euro/RSCG
15	Ammirati Puris Lintas
16	Grey Trace
17	La Banda de Agustín Medina
18	Vitruvio Leo Burnnett
19	Saatchi & Saatchi
20	Ruiz Nicoli

Source: Estudio de Imagen de las Agencias de Publicidad Española. Estudio de Consultores de la Publicidad

Table 3: Agency Ranking

Agency		Gross Income	Employees	Income per Employee
1	McCann Erickson	11,625.00	774	15.02
2	Young & Rubicam	9,375.00	460	20.38
3	FCB Tapsa	8,545.00	277	30.85
4	Tiempo BBDO	8,008.00	332	24.12

Table 3, continued

5	Bassat, Ogilvy &Mather	7,914.00	429	18.45
6	Lorente Grupo de Comunicación	7,843.00	367	21.37
7	Publicis	7,515.00	138	54.46
8	TBWA	7,350.00	248	29.64
9	Grey Trace	7,082.00	279	25.38
10	Delvico Bates	6,687.00	347	19.27
11	Tandem DDB	6,431.00	165	38.98
12	Vitruvio Leo Burnnett	5,146.00	221	23.29
13	Lowe Lintas	3,915.00	193	20.28
14	J.W. Thompson	3,575.00	127	28.15
15	D'Arcy/Grupo K-IMP	3,519.75	191	18,43
16	Saatchi & Saatchi	3,227.00	63	512
17	Contrapunto	2,548.00	200	12.74
18	Publicis Casadevall, P. & PRG	2,396.00	104	23.04
19	Creativos de Publicidad	1,573.00	25	62.92
20	Remos Asatsu	1,569.00	56	28.02

Source: Anuncios

2.2.2 Advertisers

The majority of big brands from different sectors use advertising as a means to let the public know about their products. Nevertheless, there are a series of companies that year after year are configured to have more expenses in advertising fueled into the Spanish economy. The more important advertisers are presented in this table.

Table 4: Top Spanish Advertisers

	Advertiser	Spending (Mln. PTS.)		Advertiser	Spending (Mln. PTS.)
1	Telefónica Servicios Móviles, S.A.	14,562.0	26	BBVA	4,486.70
2	El Corte Inglés, S.A.	12,285.9	27	SEAT	4,389.50
3	Telefónica, S.A.	11,418.7	28	Unilever	4,256.20
4	Fasa Renault, S.A.	9,351.9	29	M Economía y Hacienda	4,241.80
5	Procter&Gamble España, S.A.	9,224.3	30	Cosmética Selecta	4,043.00
6	Volkswagen-Audi España, S.A.	8,952.5	31	Viajes Halcón	3,963.60
7	Organización nacional de Ciegos de España	8,647.1	32	Henkel	3,909.20
8	Airtel Móvil. S.A.	8,420.8	33	Nissan Motor	3,749.80

Table 4, continued

9	Peugeot Talbot España, S.A.	7,493.0	34	Terra Networks	3,631.5
10	Danone S.A.	7,435.2	35	Bacardi-Martini	3,493.8
11	Nestlé España, S.A.	6,966.2	36	Recoletos Cia Editorial	3,433.6
12	UDV	6,818.1	37	BMW	3,402.7
13	Ford España, S.A.	6,417.3	38	Diario El País	3,302.5
14	Lince Comunicaciones S.L.	6,255.1	39	Altadis	3,241.3
15	Distribuidora Televisión Digital, S.A.	6,056.4	40	Eresmas	3,201.1
16	Leche Pascual S.A.	5,821.3	41	Cable Europa	3,013.2
17	Retevisión Móvil S.A.	5,687.7	42	Reckitt Benckiser	2,922.1
18	Cía Coca Cola de España S.A.	5,639.4	43	Canal Satélite Digital	2,856.0
19	Centro de Estudios CEAC S.A.	5,568.8	44	RTVE	2,846.6
20	Opel España S.A.	5,429.9	45	Home English	2,825.6
21	FIAT	5,367.8	46	Opening	2,822.2
22	Onda Digital	5,271.8	47	CCC	2,762.0
23	Arbora&Ausonia	4,941.5	48	Retevisión	2,735.5
24	Citroen	4,650.5	49	Ericsson	2,551.9
25	L'Oreal Prod. Publico	4,486.8	50	Nokia	2,544.6

Source: Anuncios

Table 5: Ranking of Advertising Groups

	Group	Spending (mill. ptas)
1	Grupo Telefónica	39,095.22
2	Grupo Auna	18,774.43
3	Grupo El Corte Inglés	15,260.39
4	Grupo Prisa	14,882.60
5	Grupo Volkswagen	14,456.55
6	Grupo PSA	12,413.53
7	Grupos Danone	10,714.72
8	Grupo L'Oreal	9,661.03
9	Grupo Once	9,551.35
10	Grupo Renault	9,375.78
11	Procter&Gamble España	9,224.23
12	Ford Motor Company	9,124.01
13	Grupo Airtel	8,423.54
14	Grupo Unilever	8,220.77
15	Diageo	7,881.12
16	Grupo Nestlé	7,773.28
17	Grupo BBVA	6,807.33
18	Grupo Uni2	6,558.09
19	Grupo Pascual	5,821.32

Table 5, continued

20	Grupo Sony	5,762.87
21	Cia Coca Cola de España	5,639.44
22	Grupo Fiat	5,572.62
23	Centro de Estudios CEAC	5,568.82
24	Opel España	5,429.91
25	Grupo Repsol	5,412.13

Source: INFOADEX

Table 6: Concentration of the Number of Brands per Sector

Sector	Spending mill. ptas.	% of total	Number of brands per sector
Food	59,293	6.55	2,860
Automobile	89,604	9.89	4,685
Drinks	48,894	5.40	1,526
Beauty, Hygiene and Health	71,750	7.92	3,241
Construction	21,159	2.34	5,450
Culture, Education and Communication Media	146,922	16.22	19,381
Sports and Leisure Time	16,926	1.87	3,054
Distribution	59,089	6.52	12,291
Energy	9,220	1.02	536
Office, Commercial and Telecommunications Equipment	99,661	11.00	5,225
Finance and Insurance	42,146	4.65	4,290
Homes	25,352	2.80	3,588
Industrial, Material and Agricultural Equipment	3,416	0.38	3,078
Cleaning	15,915	1.76	311
Personal Objects	10,859	1.20	1,783
Public and Private Services	46,452	5.13	14,387
Tobacco	10,360	1.14	130
Textiles and Clothing	15,141	1.67	1,662
Transportation, Trips and Tourism	25,995	2.87	3,976
Others	87,485	9.66	1,856

Source: INFOADEX

2.3   Services for the Advertising Sector

In the world of advertising there is a chain of companies that offer related services within the sector. Depending on the type of concrete activity that they do, we have:

2.3.1   Institutions That Get Data Related With the Sector

A group of institutions exist in Spain that develop research works in media, a branch of commercial research that occupy the study of these means of communication as vehicles for advertising. Some of the more important ones are:

OJD: Oficina de Justificación de la Difusión, founded on 1964, is an association of media, agencies and advertisers, of private character. It obtains and facilitates information about the distribution and the diffusion of period publications that are voluntarily given to the advertisers, advertising agencies, editors and other persons or among organizations. The editorial company of the publication presents to OJD a declaration of its print run, subscriptions, sales, services, and publication distribution for a period. The data are declared to the editor for him to examine, revise, and review by means of an audit that requires physical proofs, documentation, testimonials and analyses. When the data has been sufficiently proven an Annual Act Justifying the Diffusion of the Publication is released.

Nevertheless, the analysis of the quantity and quality of the advertising is inserted in every medium is short because they can only make by means of observation. The control of the advertisements that has truly been inserted in the media needs qualitative and quantitative research. The qualitative research is done when one wants to investigate the advertising and if the analysis is from the point of view of creative work.

The quantitative research is done when one is interested in analyzing the number of times an advertisement is seen and the cost of each placement, in order to determine the advertising investment of the advertisers. A company that dedicates itself to analyze the content and the advertising investment in media is INFOADEX.

INFOADEX: A company that offers qualitative and quantitative research of the advertising sector in Spain. They study the controls, the investments, and the advertising content in our country. They proportion ample quantitative information on all the figures of the advertising sector, their number, and their size, situations, costs and frequency of whatever advertisement of the superior press has. Information ranges from the size of a page until the total spots broadcasted for whatever chain of television stations. The analysis of advertising investments is done by medium: television, magazines, newspapers, supplements and Sunday magazines, outdoor advertising, radio and movie advertising. In each one it gives complete detailed information on the medium: from advertising fragmentation to the prices of tariffs of each support mean, general investments of each advertiser, brand investments, products, groups of media, different types of advertising (spot, sponsorship, microspaces), weighing the results.

On the part of quantitative information it possesses the best database for creative advertising in Spain. It includes all the television, movie, magazine, newspaper, and outdoor advertising in its original format which can be segmented by sector, category, products, brands, advertisers, media, and supports. The database is connected to other qualitative databases from all over the world to facilitate study and campaign comparisons.

Both institutions do research by observing the media, studying the structure, the contents and advertising investment.

Other types of institutions exists which do research through interviews, basic techniques of the media research that defines the audiences, how many people and what types are exposed to the media, with the objective of trying to know, for sure who are impacted by the messages.

General Council of Media (EGM): The EGM was born in 1968, although it 1989 it changed character into a non-profit organization called the Association for Media Research (AIMC). The AIMC was founded for other advertisers, and more importantly, for the advertising agencies, all of the media centers, the bigger part of media and the more professional agencies. Its main objective is to make studies of the audience and the structure of media and its principal supports, establishing comparisons and analyzing tendencies, which are very important data for media planning. The media financed 75% of this work and remaining 25% was obtained through membership subscriptions. The EGM made this research and reached the majority of persons in Spain after 14 years. 40.000 interviews are done annually, with questions that deal with the sociodemographic characteristics of the persons, exposure to media, equipment, product consumption and life styles. The EGM controlled the quantity of the audience of approximately 63 newspapers, 14 supplements, 26 weekly magazines, 2 quarterly magazines, 85 titles of monthly publications and proportional information to separate 35 radio station and 15 television channels.

Strong competition existed in the television medium as a consequence of the multiplication of channels, the rapid diversification of advertising spaces, and the advertising hiring has provoked a great interest in knowing the media audience, with more sophisticated perspectives. The coexistence of quantitative studies (Quantity, what and when) and qualitative (who) permits a more exact knowledge of the profile of the television viewer, which is essential for television programmers, and central to buying, agencies or advertisers. The media centers are across the research institutions that have created statistical studies of the television audiences. The system of measuring audiences is more advanced and practiced in place up to the moment the audiometrics is done by SOFREX.

SOFREX: Focusing on the audience of the private, public, national, and autonomous chains which includes cable television and satellite television with data on viewers, tape playback, video games and the computer. It allows one to know the general audience in a second, and go down to details obtaining specific data by target, region, days, and programs, spot by spot.

To investigate what we usually call new media, they are companies whose job is to explore these forms of disseminating advertising. These companies are in charge of following up this fundamental information, in order to offer their profitable and efficient services. Nevertheless, the companies dedicated to the research of conventional media have been exerting force to respond to the new needs and demands of the market.

2.3.2 Advertising Regulation

The economic importance of advertising and its increasing capacity to influence society justifies the existence of specific legislation and juridical norms that regulate advertising activity: This complements the norms configured in the Advertising Law. In 1964 the Statutes of Advertising started. This was abolished by the General Law of Advertising of 1988, which was concerned about the need to adapt normatively to community legislation. Concretely to the Directive 84450 of the European Council, of 1984 which refers to the approximation of legal regulations, rules, and administration of the State members in matters of advertising deceptions.

Actually, the legislation that is applicable to advertising is contained within the General Law of Advertising, The Law of Activities of Television and Radio Broadcast (Television without frontiers) and with a subsidiary character in the General Law for the defense of Consumers and Users (LGCU).

The general law of advertising LGP of 1994. Law 34/1988 of the 15th of November: Responds completely to the adaptation of communal norms with regard to the suitability of new circumstances of all types within the advertising ambit. The more important innovations of the LGP refer to the legal treatment of illicit advertising and the perfection of the procedural norms. Its scope of application is advertising communications without regulation as well as other activities of the same nature. In the Law, the advertising subjects are the advertisers, the advertising agencies, the communication media and the payees. The law offers general regulations, defines and categorizes illicit advertising and the different means of administrative interventions. It treats in almost the same way advertising contracts, which expressly regulate advertising, the diffusion of advertising, the creation of advertising, and sponsorship. The law sanctions and reprimands illicit advertising and at last attempts to maintain norms that regulate the advertisement of sanitary products, products risky to the health, the security, or the patrimony of persons and gambling.

The Law of Television without Frontiers: The Community directive about television without frontiers has been adopted for the Spanish Administration. This law regulates diverse aspects: the reception in Spanish territories of signals from other member states of the EU which requires incorporation of 50% of European productions in the programming. This protects European television production while meeting the quotas of broadcasting. This restricts the freedom of programming of the chains all in name of protecting its new members. This law almost regulates and limits the advertising or promotional activity.

2.3.3 Organisms of Advertising Self-Regulation

The majority of developed countries have created self-regulatory bodies, to reward the good work of its professionals, establish middle grounds for the participants of advertising activity. This development is not done at the national level, as there isn't actually any system of international regulation.

The apparition of these bodies of regulation have been caused by the petitions of the advertising public, the worries of advertisers for the quality of advertising and the inconveniences that exist in juridical marks that present grand lagoons and norms that quickly become obsolete before the rapid evolution of technology and communications. Its norms are of ethical character and attempt to protect the consumer of advertising from that which is not desirable or the advertisers of disloyal competition. They require the majority of advertising to be licit, authentic, true, loyal and socially responsible. Its objectives are to elevate the social image of advertising, making the public conscious about the contribution of advertising to economic development and social well being. Its social end is to keep vigil for the fulfillment of the ethical and legal norms that regulate advertising with its commercial communication, its suitability and truthfulness in its written, spoken and visual images. In Spain the Society of Self-Regulation was founded in 1977, seeded by the actual Associate of Advertising Self-Regulation. In other countries there also exist other bodies.

France: Bereau de Verification de la Publicite (BVP), 1953
Italy: Confederazione Generale Italiana della Publicita, 1964
US: National Advertising Review Council, 1971
Association of Advertising Self-Regulation, 13 June 1995

The Spanish Association of Advertisers managed the transformation of the company Advertising Self-Regulation into a professional association that assures the means of self-control, the Association of Advertising Self-Regulation. There are close to 100 members, among advertiser companies, advertising agencies, and media companies. This body is in charge of ensuring good advertising practices. It is independent of the Administration and was driven in 1977 by the AEA to achieve advertising self-control in order to avoid the necessity of legislation. The legal norms that define it obliges compliance among its members and has a recommendatory character for all the professionals and users of advertising activity. These were norms of ethical character and they help to give its members a clear and concrete guide about the limits within what advertising campaigns they can realize. They also exist to defend the rights of its partners and to realize and defend advertising actions that comply with all the legal and ethical norms that exist if they are presented before a restrictive organism. They elaborate on norms about alcoholic drinks, about advertising that affects children and teenagers, testimonial advertising, cosmetic and perfume product advertising, advertising of dietary products, the protection of intimacy, imitation, the exploitation of the commercial prestige, the identification of advertising and comparisons.

Regulatory norms that are imposed on different media/communication supports to accept advertising in their spaces.

The media and the supports of communication impose norms to accept advertising in their spaces. In Spain we find:

Regulatory norms for the broadcasting of advertising through TVE from the 20th of April 1990. These include general norms, norms that determine formats, and advertising means (Gift offerings, prizes and other incentives), use of terms and statistical data (technical or scientific mention of distinctions and testimonies), protective norms for babies, norms about determining goods and activities (alcoholic drinks, medicines, sanitary and cosmetic products, financial advertising and insurance advertising, house advertising, and motor vehicle advertising, norms about the distribution of space and sponsorships.

References

Aaker, D.A. (1991), *Manging Brand Equity*, The Free Press, New York

Boletín Mensual de Estadística, INE (Varios años)

Estudio INFOADEX de la Inversión publicitaria en España, 1996. INFOADEX

García Uceda, M. (2000), Las claves de la publicidad, ESIC, Madrid. 4ª ed.

Impacto Económico de la Publicidad en España, Asociación española de Anunciantes, AEA, 1999

Advertising in Switzerland

Prof. Dr. Maurizio Vanetti
lic.rer.pol. Ulrich Dimigen
lic.rer.pol Carlo Mondada
Seminar of Marketing - University of Fribourg

1   Introduction

"Advertising which is only designed to be published in a multilingual country would be as characterless as all compromise products"(Rizzi 1986: 84).

Switzerland as a country in the middle of Europe is characterized among other features by its multilingualism. In addition, a major consideration for everyone who is going to advertise in Switzerland is that there are not only four written languages (German, French, Italian and Rhaeto-Romanic), but in addition many dialects of the Swiss German, which may be considered a fifth language. That is the reason for the somewhat controversial introductory remark which shall be discussed in more detail in a separate chapter, although it is not possible to treat this matter exhaustively in the context of this textbook.

In order to give a descriptive overview of advertising in Switzerland, which is the aim of this essay, there are many further topics to be discussed. This shall be accomplished by moving from more general data to specific details: Beginning with a discussion of the implications of a multilingual society for advertising, the general environment for advertising in Switzerland shall be covered in the following chapter. Afterwards the focus will be on the specific environment of the advertising sector. In a fourth step the description of the branch itself will follow the logic of an assumed 'flow of action'. It begins with the advertiser, who initiates an advertising campaign, and then continues with the advertising agency, that converts the plan of the advertiser into action. Finally it reaches the advertising media. The concluding section will provide a short summary and complete the text.

2 Advertising in a Multilingual Country

As already mentioned in the introduction, every current or potential advertiser in Switzerland has to face the challenge of a multilingual and multicultural country. This may be shown by a full-page advertisement, which was published in 1987 by the French-speaking adapters of advertising in Switzerland in the most important newspapers of the German- and French-speaking part of Switzerland. It was a protest against bad translations from (Swiss-)German into (Swiss-)French advertisements and culminated in the following appeal: "Dear German Swiss, please do not forget, that we have also a feeling for language and our own culture. And that French is after all a world language. One million consumers are able to do without advertising badly translated. But you are not able to do without one million consumers" (Association des adaptateurs romands [ed.] 1987 - cited in Payer 1990: 6).

In addition advertising-communication in a multicultural country faces many other potential difficulties (Bosshart 1986: 17). Effectively there are the same problems that are widely discussed in the literature in the context of international marketing: 'extension', 'adaptation' and 'invention' of the marketing mix for an international company (Kotler 2000: 383).

Wyss says, that for Switzerland all data concerning the cultural trends, behaviors and attitudes of German Swiss and French Swiss which are available from studies demonstrate that there is a relatively large degree of agreement and a relatively small degree of divergence (Wyss 1986: 34). In addition the political and legal framework for advertising tends to be the same for the whole country.

But even if there are many cultural similarities between the different groups of languages in a country, the text of an advertisement has to be translated because of the different languages.

This means that although the other elements of the marketing mix may rest the same, at least the advertising mix has to be changed if a large share of people in Switzerland is not to be ignored. The more puns and specific cultural characteristics are used in an advertisement, the more difficult it is to find an appropriate translation. In this case the high costs for the translation has to be weighed up against the utility of an individual approach for each language. This has been termed by Wechssler the 'general untranslatability' of advertising (Payer 1990: 21).

In Switzerland there are four official languages…

With regard to the four official languages in Switzerland, there are different alternatives to consider when setting up an advertising campaign (following Payer 1990: 107):

- The advertising campaign may be limited to one language area. In this case it is possible to get the best results for the targeted language, and the costs are not too high. The main problem of adopting this solution is that the company might not be recognized as a national supplier in Switzerland.

- Another method is that the advertising campaign may be created in one language and subsequently translated into the other languages without any substantial adaptation. With this solution the whole audience will be covered, but the costs increase, and there could be a substantial mismatch of connotations, so that complaints as mentioned in the introductory lines of this chapter might appear.

- A third way to implement a national advertising campaign is to create the text in one language, followed firstly by a translation and secondly by an adaptation. The costs will increase further, and it is not certain that the adaptation will meet the expectations of the consumers.

- The fourth possibility is the most expensive, but may be the most effective: Each language region gets its own tailored advertising campaign. It is of note, however, that even if there is a common advertising strategy, the costs are fairly high, and there are very few cases where it is possible to design an individual campaign for the German Swiss and the French Swiss (Widmer 1986: 60).

The main problem of the former approaches is a lack of understanding of the different needs caused by lingual and cultural differences.

In contrast the main problem of the latter approaches is that the French-speaking part of Switzerland of one million consumers is rather small for a tailored, often expensive advertising campaign (Payer 1990: 6), and the Italian-speaking part is even smaller. As a result the expenditure per consumer may rise in order to fulfil the actual linguistic and cultural expectations and the increasing costs may not be covered by the revenues generated as a result of further individualization (Widmer 1986: 60).

The problem mentioned above can be illustrated by an advertisement from Swisscom, the former state-owned monopolistic telecommunications company, which is facing increasingly tough international competition. This competition has led to a reduction in price, particularly in the mobile telecommunications sector. Swisscom followed this trend and tried to illustrate the decrease of its prices for mobile communication (called 'Natel', a brand name of Swisscom) with the advertisement shown in Figure 1.

Figure 1: Example of Multilingual Advertising
Source: Swisscom 1999

The advertisement uses the association of diving with decreasing prices, which is illustrated by people wearing diving masks while using a mobile phone. In the TV-Spot, the impression was strengthened by the sound of a diver breathing.

Although the association of this advertisement (diving-decreasing) can be easily understood in French (diving is expressed by the correct translation 'plonger') and in German (diving is expressed by the correct translation 'tauchen'), there is no word in Italian which really covers both the sense of swimming under the surface and a decrease in prices. That is why for the Italian translation the term 'vanno sotto' was used, which means to 'go down'. Although it is possible for the Italian-speaking people of Switzerland to understand the advertisement, the association is less direct, much weaker and it might take more time to understand the intended meaning of the advertisement.

... and even a lot more dialects

"It is known that in German-speaking Switzerland there is a tradition, 'a kind of bilingualism within the language': you write mainly in High German standard language, but you speak dialect. Publicity is therefore mostly written in High German and not Swiss German, which is the real native language. Consequently a German Swiss expresses, when he writes, or – in certain cases – speaks in High German, in an 'acquired' language and not in an 'innate' language" (Löffler 1985: 79 - cited in Payer 1990, 12) and (Payer 1990, 12).

In addition there is not one Swiss German dialect, but many, which differ strongly from canton to canton, even from town to town. Advertising, which uses the 'innate' language, is therefore automatically aimed at a certain region of Switzerland.

Nevertheless there are solutions for the problems mentioned above. Some people think that the difficulties are merely caused by badly designed advertisements - good conceptions may be therefore adapted easily (Widmer 1986: 60).

Swiss media agencies may solve the problems of multilingualism and different cultures
- by establishing subsidies in the other language regions,
- by learning to think multilingual, and
- by encouraging the employment of colleagues from other parts of the country (Widmer 1986: 57).

Finally adaptations to the attitude of mind in another cultural region and consequently a clever lingual translation may pay off by an increased creativity and higher sales as a result of the identification with a certain subculture (Wyss 1986: 42).

The introducing statement of this article criticized homogenous advertising that is designed for a multilingual country. The experience shows for Switzerland that despite all troubles, which come along with four languages and a lot more dialects, it may be advantageous to create an advertisement in one language and to translate it afterwards. Nevertheless it should be considered that a thorough understanding of the different languages and cultures in a country helps at least to translate, perhaps even to design a generally accepted and appreciated advertisement.

3 General Framework for Advertising in Switzerland

Surrounded by five countries consisting of members of the European Community and Liechtenstein, Switzerland is one of the smaller countries in central Europe. Its geography is roughly characterized by three major areas: the 'Jura Mountains' in the north-west, the 'Mittelland' in between and the 'Pre-Alps/Alps' in the south (www.mediatime.ch/stadt/info.html, July 2001).

3.1 Demographic Environment

With slightly more than seven million inhabitants, Switzerland is also in demographic terms a rather small country. A number of just over three million households means, that the average size of household is about 2.3 people. As in many developed countries there is a clear trend towards an ageing society which has been apparent in the twentieth century, and the forecast for the next 50 years confirms this trend (www.statistik. admin.ch/stat_ch/ber01/eufr01.htm, July 2001).

The population of Switzerland consists of three major parts: German-, French- and Italian-speaking regions. Roughly two thirds of the population speaks German, a fifth speaks French and a tenth speaks Italian. Rhaeto-Romanic and other languages make up the remainder (Swiss Federal Statistical Office [ed.] 2001: 693).

3.2   Economic Environment

The gross domestic product of USD 240 billion[1] is approximately equal to that of Belgium. In contrast the gross domestic product per inhabitant is at USD 33,464 higher than in many other European countries. It is comparable to that of the United States or Japan, so that even in an international context Switzerland may be considered a highly productive country. The buying power is accordingly strong (UBS [ed.] 2001b).

3.3   Political Environment

Since 1848, Switzerland has been a confederation, currently with 26 cantons. The Government (Federal Council) is a collegial body consisting of 7 members, which since 1959 has consisted of the same combination of parties. The Swiss political party environment is also extremely stable: for over 50 years, the center/right-wing parties have had 60% to 65% of the votes between them, left-wing (and green) parties between 25% and 30%. The Swiss political system is also characterized by far-reaching popular rights (initiatives and referendums) and national votes (www.statistik. admin.ch/stat_ch/ber17/eufr17.htm, July 2001).

4   Industry-Specific Framework for Advertising in Switzerland

The communications industry in Switzerland is well organized and developed. Switzerland is perhaps one of the most developed countries in the world in terms of associations, with many professions dedicating considerable resources through research institutions, schools and societies.

   Numerous complementary associations are linked through complex self-regulating systems that operate within the framework of rather liberal legislation. Associations develop relationships and finance the necessary structures providing basic information whilst also developing tools for media research and planning.
   Consequently the first part of this chapter concentrates on the institutions. In addition advertising regulation will be discussed in the second part of this chapter.

---

[1] Basis for Conversion of Currencies: 1 USD =1.6886 CHF (Average for 2000)

4.1 Institutions

A large number of well-organized professional institutions are presently working in Switzerland.

4.1.1 Associations

The BSW (Bund Schweizer Werbeagenturen) is one of the most powerful associations in the Swiss advertising industry. Most of the large Swiss agencies (in part subsidiaries of multinational firms) are BSW members. On the other hand numerous small, management owned agencies are members of the ASW (Allianz Schweizer Werbeagenturen). Both organizations take care of collective public affairs, help their members in recruiting staff, and also classify documentation, for example in the form of video archives, with television commercials since 1964 being stored. They also commission market or general studies about industry developments and scenarios. As well as the above general organizations there are also many specialized professional institutions that provide specific services for individual sectors of activity. Examples include organizations for graphic designers, PR specialists (BPRA Bund der Public Relations Agenturen der Schweiz), media intermediaries (VSW Verband Schweizerischer Werbegesellschaften), art directors (ADC Art Directors Club Schweiz), direct marketing and communication (SDV Schweizer Direktmarketing Verband) and sponsorship (SASPO Schweizerische Arbeitsgemeinschaft Sponsoring). A comprehensive list of the professional institutions is given at the end of this article.

As Switzerland is a multilingual country the consequence is that each association is subdivided into independent German- and French-speaking sections and sometimes even into Italian-speaking ones. Interests of all these branches may sometimes converge or may sometimes be in conflict.

4.1.2 Research Institutes

Wemf (Werbemedienforschung AG, known as Remp in French) is another important institution in the advertising industry. It is a collective, private institution owned by media editors. For approximately 20 years it has provided authoritative research on press, media customers and audience. So as to quantify the audiences of newspapers and magazines about 25,000 randomly selected people are interviewed in four sessions each year (Mach

Basic Research). An additional research on consumer habits (Mach Consumer) is also done on 4.000 people. Other major media such as TV, radio, Internet and billboard are also covered by different Wemf audience researches. Since 1997 Wemf has extended its official research to the radio and television market. Audience and media surveys on 18.000 people are done yearly. Since 1999 a further official survey on the Swiss Internet Market (MA Net) is also organized. Currently, advertisers can access the data research directly with their computers by hiring special software. Subsequently they are able to program on-line press, broadcasting and billboard media plans. According to a specific target group, they may define the media mix in order to reach precise penetration and contact objectives.

In addition SRG SSR (Swiss Broadcasting Corporation) organize an electronic panel (Telecontrol) with 850 households disposing on a special audience measurement tool.

Announcers can access the data research directly in their computers by hiring a specialized software and program, on line press and billboard media plans. According to a specific target they define the media mix in order to reach precise penetration and contact objectives.

4.1.3   Schools

SAWI is the most important professional teaching center for marketing, advertising and communication. About 2500 students are presently studying at this school. After 2 years practical work in an advertising agency, students may enroll and follow the courses so as to obtain professional competency certificates.

4.1.4   Limitations on the Swiss Advertising Market

As in other industrialized countries, there is no unified advertising law in Switzerland. Therefore a quite complex advertising limitations framework formed by heterogeneous public and private regulations limits directly or indirectly the activities of this industry.

4.1.5   Public Regulations

Public limitations (codes, laws, regulations) are established by the Swiss Confederation, by the 26 cantons and at a communal level. The regulation of both advertising duration and content is more a matter for the Confederation. Cantons and communes have a higher degree of freedom in the regulation of outdoor advertising.

A federal law concerning radio and television (LRTV) organizes the whole public radio and TV sector. On the basis of this law, concessions for private broadcasters (both for radio and TV) are permitted.

A federal ordinance on radio and television (ORTV) specifies the present legal limitations on TV and Radio. According to article 13 of the federal ordinance, advertising in both public TV and radio (SRG SSR) is limited to 8% of the daily broadcasting time. Commercials cannot last more than 12 minutes on a broadcasting period of 1 hour. Advertising time for private broadcasting is limited to 15% of the corresponding broadcasting time.

On the basis of article 15 of the federal ordinance advertising both for public and private broadcasters is prohibited for the following themes:

- religion and politics
- alcohol and tobacco
- drugs.

Lies and falsehoods as well as subliminal advertising are also forbidden along with advertising that seeks to exploit the naivete of children.

News broadcasts and TV programs related to political elections cannot be sponsored. Sponsoring is allowed, however, for entertainment programs and weather forecasts.

4.1.6 Private Regulations

Apart from public regulation, there are also two types of private collective regulations: private rules edited by branch organizations and private cartel agreements (which are more or less secret editors cartels).

The 'Schweizerische Lauterkeitskommission', (the Swiss commission for integrity of advertising) is a crucial institution in Switzerland's communications industry. It is a professional council that provides effective mechanisms for guaranteeing self-regulation in advertising and for settling conflicts between consumers and the advertising industry. It edits and implements a catalogue of rules based on the Swiss legal codes and the Swiss legislation as well as general principles of the International Chamber of Commerce (Code of Advertising Practice [1998], International Code of Sponsorship [1991], Rules on Advertising and Marketing on the Internet [1998]).

The 'Rules on the integrity of commercial communication' specify for example at point 3.2.2 that testimonials (intended as natural persons who give advice about products) have to limit their comments to the product context itself. Obviously this information has to be true. The use of imaginary characters as testimonials is forbidden. A specific rule states that the term 'Swiss' may only be used in advertising for goods if at least 50% of the production costs are generated in Switzerland.

Rule 3.14 states that sponsoring is forbidden in editorial parts of articles and programs when people cannot distinguish if the article or program has been sponsored or not.

Comparative advertising is in principle allowed (according to rule 3.3). A further rule states that comparisons have to be true and must not needlessly belittle competitors. Comparative advertising is not frequently used in Switzerland, however, principally because of the opposition of media themselves.

5   Swiss Advertising Industry

As in the other industrialized countries, there has been an advertising surplus in recent years in Switzerland. The growth rate of advertising expenditure has slowed down in the last few years and signs of saturation have become more evident especially in classical media advertising. Clearly there is increased competition for revenues between off line and on line advertising and classical mass media communication.

Nevertheless advertising expenditure per capita is still on a very high level in Switzerland in comparison with other countries. Some sources rank Switzerland even as the country with the highest expenditure per capita in the world (Publicitas [ed.] 2001: 10). On the one hand this may reflect to a certain degree the complexity of advertising in Switzerland caused by the multilingualism, on the other hand it may result from the relatively high level of costs, productivity and gross national product per capita of Switzerland in general.

Detailed advertising expenditure figures are available for classical media, as well as for direct and Internet communication (which is less precise, however). As shown in the following tables, classical media expenditure presently accounts for approximately USD 2.5 billion. This represents about 1% of the Swiss GNP. Direct communication and POS expenditure has been estimated at about USD 2 billion. Internet advertising expenditure is no more than USD 0.3 billion of the overall media expenditure - this figure is somewhat low, but in line with other countries. Together these three expenditure categories account with more than USD 4.5 billion for about 2% of the GNP. It has to be noted that these statistics are not too precise and do not include the substantial Internet expenditure dedicated to creating home web pages.

Table 1: **Classical Media Expenditure in Switzerland in 2000 –2001 (Million USD)**

Medium	2000	Share of total
Daily Newspaper	1,045	44%
Magazines	416	18%
Professional Magazines	149	6%
TV	385	16%
Radio	80	3%
Cinema Advertising	23	1%
Others Media	29	1%
Outdoor Advertising	241	10%
Total	2,368	100%

Sources: www.publimedia.ch, July 2001

If classical media are considered only, print media has a dominant market share. If direct communication is included in the statistics the two dominant media of print and direct media appear approximately with equal value. It may also be noted that in Switzerland, unlike other European countries, TV is by no means the most important national advertising medium, whereas magazines and billboard advertising have a clearly higher significance (Publicitas [ed.] 2001: 10).

Despite signs of saturation in the past mentioned above, the advertising sector as a whole is expecting a sustained uptrend in the near future (UBS [ed.] 2001a: 39).

5.1   Swiss Advertisers

Large distributors in the food and non-food sectors are clearly leaders in advertising spending. This fact is unsurprising given the strength and concentration of the Swiss food and convenience goods distributors. Table 2 summarizes the 25 major advertisers in Switzerland. Additional information relating to these figures such as detailed expenditure by each advertiser in each medium can be obtained by contacting the Internet sites listed below.

Table 2: Top Swiss Advertisers 2000 (in Classical Media only, Million USD)

Ranking	Company	Total Million USD	Share
1	Migros	121.5	5.1%
2	Coop	109.3	4.6%
3	Swisscom	47.1	2.0%
4	UBS	26.6	1.1%
5	Tamedia	26.3	1.1%
6	Diax	26.1	1.1%
7	Orange	25.2	1.1%
8	Nestlé	23.9	1.0%
9	Effem	20.7	0.9%
10	Procter & Gamble	19.5	0.8%
11	Blick	18.2	0.8%
12	Fust	16.9	0.7%
13	B.A.T.	16.6	0.7%
14	Philip Morris	15.7	0.7%
15	Media Markt	15.4	0.7%
16	Occasional Political Advertising	15.3	0.6%
17	Opel	15.1	0.6%
18	Credit Suisse	14.8	0.6%
19	Ringier	14.6	0.6%
20	Denner	14.3	0.6%
21	Tele 2	13.9	0.6%
22	Renault	12.6	0.5%
23	Frimago	12.4	0.5%
24	Mercuri Urval	12.4	0.5%
25	Publicitas	12.4	0.5%
	Total Ranked Groups	**666.8**	**28.2%**

Source: www.publimedia.ch, July 2001

Table 3: Advertising According to Business Branches (Million USD)

Ranking	Branch	Total Million USD	Share
1	Car	199.2	8.4%
2	Mass Media	169.4	7.2%
3	Telecommunication	150.7	6.4%
4	Trade Organization	145.3	6.1%
5	Finance	127.1	5.4%
6	Service	123.0	5.2%
7	Publishing	76.2	3.2%

Table 3, continued

8	Associations	74.3	3.1%
9	Tourism	72.7	3.1%
10	House	69.2	2.9%
11	Clothing	68.9	2.9%
12	Computers	65.0	2.7%
13	Insurance	55.1	2.3%
14	Food	48.0	2.0%
15	Chocolate	45.7	1.9%
16	TV/Radio	45.5	1.9%
17	Consultancy	42.9	1.8%
18	Tobacco	42.3	1.8%
19	Milk Products	41.9	1.8%
20	Body Care	41.6	1.8%
21	Alcohol Free Beverages	41.3	1.7%
22	Pharmacy	31.3	1.3%
23	Transport	30.3	1.3%
24	Bread	26.6	1.1%
25	Construction	25.6	1.1%
	Total Ranked Groups	**1,859.1**	**78.5%**

Source: www.publimedia.ch, July 2001

A breakdown of advertising expenditure by industry sectors is shown in Table 3. It may clearly be seen that expenditure is spread over all sectors. The car industry, media editors, telecommunications industry along with distribution and commerce spend the largest amounts on advertising.

5.2 Swiss Advertising Agencies

The Swiss advertising agencies industry is changing rapidly. Start-ups, mergers and closings make it difficult to get a comprehensive overview of the market. In addition there is no clear definition for advertising agencies.

Nevertheless it may be estimated that there are about 800 companies in the market: about 100 are members of the two most important advertising agency associations each, and 600 are independent, that means not linked to an association.

Table 4 provides a general picture of the most important advertising agencies in Switzerland, although it may not be representative, because there is no obligation to publish figures, particularly the gross operating income, which is used as a measure of importance.

Table 4: Top Swiss Advertising Agencies 2000

Ranking	Agency/Group	Place	Gross operating income 2000 in Million USD
1	*Young & Rubicam Schweiz*		**30,091**
	Advico Young & Rubicam	Zurich	18,546
	Burson-Marsteller	Bern	5,845
	The Media Edge	Zurich	0,958
	Young & Rubicam BC	Geneva	4,742
2	*Publicis Gruppe Schweiz*		**25,454**
	Publicis Zürich	Zurich	19,607
	Publicis Lausanne	Lausanne	2,673
	Saatchi & Saatchi	Nyon	3,174
	Optimedia Schweiz AG	Zurich	N/A
3	*McCann-Erickson Schweiz*		**24,443**
	McCann-Erickson SA/AG	Geneva/Zurich	23,104
	Target-Group AG	Zurich	1,338
4	Wirz Werbung AG	Zurich	14,716
5	Lowe Lintas GGK	Zurich	12,044
6	*EURO RSCG Gruppe Schweiz*		**10,882**
	EURO RSCG Schweiz	Geneva / Zurich	8,801
	Catapult AG	Zurich	2,081
7	IMPULS@TBWA AG	Küsnacht	9,209
8	Grey Worldwide AG/SA	Zurich / Geneva	8,765
9	Fisch.Meier.Direkt AG	Zurich	8,440
10	FCB Leutenegger Krüll AG	Wallisellen	6,245

Source: www.bsw.ch/d/rangliste_frame.htm, July 2001

5.3   Swiss Advertising Media

The Swiss media landscape is very rich and diversified. The high number and diversity of press titles as well as TV and radio programs may be attributed to socio-cultural and ethnical factors. The main elements of these are Switzerland's political federal structure as well as the ethnical and linguistic heterogeneity, which explain the diversification into German, French, and Italian and to a lesser extent into the Rhaeto-Romanic media. When this is combined with the high levels of advertising expenditure the result is that in Switzerland, as in other countries media are strongly financed by advertising.

The breakdown of advertising expenditure through the media has already been indicated at the beginning of this chapter. The following section provides additional details of each particular medium.

5.3.1 Newspapers

In the year 2000, the press included 2736 publications - more exactly 238 newspapers (about 10 for each canton), 406 official sheets, 1012 professional revues, 1014 specialized and 66 general public magazines.

Tables 5 and 6 give a breakdown of daily and weekly newspapers for the year 1999.

Table 5: Major Daily Newspapers (1999)

Daily Newspapers	Circulation	Readership
Blick	314,179	742,000
Tages-Anzeiger	279,912	616,000
Neue Zürcher Zeitung	169,118	308,000
Südostschweiz	138,563	232,000
Berner Zeitung	135,723	255,000
Neue Luzerner Zeitung	133,563	273,000
Aargauer Zeitung	119,680	221,000
Basler Zeitung	115,409	218,000
St. Galler Tagblatt	110,485	220,000
24 heures	89,621	232,000
Tribune de Genève	78,402	195,000
Der Bund	68,175	155,000
Le Matin	66,393	274,000

Source: MACH-Basic 2000

Table 6: Major Weekly Newspapers (1999)

Weekly Newspapers	Circulation	Readership
Brückenbauer	1,809,039	1,916,000
Coop-Presse	1,879,660	2,243,000
Sonntags Blick	334,693	1,003,000
Le Matin Dimanche	220,451	613,000
Sonntags Zeitung	220,102	752,000
Weltwoche	92,337	339,000
Cash	70,311	376,000

Source: MACH-Basic 2000

5.3.2   Consumer Magazines

Following the same classification structure, Table 7 shows expenditure structure for magazines.

Table 7: Major Consumer Magazines (1999)

Magazines	Circulation	Readership
K-Tip	382,213	1,133,000
Beobachter	333,218	1,076,000
Schweizer Illustrierte	251,251	1,013,000
Schweizer Familie	155,324	607,000
Facts	104,598	545,000
Bilanz	57,110	461,000
L'Hebdo	56,120	232,000

Source: MACH-Basic 2000

5.3.3   TV Channels

As already shown by statistics in this article, television is far from being the major advertising medium in Switzerland. Television market share varies according to different statistics, but may be estimated at about 10%.

The Swiss TV market is dual, as in many other industrialized countries, and there is a majority of advertising expenditure directed towards public TV. In Switzerland the public TV's broadcasting monopoly ended with the telecommunications law of 1991, but private TV and therefore private TV advertising has not to date resulted in real competition for public broadcasters.

There are three national broadcasters in Switzerland (one for each major language) with 10 'national' public TV chains; there are also 85 local private TV chains, mostly concentrated in German-speaking Switzerland. Moreover TV subscribers can access 150 foreign chains, 15 of them (called 'open windows') with advertising targeted to the Swiss market. In addition, there are 14 'national' public radio and 47 private local radio chains. About 1,500 foreign radio channels may be received, with 20 of them sending advertising specifically to the Swiss marketplace.

The major private Swiss broadcasters are Tele24, TeleZüri, telebaern, TeleM1, TeleTell and TV3. The most important foreign broadcasters with specific advertising to Switzerland are RTL, RTL2, SAT1, PRO 7, and Kabel 1.

Public sector radio and TV represent two distinct but well co-ordinated activity fields of a single publicly owned company.

More detailed statistics showing the breakdown of the audience according to the three Swiss cultural regions may be seen in the following scheme.

Table 8: Audience Market Share of the Swiss TV Chains (2000)

	German Swiss	French Swiss	Italian Swiss
SRG SSR	33.3%	34.9%	34.0%
other*	66.7%	65.1%	66.0%

*private and foreign TV
Source: SRG SSR Telecontrol

TV advertising expenditure is spread among the three broadcasters as follows:

Table 9: Share of Advertising Expenditure for TV-Groups and Areas of Business

Industry	SRG SSR	Swiss Windows	Private TV
Food	72%	24%	4%
Cosmetics	58%	40%	2%
Transport	78%	16%	7%
Office/Computer	72%	22%	5%
Drink	74%	25%	1%
Finance/Insurance	75%	19%	6%
Trade	76%	16%	7%
Home/Garden	72%	13%	15%
Industry/Investments	60%	32%	8%
Media	52%	39%	10%
Cleaning Products	68%	31%	0%
Pharmaceutical/Health	68%	30%	3%
Leisure/Tourism	67%	25%	7%
Household Appliances	91%	7%	2%
Clothing	62%	19%	19%
Consumer Electronics	58%	21%	21%
Services	72%	9%	19%
Tobacco	0%	0%	0%
Total	**70%**	**25%**	**6%**

Source: www.publisuisse.ch, July 2001

Table 9 shows that public broadcasting accounts for about 70% of advertising with 'foreign windows' having 25% and only about 5% derived from private local television stations.

The above data may also be further analyzed according to branches of activity. The result is that public broadcasters are dominant in all branches. Advertising in private broadcasting is significant in the following sectors: 'consumer electronics', 'clothing', 'services' as well as in the 'home and garden' industry.

The price of TV spots depends on many factors such as
- duration (short spots of 5-14 seconds, current spots of 15-119 seconds, long spots of 2-6 minutes),
- audience (according to media research date, with price calculation per 1000 contacts) and
- season (prices vary per month - in august when demand is weak prices are often lowered).

5.3.4 Radio Channels

It is well known that radio may be used as a complementary advertising medium. It is often used to complete multimedia campaigns in order to create a special atmosphere, which could be for example lively or nostalgic. It is more important for local and regional advertising.

In Switzerland radio is a rather young advertising medium, and was introduced many years after TV advertising.
As for TV one can distinguish between public and private radios, as well as foreign radios with Swiss advertising.

In Switzerland there are the following channels: Swiss public radios (SRG SSR), Swiss private radios and foreign radios.
The public radio sector, in the same way as TV, is subdivided into German-/Swiss German-/Rhaeto-Romanic-speaking, French-speaking and Italian-speaking radio stations. The first of these categories includes DSR1, DSR2, DSR3, MW 531 and Virus chains. French-speaking public radios are Les infos, La première, Espace 2, Couleur3 and Option musique. There are also three Italian-speaking radio stations Rete 1, Rete 2 and Rete 3.
Private radio stations, which will not be specified, are numerous and often have a typical cantonal and regional character.

The market share according to the audience of these three broadcasters is presented in the following scheme:

Table 10: Radio Audience Market Share (2000)

	German Swiss	French Swiss	Italian Swiss
Public Radios (SRG SSR)	51%	46%	75%
Private Swiss Radios	38%	37%	8%
Foreign Radios	11%	18%	17%

Source: SRG SSR Medienstudie 2000

5.3.5 Outdoor Advertising

Outdoor advertising consists of about 150,000 places all over the country. From a geographic point of view it is a very flexible medium, always present in multimedia campaigns. In Switzerland the quality of billboards and the timing of the issues ensures that this medium is a very dynamic one. Its market share has been stable over time but has not increased significantly due to strong political limitations on permitted space.

Further details according to the main outdoor advertising categories can be seen in Table 11.

Table 11: Expenditure in Main Categories of Outdoor Advertising 2000 (Million USD)

Medium	2000
Billboards	210.2
Transport Advertising	21.3
Sport and Stadium Advertising	19.0
Neon	91.8
Other Outdoor Advertising	8.3
Total	**350.6**

Source: Fondation Statistique Suisse en Publicité, 2001

5.3.6 Other Media

There are 419 cinema and many hundreds of Internet sites with banners and other forms of on-line advertising. A ranking shows that sites of providers are the most frequently visited. A new development is that advertising fees are now no longer paid according to time but according to the contacts (clicks). UBS expects, that the ongoing Internet boom will mean further funds earmarked for banner advertising in 2001 (UBS [ed.] 2001a: 39).

Fairs and exhibitions constitute a very interesting communication medium for both business to consumer and business-to-business. In Switzerland there are three main international locations (Geneva, Basle and Zurich) for fairs. There are also four national and many more regional and local locations, although the trend is towards merging and segmenting so as to be able to cope with increasing international competition.

6 Summary

Switzerland is one of the smaller countries in terms of population and geography in central Europe. Nevertheless it is an interesting object for research in advertising. Characterized by its multilingualism with four official languages, there are many more dialects in Swiss German, which are scarcely written, but which represent the native language for a large part of the population. In the German-speaking part publicity is consequently written in High German, an 'acquired' language and not in Swiss German, the 'innate' language of the German Swiss.

Beside a wealthy economy and a stable political situation a large number of well organized associations in the industry sector build an advantageous environment for advertising in Switzerland. In addition complex self-regulating systems within the framework of a rather liberal legislation characterize the position of advertising in Switzerland. The high expenditure for advertising per capita may reflect on the one hand the wealth of the country, on the other hand it may be generated by the additional expenditure in order to cope with the multilingualism of the country. The absolute annual expenditure for advertising amounts to about USD 4.5 billion or 2 per cent of the GNP.

The media landscape of Switzerland is rich and diversified. Despite tailored advertising for Switzerland in foreign TV-Channels, TV as a medium is less important in comparison to other European countries. On the other hand magazines and billboard advertising have a clearly higher significance as media for advertising in Switzerland.

Differences in language and culture characterize the advertising in a country, which is nevertheless held together by a relatively large degree of agreement with regard to cultural trends, behaviors and attitudes. Different approaches of advertising, which are known from market segmentation as well as from international marketing, have to be weighed up with regard to costs and utility: Advertising limited to one language area, translation without substantial adaptation, translation and adaptation or a tailored advertising campaign for each part of the country. For the decision it has to be considered, that the French-speaking part of Switzerland is rather small, the Italian-speaking part is even smaller for a tailored advertising campaign. It has to be estimated if the additional costs for a differentiated approach are offset by an improved quality of the approach and finally a higher acceptance and revenues in all parts of the country (Kühn 1986: 143).

Despite all problems that come along with multilingual advertising, the lingual and cultural diversity means a chance for Switzerland – and for advertising in Switzerland too.

References

Association des Adaptateurs Romands (ed.): Advertisement 'Die Welschen haben die krachlederne Werbung satt.'; 1987 - cited in Payer 1990: 6

Bosshart, Louis: 'Kulturübergreifende Kommunikation' in Bund Schweizerischer Werbeagenturen (Hrsg.): ‚Werbung in einem mehrsprachigen Land', Freiburg (Schweiz): Universitätsverlag Freiburg Schweiz, 1986

Fondation Statistique Suisse en Publicité (ed.): 'Werbeaufwand Schweiz', Zürich: 2001

Kotler, Philip: 'Marketing Management', Upper Saddle River: Prentice Hall, 2000

Kühn, Richard: 'Werbung in einem mehrsprachigen Land: Versuch einer Synthese' in Bund Schweizerischer Werbeagenturen (Hrsg.): ‚Werbung in einem mehrsprachigen Land', Freiburg (Schweiz): Universitätsverlag Freiburg Schweiz, 1986

Löffler, H: 'Germanistische Soziolinguistik', Berlin: 1985 – cited in Payer 1990: 12

Payer, Gabriele: 'Adaptionen in der Werbesprache', Zürich: 1990 (Thesis)

Publicitas (ed.): 'Print-Media-Planer 2001', Zürich: 2001

Ringier (ed.): 'ABECEDAIRE PUBLICITAIRE 2001', Zürich: 2001

Rizzi, Silvio: 'Die Bedeutung der Sprach- und Kulturunterschiede für die Kreation und Realisation von Werbemassnahmen' in Bund Schweizerischer Werbeagenturen (Hrsg.): ‚Werbung in einem mehrsprachigen Land', Freiburg (Schweiz): Universitätsverlag Freiburg Schweiz, 1986

Swiss Federal Statistical Office (ed.): 2001: 'Statistisches Jahrbuch Schweiz 2001, Zürich: Verlag Neue Zürcher Zeitung, 2001

UBS (ed.): 'Swiss Sectoral Trends', edition 2001: 2001a

UBS (ed.): 'Switzerland in Figures', edition 2001: 2001b

Widmer, Bruno: 'Die Probleme der Werbung in einem mehrsprachigen Land aus der Sicht einer deutschsprachigen Werbeagentur' in Bund Schweizerischer Werbeagenturen (Hrsg.): ‚Werbung in einem mehrsprachigen Land', Freiburg (Schweiz): Universitätsverlag Freiburg Schweiz, 1986

www.mediatime.ch, July 2001

www.publimedia.ch, July 2001

www.publisuisse.ch, July 2001

www.statistik.admin.ch, July 2001

Wyss, Werner: 'Schweizer diesseits und jenseits der Saane' in Bund Schweizerischer Werbeagenturen (Hrsg.): ‚Werbung in einem mehrsprachigen Land', Freiburg (Schweiz): Universitätsverlag Freiburg Schweiz, 1986

Useful Addresses

Although many of the following organisations have parallel structures in French-, German- and Italian-speaking parts of Switzerland, for reason of simplification only the German-speaking part is listed.

ADC Art Directors Club Schweiz
Association of art directors, copywriters, photographers, producers, designers, illustrators, journalists etc. in the advertising industry and related branches in Switzerland.
Oberdorfstrasse 15
CH-8001 Zurich
Tel ++41 (0)1 262 00 33
Fax ++41 (0)1 262 02 74
www.adcschweiz.ch
adc@bluewin.ch

ASW Allianz Schweizer Werbeagenturen
Swiss Advertising Agencies Alliance
Association of management owned communication agencies in Switzerland
Ankerstrasse 53
CH-8026 Zurich
Tel ++41 (0)1 240 56 56
Fax ++41 (0)1 240 56 57
www.asw.ch
info@asw.ch

BPRA Bund der Public Relations Agenturen der Schweiz
Association of the PR-Agencies of Switzerland
Geschäftsstelle c/o Hugo Schmid AG
Schützenstrasse 6
CH-6000 Luzern 7
Tel +41 (0)41 249 48 00
Fax +41 (0)41 249 48 48
www.bpra.ch
info@bpra.ch

BSW Bund Schweizer Werbeagenturen
Association of Swiss Advertising Agencies
Winkelriedstrasse 35
CH-8033 Zurich

Tel +41 (0)1 361 37 60
Fax +41 (0)1 361 38 10
www.bsw.ch
info@bsw.ch

GfM Schweizerische Gesellschaft für Marketing
Swiss Association for Marketing
Bleicherweg 21
Postfach
CH-8022 Zurich
Tel +41 (0)1 202 34 35
Fax +41 (0)1 281 13 30
www.gfm.ch
gfm@ihagfm.ch

IGEM Interessengemeinschaft elektronische Medien
Syndicate of electronic media
c/o Ueli Custer
Dorfstrasse 2c
CH-4514 Lommiswil
0878 888 680
www.igem.ch
info@igem.ch

publisuisse
Purpose: Acquisition and implementation of television advertising for the benefit of the Swiss Broadcasting Corporation
Giacomettistrasse 15
CH-3000 Bern 31
Tel ++41 31 358 31 11
Fax ++41 31 358 31 00
www.publisuisse.ch
webteam@publisuisse.ch

SASPO Schweizerische Arbeitsgemeinschaft Sponsoring
Swiss Sponsoring Association
Oberdorfstr. 20
CH-8820 Wädenswil
Tel ++41 (0)1 783 20 24
Fax ++41 (0)1 783 20 21
www.saspo.ch
info@saspo.ch

SAWI Schweizerisches Ausbildungszentrum für Marketing, Werbung und Kommunikation
Swiss centre for education in marketing, advertising and communication
Zentralstrasse 115 Ost
CH-2500 Biel
Tel +41 (0)32 366 70 40
Fax +41 (0)32 366 70 49
www.sawi.com
info@sawi.com

Schweizerische Lauterkeitskommission
Swiss Commission for integrity of advertising
Kappelergasse 14
CH-8022 Zurich
Tel +41 (0)1 211 79 22
Fax +41 (0)1 211 80 18
www.lauterkeit.ch
info@lauterkeit.ch

SDV Schweizer Direktmarketing Verband
Swiss Association for Direct Marketing
CH-8708 Männedorf
Tel +41 (0)1 790 34 70
Fax +41 (0)1 790 34 71
www.sdv-direktmarketing.ch

SFVP Schweizer Film und Video Produzenten
SFVP Swiss Film and Video Producers
Weinbergstrasse 31
CH-8006 Zurich
Tel +41 (0)1 266 64 46
Fax +41 (0)1 262 29 96
www.filmproducers.ch
info@filmproducers.ch

SGD Swiss Graphic Designers
Limmatstrasse 63
CH-8005 Zurich
Tel (+41) 1 272 45 55
Fax (+41) 1 272 52 82
www.sgd.ch
info@sgd.ch

SGV Schweizer Grafiker Verband
Swiss Association of Graphic Designers
Schulhausstrasse 64
CH-8002 Zurich
Tel +41 (0)1 201 07 37
Fax +41 (0)1 201 07 37
www.sgv.ch
info@sgv.ch

SMC Schweizer Marketing Club
Swiss Marketing Club
Jurastrasse 20
CH-4600 Olten
Tel 062/207 07 70
Fax 062/207 07 71
www.smc-cms.ch
sekretariat@smc-cms.ch

SPRG Schweizer Public Relations Gesellschaft
Swiss Public Relations Association
c/o Farner PR
Oberdorfstrasse 28
CH-8001 Zurich
Tel 01 266 67 63
Fax 01 266 67 00
www.sprg.ch
info@sprg.ch

SPRI Schweizerisches Public Relations Institut
Swiss Public Relations Institut
Ankerstrasse 53
CH-8026 Zurich
Tel +41 (0)1 299 40 40
Fax +41 (0)1 299 40 44
www.spri.ch
spri@swisspr.ch

SRG SSR idée suisse
Swiss Broadcasting Corporation
Giacomettistr. 3
CH-3006 Bern
Tel +41 (0)31 350 91 11

Fax +41 (0)31 350 92 56
www.srg.ch

ST Schweizerischer Texterverband
Swiss Copywriters Association
Postfach 223
CH-8057 Zurich
Tel +41 (0)878 878 326
Fax +41 (0)878 878 327
www.texterverband.ch
text@access.ch

SUISA
Corporation which manages royalties for composers, lyricists and music publishers.
Bellariastrasse 82
Postfach 782
CH-8083 Zurich
Tel +41 (0)1 485 66 66
Fax +41 (0)1 482 43 33
www.suisa.ch
suisa@suisa.ch

SW Schweizer Werbung
Swiss Advertising - Umbrella Organisation for Commercial Communication
Kappelergasse 14
CH-8022 Zurich
Tel +41 (0)1 211 40 11
Fax +41 (0)1 211 80 18
www.sw-ps.ch
info@sw-ps.ch

Verband Schweizer Presse
Swiss Press Association
Baumackerstrasse 42
Postfach
CH-8050 Zurich
Tel +41 (0)1 318 64 64
Fax +41 (0)1 318 64 62
www.schweizerpresse.ch
contact@schweizerpresse.ch

VISCOM Schweizerischer Verband für visuelle Kommunikation
Swiss Association for Visual Communication
Leading association for employers and businesspeople in the visual communications industry
Alderstrasse 40
CH-8034 Zurich, Switzerland
Phone: ++41 (0)1 421 28 28
Fax: ++41 (0)1 421 28 29
www.viscom.ch
visc.schweiz@viscom.ch

VSD Verband der Schweizer Druckindustrie
Swiss Graphic Industry Association
Schosshaldenstrasse 20
CH-3006 Bern
Tel +41 (0)31 351 15 11
Fax +41 (0)31 352 37 38
www.vsd.ch
office@vsd.ch

VSW Verband Schweizerischer Werbegesellschaften
Association of advertising intermediary companies
Weinbergstrasse 11
CH-8001 Zurich
Tel +41 (0)1 261 30 33
Fax +41 (0)1261 30 44
www.vsw-assp.ch
gs@vsw-assp.ch

WEMF AG für Werbemedienforschung
Advertising Media Research Association
Bachmattstrasse 53
8048 Zurich
Tel +41 (0)1 431 68 08
Fax +41 (0)1 432 84 33
www.wemf.ch
wemf@wemf.ch

Advertising in the United Kingdom

Prof. Dr. Paul O' Sullivan
Dublin Institute of Technology

1 Introduction

The year 2000 has seen a deepening crisis for the UK advertising industry mirroring the increasingly difficult business environment and deteriorating economic situation. Fears of a slump leading to a full recession have grown since the turn of the year with the American economy faltering and indications that growth in the Euro zone would slow further. A number of interest rate cuts in the Spring and early Summer of 2001 served to give a temporary boost to confidence and to perhaps mask the underlying trends. The inescapable conclusion is that both Wall Street and London have been experiencing a Bear market for some two years commencing mid '99 and the collapse of the dot.com sector and negative sentiment regarding the Telecom sector have seen a huge reduction in the value of shares in these sectors and a heavy blow to the overall performance of major players with direct consequences for advertising spend.

Compounding the problem is the fact that the first six months of 2000 saw quite exceptional growth in advertising spend with growth rates between 11 and 15% year on year, driven by strong demand from new technology sectors. The dot com collapse and poor demand in the car industry inevitably saw a major correction. Figures released by AC Nielsen MMS for the twelve months to June 2001 show that two thirds of the top thirty creative agencies and half of the top thirty media buying houses experienced a fall in billings. For instance, the largest agency in the UK, Abbot Mead Vickers BBDO, has seen a drop of 8% in billings and the largest media house in the UK, Zenith, has seen billings fall by almost 14%. All of this precedes recent international difficulties.

Increasing international tension and the likelihood of military action in the Middle East and Central Asia will add greatly to recessionary pressures. Sectoral problems in the insurance, air-line and tourism industries will limit the options for investors and are likely to have a direct impact upon advertising spend. Negative signs were already visible in the UK market-place prior to the deterioration in the international arena. British commercial television companies had seen a sharp and alarming decline in the level of bookings of advertising time for November and December 2001. This can only deteriorate further in the present conditions.

2 Overview of Advertising Spend in the UK

Depending on the source and currency of the data and the definition of what constitutes 'advertising', national advertising spend in the UK is reported as ranging from £8 billion to £17 billion in the year 2000. The latter figure provided by the *Advertising Statistics Yearbook 2001* represents 1.82% of GDP (up from 1.74%in 1999) though it should be noted that some 25% of this figure refers to 'Classified Advertising' (Fig 1), financial and legal notices, company announcements and recruitment advertising. An estimated further 25% relates to advertising services and other billings charged to advertisers by their agencies and some 13% relates to Direct Mail. It is worth noting inter alia, that very few agencies rely upon the traditional media commission for their total revenue and most major accounts involve billings for service provision as well as commissions.

Table 1: Overall Advertising Expenditure UK 1998

	Display Advertising £M	Classified Advertising £M
Television	4029	-
National Newspapers	1351	442
Regional Newspapers	826	1563
Consumer Magazines	553	157
Business and Professional Journals	756	453
Directories (including Yellow Pages)	-	780
Press Production Costs	610	-
Outdoor and Transport	563	-
Radio	463	-
Cinema	97	-
Direct Mail	1666	-

Source: Advertising Association UK

In terms of overall advertising spend, press/magazines is the single largest category at approximately 42% of the total (with production costs add-

Advertising in the UK   301

ing a further 4%). Television is in second place accounting for 28%. However there is a strong argument for excluding classified advertising and directories and this would make television the dominant player in 'Display advertising'.

Table 2: Distribution of Advertising Spend by Top Fifteen Sectors 1998

Advertiser	£M
Retail and Mail Order	1093
Motors	631
Food	625
Financial	481
Toiletries & Cosmetics	356
Leisure Equipment	327
Drink	245
Household Stores	244
Holidays, Travel and Transport	242
Publishing	217
Pharmaceutical	217
Entertainment	182
Institutional & Industrial	142
Government	87
Charity & Educational	49

Source: Advertising Association UK

Table 2 shows the distribution of the *Advertising Yearbook* global figure in terms of the top twenty sectors. Not surprisingly retail, motors and food feature prominently. However the difficulties of dis-aggregating Direct Mail and other categories makes it difficult to arrive at a clear picture of advertising activity by sector or by medium. Therefore, for purposes of this discussion the current and reliable media spend data provided by Admap/World Advertising Research Center are utilized.

Table 3: UK Media Adspend

	2000 £000	2000 % Yr/Yr	Last 3 mths * % Yr/Yr
Total Spend	8,010	5.5	3.8
TV	3,842	6.7	-0.9
Press	3,124	3.9	6.1
Radio	555	4.8	6.7
Outdoor	403	10.4	28
Cinema	86	-6.7	36.6
*Dec 01 – Feb 01			

Source: AC Nielsen MMS

Just over £8 billion was spent on media advertising in the UK in the year 2000, representing a 5.5% year on year increase over '99. Television (including terrestrial and satellite) with 48% share of revenue, represents the largest share of advertising spend in the UK market, followed by Press (newspapers and magazines) with an aggregate 39%. The other main components are made up by outdoor (5%) and radio (7%).

3   Analysis of UK Media

3.1   Television

Commercial television regulated by the Independent Television Authority ITV (later the ITC) was established in the U.K. in the early 1950s through the mechanism of renewable regional franchises networked into a national presence as ITV. Subsequent developments included the creation of ITN (Independent Television News) and a national breakfast-time station GMTV. There is a strong trend towards consolidation of ITV station ownership and there are now three large players in the field – United News and Media, Carlton, and Granada.

In the 1970s the ITV contractors played a somewhat reluctant role as foster parent to a new state owned service, Channel 4, which is dependant on commercial earnings, largely from advertising. In 1997 a further national terrestrial station license, Channel 5, was granted to a consortium of media interests. This is a low cost operation relying on US imports for up to half its output and it has a young, mid-market, male bias attractive to advertisers. It has now won more than 7% viewing share and 5% share of television advertising revenue, largely at the expense of existing terrestrial stations.

Today the Independent Television Commission (ITC) is responsible for the regulation of all commercial terrestrial television, satellite uploaded programming and cable delivered commercial television programming in the UK, whether in analogue or digital formats. The principal players within the ITC remit are TV3 (i.e. the original ITV network of regional franchises with the addition of GMTV breakfast television), Channel 4 and Channel 5 as well as services uplinked to satellite from the UK.

Advertising sales are achieved through Sales Houses, owned by the main ITV ownership interests and selling on behalf of a group of financially linked stations. GMTV, Channel 4, and Channel 5 handle their own sales.

The three main ITV sales houses account for over 95% of all ITV airtime sales and full service advertising agencies and specialist media buying houses (usually associated with major agency groups) purchase airtime to order from these sources. UK media houses do not act as brokers buying and reselling airtime.

The United Kingdom enjoys 98%+ penetration of its 24.75 million households by terrestrial television, with a minimum of one set per household. All such television homes receive the non commercial stations BBC1 and BBC2 as well as ITV. Almost 24 million household receive Channel 4 and 1.25 million households receive S4C (Welsh version). Channel 5 is received by almost 20 million homes. 99% of television homes have colour sets, 38% have two sets and 84% have at least one VCR. TV research data in the UK includes 'time shift' viewing via VCR.

UK households are becoming richer in their range of technologies with 70% having 2 or more television sets and 16% having wide screen televisions in 2000, up from 8% in 1999. Internet access in the population from 24% in 1999 to 34% in 2000. 24% of the population had domestic internet access and a quarter of these achieved this access via the television set. Multi channel households i.e. capable of accessing both terrestrial and satellite channels or cable channels, now represent 76% of all households and there is some indication that saturation levels may soon be reached. It is notable that the uptake of digital TV, whether driven by terrestrial, cable or direct satellite platforms, represents a much steeper adoption graph than any other technology to date.

The amount of advertising air time permitted on ITV, Channel 4, and Channel 5 is strictly regulated at seven minutes per clock hour in the run of the day and seven point five minutes per hour peak time. Air time is sold in a pre-emptive auction system which tends to maximize the yield for the station. The permissible EU average of nine minutes is allowed to satellite and cable services and there is an active debate as to whether terrestrial stations should be allowed this level of advertising. It might in fact lead to a weakening of price achieved and an increase in clutter.

The final years of the 90s saw some diversification in the sources of revenue of UK commercial television with a significant rise in subscription revenues and the emergence of other revenues such as sales of goods and program sponsorship. Nevertheless Net Advertising Revenue (NAR) remains by far the single most important component of overall television revenue and particularly of non license revenue i.e. revenue available to the commercial television sector.

In nominal terms the total revenue volume of the television sector grew from £4,205 billion in 1995 to £7,223 billion in 2000, an overall growth of 72%. Within the overall picture subscription revenue enjoyed particularly strong growth to reach £1.9 billion in 2000. Advertising revenue growth was strong throughout the period and this continued through the first three quarters of 2000. However the final quarter saw distinct signs of a slow down.

Overall Net Advertising Revenue amounted to £3.3 billion in 2000 and while the share of this achieved by multichannel has risen from 6% in 1995 to 14% in 2000, traditional 'free to air' broadcasters continue to receive the lion's share of these revenues.

Table 4: Channel Shares by Platform, in the 12 Months to December 2000

	Share in all homes	Share in multi-channel homes	Share in digital homes
ITV	29.3%	22.3%	19.0%
C4	10.5%	7.2%	6.0%
C5	5.7%	4.2%	2.8%
All Sky Channels	5.7%	13.7%	174%
All others (excluding BBC1 and BBC2)	10.9%	26.0%	30.6%

The UK broadcasting market is characterized by dynamic change and it is likely that intense competition will develop within the commercial television sector with consequences for air-time availability, audience fragmentation and media costs. ITV's average audience share fell from 31.2% in 1999 to 29.3% in 2000 and this latter figure was in fact bolstered by a strong performance in the fourth quarter. ITV's peak time share of viewing is of the order of 35% down from 36.9% in 1999. The share to non-terrestrial channels rose from 15.5% to a new high of 16.6% in 2000. Both Channel 4 and Channel 5 saw some year on year growth also.

According to a recent study by Cumberbatch, Wood and Littlejohns (2000) ITV/TV3 remained the favorite channel if viewers could pick only one. Average viewing of television was 26 hours a week with variations across the age profile and most viewers watched between 15 and 35 hours a week. Heavy viewers watching over 5 hours a day, tended to be older in socio-economic group DE and living in Scotland, Wales or the midlands with a preference for ITV. Light viewers (15 hours a week or less) were likely to be ABs living in the South and preferring BBC 1.

The distribution of television advertising spend by product category indicates the prominence of food, motor cars, retail and cosmetics (note: figures are to August 1999 when there was strong growth in many categories). Retail advertising spend has been boosted by the arrival of continental European supermarket chains who have proved to be heavy spenders in pursuit of initial brand impact as well as by competitive activity in the electrical and DIY sectors. Indication are that retail has remained relatively flat in 1999 – 2000 but the figures mask a shift in retail ad spend from press to television. Motor advertising may also see a fall in 2000 as spend shifts to press in competitive pursuit of forecourt sales rather than brand building activity.

Table 5: Top Ten Categories Television Advertisers (year to August 1999)

	Sep 98 – Aug 99 £m	+/- %
Total	3,543	7.7
Food	530	-2.9
Motors	483	9.9
Retail	416	14.1
Cosmetics & toiletries	293	1.3
Entertainment & the media	268	28.0
Drink	251	18.0
Business & industrial	244	9.7
Finance	216	5.9
Household stores	202	2.5
Leisure equipment	173	-0.9

Source AC Nielsen MMS

A notable trend which became clearly evident as 2000 progressed, was the shift of spend by major FMCG players such as Procter & Gamble and Lever Brothers away from television. The alarming decline in British Telecom spend, relating to a number of sub-brands as well as the main brand is indicative of the crisis in the technology sector and its impact upon advertising spend.

There is evidence in Table 6 that many big advertisers were already beginning to cut back dramatically on TV adspend even before January 2000. The main reasons appear to be over inflated airtime and some diversion of spend toward new media. Paradoxically it was demand from the dot.com sector and their inability to negotiate favorable rates which led to airtime inflation in the first instance. The collapse of the dot.com sector in 2000 had a direct negative impact on all media spend for the second half of that year.

Table 6: Top Ten Television Advertisers (year to August 1999)

	Sep 98 – Aug 99 £m	+/- %
Total	3,546	7.8
Procter & Gamble	135	-16.9
Ford Motor Company	60	35.0
L'Oreal Golden	58	41.3
Elida Fabserge	51	20.7
Vauxhall Motors	49	22.3
Mars Confectionery	49	1.4
Van Den Bergh Foods	48	21.6
BT British Telecom	47	-34.8
Kellogg	44	-10.1
Renault	42	-2.8

Source AC Nielsen MMS

3.2   Digital TV Channels

While terrestrial broadcasting in the UK continues to be provided on an analogue basis, government has already announced its intention to switch off the analogue signal in favor of digital provision at the end of this decade. This strong endorsement at policy level should in itself build confidence among station owners and providers and should aid the rapid diffusion of digital technology. In theory, the infrastructure for a rapid expansion of digital channels should mean a proliferation of station options and, more problematically, a widening of viewer choice.

From a greenfield situation in October 2000 Digital Television had been taken up by over 30% of UK households by the end of December 2000, representing 6.5 million UK homes. Satellite has been the main driver of digital pay television and B Sky B had sold more that 4.6 million subscriptions by the end of December 2000. Broadband cable infrastructure now covers more than half the UK population with approx. 1 million homes accessing broadband with consequent impact upon digital subscriptions. Hours of television output by multichannel providers have grown in parallel.

Already some 200 niche channels have emerged via cable and satellite technologies in the UK but the staying power and longevity of most may well be brought into question by the impending economic downturn. It now seems that most such stations do not have the power to attract significant advertising revenues and those dependent on such revenues are likely to fail in the near future. Alternative business models might involve subscription and charges for other services such as telephony, shopping or interactive gaming. FilmFour has an audience of 200, 000 viewers on a subscription model and the Emap music channel 'The Box' largely generates its revenue from peak rate telephone calls.

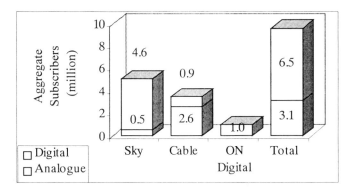

Figure 1: Distribution of Subscription Services by Platform and Technology
Source: ITC, Merril Lynch, ON Digital

Neither of these alternative models is guaranteed success. FilmFour is believed to work because it brings real added value to the Sky/ITV/Cable package to help attract subscriptions and because the films are of high quality and are exclusive. Flextech makes the point that the subscription pot has not increased proportionately with the number of channels seeking distribution, creating downward pressure on the available revenue for individual channels.

Commercial viability based on alternatives to advertising and subscription can also be difficult to achieve. Carlton Communications and Sainsbury jointly invested £10 million in an integrated food channel/web presence. The Taste Network website is now being closed down as revenues have proved disappointing and the future of the Carlton Food Network Channel may now be under review.

3.3   Press

In this discussion 'Press' is taken to subsume the two broad categories of Newspapers and Magazines though each category in turn covers a wide diversity of print vehicles in terms of their format, distribution and audience.

The past three decades have seen a major decline in aggregate circulation of daily newspapers in Great Britain, significant consolidation of ownership and a radical restructuring of production and distribution costs through the adoption of new printing technology and the facilitating of regional editions.

Table 7: Daily Newspaper – Main Titles Sales UK 1999

Daily Newspapers – Popular	
Daily Express	1,095,716
Daily Mail	2,350,241
The Mirror	2,313,063
The Star	525,734
The Sun	3,730,466
Daily Newspapers – Quality	
Daily Telegraph	1,044,740
Financial Times	385,025
The Guardian	398,721
The Independent	233,304
The Times	751,076

Source: British Rate and Data, October 1999

Two thirds of the UK population read the daily newspaper and almost three quarters read a national Sunday newspaper and a weekly local freesheet. Daily and Sunday newspapers are generally described as belonging to either broadsheet, (upscale and mid market news oriented) or tabloid (middle and largely down market, tending towards sensation, entertainment and sports oriented) categories. The UK currently has 14 national daily newspapers and 11 national Sunday newspapers. In addition there are some 18 regional daily papers, seven regional Sunday papers and 72 regional evening papers. Filling out the total picture of newspaper offerings are a further 477 local weekly newspapers.

The dependence of individual newspapers upon advertising revenue as opposed to cover price varies significantly from title to title but some broad patterns may be observed. National quality broad sheet daily and Sunday papers derive 70% of their income from advertising and 30% from sales whereas popular tabloid dailies depend upon sales for 60% of income with advertising making up the balance of 40%. The Mail on Sunday for instance is tabloid in format and popular in appeal but more upscale in its audience and measured in its tone than the 'red top' tabloids. This is reflected in an almost 50/50 balance of advertising and cover price sales in its revenue mix. The regional press is heavily dependent on advertising

(70% of revenue) with regional paid for weekly papers depending on advertising for 85% of revenue.

The magazine sector is witnessing intensifying competition with European publishers and pan-European titles having a major impact. The economics of consumer magazines are heavily dependent upon copy sales (70% approx. of revenue) though this situation is reversed in the case of business magazines.

Table 8: Total Revenue by Source - the Magazine Sector in the UK 2000

Consumer Magazines	
Advertisement Sales	£ 700m
Copy Sales	£1,708m
Other	
Business Magazines	
Advertisement sales	£1,200m
Copy sales	£ 400m
Exhibition	£ 400m
Directories	£ 300m
Electronic products	£ 350m
Other	£ 400m
Customer Magazines	
All	£ 350m
Total	£6,100m

Source: Periodical Publishers Association, Annual Report 2000/1

There are at least 10,000 magazine titles in circulation in the UK which can be usually be viewed as belonging to either the category of Consumer magazines or alternatively Business/professional/controlled circulation magazines. These latter represent approximately two thirds of all titles. In the consumer magazine category three quarters of all titles are published weekly and television listing magazines dominate the category followed by women interest magazines. A notable feature of this market has been the rapid internationalization of provision with German publishers in particular making inroads. TV related weeklies represent 5.5 million aggregate sales with the leading titles represented in Table 9.

What's on TV dominates the sector and appears to have recovered the ground lost when *TV Choice* was launched in 1999. There is a general drift towards more popular titles in this sector with the traditional *Radio Times* and *TV Times* both continuing to loose circulation and it is predicted that the more high brow titles will continue to have difficulty.

Table 9: TV Weeklies – Circulation of Main Titles

Title	Publisher	Total ABC	Period on Period	% Year on year
What's on TV	IPC	1,709,092	0.5	0.1
Radio Times	BBC	1,200,796	-5.0	-3.9
TV Choice	H Bauer	751,618	2.6	-4.2
TV Times	IPC	636,951	-7.6	-9.7
TV Quick	H Bauer	511,737	-7.5	-11.6

Source: Audit Bureau of Circulations (Jan-June 2001)

Table 10: Women's Lifestyle Segment Magazines by Circulation

Title	Publisher	Total ABC	Period on Period %	Year on Year %
Cosmopolitan	Natmags	452,176	-1.7	0.5
Glamour	CondeNast	451,486	N/a	N/a
Candis	Newhall	433,550	-3.3	-5.0
Good Housekeeping	Natmags	395,070	-2.3	3.9
Prima	Natmags	380,181	-3.8	-5.9
Marie Claire	IPC	370,089	-7.6	-11.9
Yours	Emap	350,363	4.5	11.2
New Woman	Emap	292,038	3.6	6.9
Woman & Home	IPC	238,458	-11.5	-13.5
Elle	Emap	224,410	0.0	2.3
Company	Natmags	223,121	-14.4	-3.2
Vogue	CondeNast	201,279	-0.7	0.3

Source: Audit Bureau of Circulations (Jan-June 2001)

Table 11: Women's Weeklies by Circulation

Title	Publisher	Total ABC	Period on Period % Year
Take Break	H Bauer	1,166,591	205
Hello	Hello Ltd	842,723	67.6
Woman	IPC	660,781	3.8
OK	N & S	651,513	11.1
That's Life	H Bauer	569,818	0.0
Womans Own	IPC	538,424	-208
Now	IPC	518,322	9.0
Womans Weekly	IPC	503,722	1.5
Bella	H Bauer	484,986	-90.
Chat	IPC	466,422	-0.7

Source: Audit Bureau of Circulations (Jan-June 2001)

The women's lifestyle segment saw an 18% year-on-year aggregate sales increase but it is intensely competitive. The success story of 2000 has been the Condé Nast new title *Glamour* which is now number two in the segment and number one in terms of news stand sales. The more downmarket Women's Weekly segment saw major circulation advances by the international publishers.

3.4 Radio

There is a long tradition of public radio in Britain dating back to the emergence of broadcasting in the early 1920s. The technical and organizational excellence achieved by the British Broadcasting Corporation (BBC) exclusively supported by license fee and operating within a Government sanctioned framework of regulation, may well have inhibited the development of commercial radio broadcasting in the U.K. The BBC evolved into a great national institution with authoritative news provision and a tiered station structure which was designed to cover all possible areas of public taste and need. This development was in stark contrast to the laissez faire environment for broadcasting which characterized the US in the 1920s and 30s and which led to a proliferation of commercially driven stations, unashamedly pursuing the profitable service of popular taste in areas such as music, drama and sport. It is ironic that commercial television was established in the U. K. almost two decades before commercial indigenous radio emerged.

Dramatic social and economic change in the 1960s, the rise of rock and roll and the availability of disposable income across the population and especially among the urban young, fuelled a distinctive youth culture focused in particular on music. The BBC 'light entertainment' approach was seriously out of touch with the realities of British pop culture. British advertisers wishing to speak to this new and important market were forced to rely on low quality medium wave broadcasts from Radio Luxembourg. The emergence of a number of popular offshore pirate stations forced the authorities to relent and two London commercial stations were licensed and launched in 1973. A further nineteen stations were launched over the next seven years. Radio advertising however did not have the mass market appeal which television, then in its heyday, was enjoying and the lack of a commercial national station or network of stations limited the appeal of the medium for national brand advertisers. The launch in 1989 of Atlantic 252, a long wave station based in the Irish Republic but with national coverage in Britain, was a catalyst to further change and there are now three indigenous national broadcasters - Classic FM, Virgin 1215 and Talk UK. These national offerings are supplemented by regional stations, usually FM broadcasters aiming at younger market segments and by a plethora of local stations offering niched program menus which seek to build and hold listener loyalty through a consistent well-defined diet of programs.

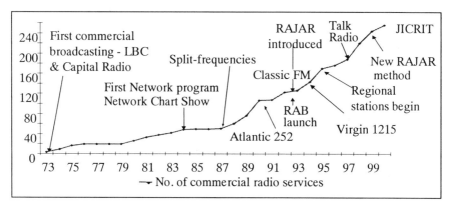

Figure 2: Growth of Commercial Radio in UK
Source: Radio Advertising Bureau 2000

There are now over 250 radio stations (public and commercial) in the UK and annual revenue from advertising reached £577 million in 2000 AD. The medium is now attractive to national advertisers because of the availability of national stations or networks of regional and local stations. This has been facilitated by the emergence of strong sales houses which have been subject to significant consolidation across the nineties and by strong trends towards consolidation of station ownership itself. This in turn has led to a number of media groups developing significant ownership positions across radio, print and television media, though monopolies legislation has to date put a break on the emergence of overly dominant media players.

The advertising industry relies on a flow of accurate consistent and timely data which can provide a trading currency for media buyers and sellers. The development of RAJAR radio audience research and its progressive refinement of its research approaches and instruments has had a significant impact in both facilitating the use of the medium by major consumer brands and increasing the overall number of commercial radio stations. The share of radio of the expanding display advertising cake has grown from 2.8% in 1992 to an estimated 6.4% in 2000.

A further important stimulus to this advertising growth has been provided by the work of the Radio Advertising Bureau. An industry funded but independently operating company, RAB is dedicated to advancing the cause of radio amongst advertisers and their agencies through awareness building, dissemination of research findings and promotion of best practice by creatives, media buyers and advertisers alike. While radio in many ways remains the Cinderella of media schedules, the medium does offer a number of special characteristics in terms of audience composition and behavior. It is argued that radio experiences a low advertising avoidance as compared to all other major advertising media; advertising avoidance for newspapers and magazines is estimated to be well over 60% as compared to 16% for radio. It is also argued that radio, as a background medium, is compatible with a range of work and domestic activities and that it is highly compatible with internet usage. Advocates also point to the exceptional Weekly Reach of radio which stands as 77% of total segment for the 25-44 year old age group and an impressive 82% for the 15 to 24 year age group. The dominant share of media consumption that radio enjoys at specific times of day makes a compelling argument for its inclusion in a wide variety of campaigns. Radio assumes even greater significance when its proportional importance in terms of time spent in the average media day is measured. At 31% share of the average media day – albeit as a background medium – it is a clear second to the dominant medium of television.

Table 12: Growth in Display Advertising Revenue by Medium 1999-2000

Radio	292%
TV	94%
Outdoor	157%
Magazines	36%
Papers	69%
Total Display Advertising	**85%**

Source: Radio Advertising Bureau

All of these factors, compellingly argued by RAB have had an influence on the growth of radio advertising revenues.

A brief overview of the advertisers currently devoting major spend to radio indicates the dominance of consumer telecom services and mobile phone retailers followed by newspaper and magazine, motor cars and government communications. The second quarter data for 2001 is largely consistent in rank order with the data for the whole of the year 2000 but it also serves to point out the early impact of recessionary conditions on key sectors. It is likely that radio will feel this impact disproportionately.

Table 13: Major Radio Advertisers by Volume Spend (Quarter 2/2001)

	Advertiser	£M's	% YoY
1	BT	2.0	-43
2	Vodafone	1.7	-24
3	Carphone Warehouse	1.6	-34
4	News international	1.5	24
5	COI Communication	1.3	-43
6	MG Rover	1.2	124
7	Coldseal	1.1	-25
8	Renault	1.1	-25
9	Reg Vardy	0.9	26
10	Marks & Spencers	0.9	22

Source: Radio Advertising Bureau

All of the major media buying houses are represented in the spending league table for radio in much the same way as they would appear in a television advertising spending league. This suggests that radio is now an accepted element in the media schedule for major national brands, their agencies and their media buyers.

Table 14: Radio Spend by Agency (Quarter 2/2001)

	Agency	£M's	% YoY
1	Zenith	7.5	-23
2	Carat	6.6	-33
3	OMD	5.7	-10
4	Media Com	4.6	74
5	Mindshare	3.6	30
6	PHD	3.3	-31
7	Starcom Motive	3.2	-29
8	Intitiative	2.8	20
9	Optimedia	2.7	-23
10	MGM	2.1	-8

Source: Radio Advertising Bureau

3.5   Cinema

The restructuring of cinema distribution in the nineties - partly in response to changing attendance profile and customer demands, partly responsible for and fuelling those very factors - has seen a significant resurgence in the U.K. cinema audience. Currently some 23% of the total population visit the cinema at least once a month and the average cinema attendee is currently making eight visits a year, up almost one third since the mid nineties. Cinema has withstood the challenge of DVD and emergent home cinema technologies just as it previously saw off the pre-recorded video tape and in the very first wave of competition, the advent of television itself. The average British cinema goer is well informed and committed to the medium and enjoys his cinema experiences in Multiplex high comfort environments which offer a range of food service options and credit card booking. The regular cinema audience now approaches a 150,000,000 ticket sales per annum with a strong bias towards the 15-34 year olds (two thirds of total audience) and towards ABC1 status (a similar two thirds of total audience). The distinctive attendance profile makes for effective targeting and the ability to buy space screen by screen can mean a very high quality fit between an advertisement and the film environment in which it is embedded. CAVAIR data allows media buyers to predict the likely audience type for a forthcoming movie release and exceptional technical quality can give scope for exceptional creative treatment. Nevertheless, cinema lacks strength in terms of reach and adequate frequency can be very difficult to achieve in a campaign which relies heavily on cinema.

3.6   Ambient Media

Ambient media is one of the sub sectors which has clearly enjoyed growth in the past two years. There is no doubt that the term is often used to capture any advertising technique which doesn't fit in the traditional media sectors (TV, press, etc.) and this may account for some of the reported growth. There is also a lack of clarity of definition as many one off external ambient placements smack more of a PR or sales promotion stunt.

There are over 400 companies offering ambient advertising in the UK – an increase of more than 25% on the same period in 2000. Players provide a range of media including giant banner advertising, TV ads in taxis, advertising messages on petrol pump nozzles or till receipts, posters in university toilets, giant slide projections onto major buildings amongst others. Some of the media involved are clearly accountable while others are less so. It is anticipated that there will be a shake out in the sector over the coming years, and this will be accelerated by recession. The key to survival of the option will be accountability and the sales houses will themselves have to turn their attention to measurement issues. Reliable measurement should be easily achieved, particularly those that perform in retail environments such as petrol stations. A message is delivered close to point of purchase prompting impulse buying and this should register in the EPOS data. Similarly petrol nozzle prompts to seek information about car products or cars can be regarded as effectively targeted and delivered within an environment for positive reception.

The single biggest draw back for inclusion of the medium in strategically focused campaigns is the inability to achieve precise targeting. In a world of clutter, ambient media may well have a real future in prompting enquiry or sale.

3.7 Internet Advertising

Internet penetration figures in the UK suggest that 34% of the population have access to the web with 24% having that access in a domestic setting. A quarter of this later group appear to access the web through the television set.

A research study by the Chartered Institute of Marketing (April 2001) suggested that the internet and other new media have moved into the mainstream as an essential elements in the marketing mix but it is notable that three quarters of the respondents in the CIM study said that they never saw adverts on digital TV, mobile phones or internet banners.

Internet advertising faces an uphill struggle to become a media option in a period of industry recession. It is now evident that the use of offweb advertising to build web traffic will not be financially feasible in most instances. Sales of advertising on the web are by definition driven by the attraction of significant traffic. Another difficulty lies in verifying levels of traffic. In the UK alone there are three different competing audience measurement services – Nielsen e-Ratings, Jupiter MMXI and NetValue. The three competitors use different methodologies employing panels of users but the industry still lacks a common currency to drive the interest of media buyers.

While all technology pundits suggest that convergence of media technologies (television, PC and telephony) the reality of integration may lie somewhere in the future. Recent qualitative research by CIA MediaLab (October 2000) explored usage and attitudes towards interactive TV. It is clear that existing users feel overloaded with multiple messages and the need to co-ordinate a range of functions on the remote control. Preferred response options very much favor traditional roots such as the telephone. Interactive services were not a primary motivator for subscribing to a digital package. Children are more technologically receptive and are the key group in terms of promoting uptake by households.

4 Data for Advertising Decision-Making

A complex media research infrastructure has evolved to provide data which are accurate, relevant and timely for media buyers in the UK industry. The move to refine research tools across the last decade has been driven by the maturing of new media options (radio), the rising costs and increasing audience fragmentation of terrestrial television, and the emergence of new media technologies such as satellite broadcasting such as satellite and digital. The research infrastructure has been reconfigured to reflect these emerging needs and it is generally credited with providing rebust data and a high quality of service to the industry.

4.1 Television Audience Research

The Broadcaster's Audience Research Board (BARB) is a consortium of the BBC, ITV, Channel 4, Channel 5, B Sky B, Flextech and the Institute Practitioners of Advertising.

BARB commissions research through designated sub contractors. It conducts an Annual Establishment Survey of 40,000 individual interviews each year to provide overall profile data of television households and to provide a source from which the main panel can be drawn, maintained and quality controlled.

A sample of 4,485 households is drawn from the Establishment Survey for purposes of audience measurement and audience reaction measurement. Electronic monitoring of television sets, VCR's and satellite decoders is implemented by Taylor Nelson Sofres on behalf of BARB. The in house meter system collects and stores viewing information on a minute by minute basis and the data is retrieved over night by landline. Full reports are available on a daily basis to subscribers. Audience reaction data is gathered by means of questionnaire on a weekly basis. Since 1977 the ITC has placed questions in the survey to identify viewer reaction to outstanding programs, to items of which they disapproved and to items which they feel should not have been shown. This data is now available in the public domain on a quarterly basis.

Innovations which BARB pioneered include metered monitoring of all television reception in the UK, disproportionate sampling of market segments of particular appeal to advertisers and monitoring of 'time-shift' viewing via VCR.

4.2   Radio Audience Research

Since the advent of commercial broadcasting in 1973 various arrangements
have been put in place for measuring the radio audience. However it was
not until the Radio Joint Audience Research (RAJAR) was inaugurated in
1992 that an effective basis for media buying decisions was available to
facilitate the growth of commercial radio as a medium. Previously radio
had been treated as comprising of two distinct sectors, Public Radio serviced through the BBC Daily Survey, and Commercial Radio serviced
through the Joint Industry Committee for Radio Audience Research
(JICRAR). Now it was possible to evaluate the performance of a given
station in terms of the total radio audience rather than simply the commercial radio audience.

 RAJAR is owned by a consortium of BBC and the Commercial Radio
Companies Association and it provides a single source of radio data for all
services in the UK including both commercial and non commercial stations. This has increased media buyers confidence in the medium and has
allowed for a meaningful survey of audience for each of the 250 national,
regional and local commercial and public radio stations in the UK. Three
thousand profiled respondents are asked to keep a weekly diary of listening
habits. The figures for all stations are reported on every three months by
the contractor IPSOS- RSL.

4.3   Print Media Research

The Audit Bureau of Circulations (ABC) certifies circulation figures for
print media on an independent basis. The bureau has as its key members
advertisers, agencies and publishers and its audits cover print media which
account for over 90% of all press advertising expenditure. Audit figures
are published periodically (e.g. monthly for the national newspapers, twice
yearly for magazines) and the Bureau also certifies free circulation print
media (Verified Free Distribution) and exhibition attendance (Exhibition
Data Forms). ABC can also provide customized data relating to the readership profile of certain magazines.

 The National Readership Survey is a commercial provider of data relating to the readership of UK newspapers and consumer magazines. It is an
independent body funded by subscription by the International Publishers
Association, Newspapers Publishers Association and Periodical Publishers
Association. Its surveys provide a common currency of readership research

data relating to over 250 different publications involving personal interviews with 38,000 adults in their own homes, each year. Data is published in full format twice a year and members also have access to monthly data updates.

The Joint Industry Committee for Regional Press Research (JICREG) provides data on over 1,000 regional press titles generating its key data through examining circulation breakdowns (usually at postcode level) through an analysis of readers per copy – the latter norms increasingly being established by customized market research.

4.4   Outdoor Advertising Research

POSTAR provides detailed poster research covering both opportunity to see and likelihood of viewing for 100,000 sites in the UK. The research is conducted by a consortium which represents both the media buyers and the specialist outdoor agencies and site providers. The basis of the research lies with Local Authority traffic count estimates for some 10,000 sites and customized research on traffic movement for a further 9,000 sites. The data would provide the media planner with site and positioning specifics, a model of pedestrian traffic and an estimate of the likelihood of the poster site actually being seen. POSTAR also seeks to provide profiling data of likely audience through tracking large numbers of respondents across typical journeys.

4.5   Cinema Audience Research

The placement of cinema advertising is concentrated almost exclusively in the hands of two contractors who negotiate directly with the cinema owners for advertising time and then create and produce the individual packages either on a screen by screen basis or against audience targets.

Gallup Admissions monitor provides a continuous weekly audit of admissions based on ticket count and questionnaire responses from a representative sample. Cinema and video industry audience research provided by the Cinema Advertising Association, seeks to predict the likely appear of future releases and the audience profile which they are likely to attract.

5   Regulatory Environment

A complex set of elective and statutory arrangements provides a regulatory framework for advertisements and for the media which carry them. Present arrangements have evolved over the past half century and it is likely that an integrated statutory framework for all communications media will be in place by 2003. Currently there are two broad strands of provision involving statutory control of licensed media and elective self-regulation of advertisements in other media.

Statutory bodies license and monitor the performance of television (including satellite and cable delivered programming) and radio. Television advertising has been controlled through the Broadcasting Act since commercial broadcasting began via the ITV network in 1955. The introduction of commercial radio in 1972 resulted in the creation of a parallel regulatory framework for the medium. Today television advertisements are regulated by the *Independent Television Commission* and radio advertisements by *The Radio Authority*.

5.1   The ITC

The main responsibilities of the ITC are to
- issue licenses that allow commercial television companies to broadcast in/from the UK – whether the services are received by conventional aerials, cable or satellite: and whether delivered by analogue or digital means. These licenses vary according to the type of service, but they all set out conditions on matters such as standards of programs and advertising;
- regulate these services by monitoring broadcasters' performance. There is a range of penalties for failure to comply with them;
- ensure that a wide range of television services is available through the UK
- ensure fair and effective competition in the provision of these services
- investigate complaints and regularly publishes its findings

The ITC publishes and applies codes and rules on the content, amount and distribution of television advertising and on program sponsorship. The ITC also considers complaints relating to these issues.

The advertisements which they carry comply with the *ITC Code of Advertising Standards and Practice* (including associated Guidance Notes) and *ITC Rules on Amount and Scheduling of Advertising*. These are kept under regular review with the help of an independent advisory committee comprising of both consumer and advertising interests.

The main objectives of the Code are to ensure that television advertising:
- is not misleading
- does not encourage or condone harmful behavior
- does not cause widespread or exceptional offence

The frequency and duration of commercial breaks are restricted. Advertisements also have to be clearly separated from programs.

Sponsorship
Program sponsorship has only been allowed in the UK since 1991. Sponsors pay to receive a credit associating them with a particular program, but they should not exert influence on the editorial content of programs. The ITC's *Code of Program Sponsorship* sets out the rules in this area.

5.2   Self-Regulation

Non-broadcast advertising, by way of contrast has been subject to a system of self-regulation since 1961 when the first edition of the Advertising Code was published. The Advertising Standards Authority which was established in 1962, is responsible for supervising the system and for applying the Codes to make sure that the public are not misled or offended by advertisements. The Sales Promotion Code was added in 1974 and the two Codes were brought together in 1995 into one comprehensive set of rules for advertisements and sales promotions. The ASA is independent of both the Government and the advertising industry. It is undoubtedly the case that the industry moved to put a self-regulatory regime in place in 1961 in order to anticipate and prevent statutory controls being extended from television advertising to other media. The spirit of self regulation has been an accepted part of British professional life in areas such as Accountancy and the Law and it is felt that a self regulatory approach offers distinct advantages. For one thing both the spirit and letter of the Codes are in fact significantly more strict than comparable areas of consumer protection law. Nonetheless self regulation allows for flexibility and creativity and a more immediate response to emerging forms of advertising and changes in public attitude and taste.

The Codes of Advertising and Sales Promotion are written by the Committee of Advertising Practice (CAP) whose membership includes the main organizing bodies representing advertisers, media, agencies and service providers. Funding comes through a levy on display advertising and direct mail expenditure and this levy is collected by an independent body, the Advertising Standards Board of Finance. All advertisements and promotions in non-broadcast media are covered by the British Codes of Advertising and Sales Promotion and are regulated by the ASA. These include: Press, Outdoor, Direct Marketing, Cinema commercials, Sales promotions, Internet and other electronic media.

The basic principles of the Codes are that advertisement should be:

a.   legal, decent, honest and truthful
b.   prepared with a sense of responsibility to consumers and to society
c.   in line with the principles of fair competition generally accepted in
       business.

There is a high degree of voluntary compliance with the codes. ASA research indicates that 97% of the 30 million press advertisements published in the UK annually are fully compliant as are 98% of posters and 85% of direct marketing material.

Operation of the Code
The ASA will act upon a complaint from a member of the public of third party but can also take a pro-active stance to have an advertisement changed or withdrawn even if a complaint hasn't been made. Around 10,000 advertisements a week are spot checked by the ASA's staff. The checks help the Authority to keep an eye on trends and to act quickly to have an advertisement stopped if it raises problem under the Codes. Many advertisers, agencies and publishers use the free pre-publication advice service provided by CAP to check advertisements against the Codes to avoid problems prior to publication. The ASA also receives about 12,000 complaints each year. Most of these are from members of the public who have felt misled or offended by an advertisement but some are from consumer groups or competing companies. If an advertising is found to break the Codes the ASA will ask the company to withdraw or change it.

The ASA has a number of sanctions it can use to ensure that advertisements that break the Codes are amended or withdrawn. The ASA and CAP rely on persuasion and consensus: in the vast majority of cases companies act quickly to make any changes necessary to bring their advertisements into line with the Codes. It is not in an advertiser's best interests to mislead or offend consumers. For the few companies who do not change or withdraw their advertisement, the ASA can draw on a range of sanctions.

6 Prospect – What Lies Ahead for the UK Advertising Industry

Traditionally a downturn in advertising precedes a downturn in the economy. As noted above the supply side-driven advertising boom of 1999 and early 2000 inevitably led to media inflation which in turn required a correction. However business confidence in economic prospects have seen a freezing and in some cases a reduction in marketing budgets – particularly by multi-national companies, which has had the effect of deepening the cutback. International tension may now see the industry enter a crisis phase.

A review of IPA (Institute of Practitioners of Advertising) census data over 40 years reported by Claire Beale in Campaign magazine (7th September 2001) noted that the industry has been quick to respond to recessionery and expansionary trends in the economy. This has meant a rapid downsizing and shedding of staff in poor economic conditions but also a speedy gearing up when things improved. Nevertheless staff numbers have not returned to previous levels as each upturn in the cycle arrives. This in effect means an overall contraction in the industry over time. Agency consolidation and the widespread deployment of information technology no doubt contribute to this but it is unarguable that each economic downturn brings further contraction.

The figures support this contention. A total UK advertising workforce of 17,200 had shrunk to 13,900 by 1975; 1980 saw some 15, 500 people at work in advertising but this dropped to 13,500 in 1983. Recovery saw 15,400 employees at the end of the 80s but this dropped to an all time low of 11,100 by 1994. Similarly the number of agencies has fluctuated from 280 in 1970 to a high of 310 in 1979 with some 220 agencies today. As Beale remarks "If the current recession has a similar impact, the advertising industry could be supporting 10,000 people within a year or so" (p. 25).

Advertising faces many challenges in the coming years. A fragmented media scene with digitally driven expansion of channels and programming will see intense competition for audience share rather than any expansion of total audience itself. Major brand owners are likely to seek value in switching their media mix, in employing new media options or in shifting spend below the line. The early experience of convergent technologies would seem to suggest that there are many problems to resolve before revenue generating solutions are achieved. Finally the UK ad industry will deliver it's communication through a significantly de-regulated media environment with increasing pan-European and Global competitive pressure.

References

Beale, C.: *Campaign Magazine* pp. 24-25, September 7th 2001
Cumberbatch, G –Wood & Littlejohn: *Television: The Publics View 1999*
Independent Television Commission, London, 2000
Independent Television Commission *Annual Report 2000*, London, 2001

Useful Addresses

World Advertising Research Center
Farm Road
Henley-on-Thames
Oxfordshire RG9 1GB
Tel: 01491 441 000
Fax: 01491 571 188
Website: http://www.warc.com
eMail: enquiries@warc.com

The Advertising Association
Abford House
15 Wilton Road
London SW1V 1NJ
Tel: (+44) (0) 207 828 2771
Fax: (+44) (0) 207 931 0376
Website: http://www.adassoc.org.uk
eMail: aa@adassoc.org.uk

The Independent Television Commission
33 Foley Street
London W1W 7TL
Tel: 020 7255 3000
Fax: 020 7306 7800

Radio Authority
Halbrook House
14 Great Queen Street
Holborn
London WC2B 5DG
Tel: +44 (0)20 7405 7062
Fax: +44 (0)20 7405 7062
Website: http://www.radioauthority.org.uk
eMail: reception@radioauthority.org.uk

Case Study:
Barclaycard International

Ron Boddy
Commercial Director Barclaycard International

1 Background

Unlike most other European countries, bank-issued revolving credit cards preceded debit cards in the UK by about 20 years.

Launched in 1966, Barclaycard pioneered the UK credit card and for 6 years enjoyed uncontested growth. It was not until 1972 that competition, in the shape of a banking consortium operating under the 'Access' brand, finally emerged.

Needless to say, the powerful combination of a modern and relevant product, Barclays' substantial customer base and distribution network, and the absence of a direct competitor during the early years fuelled rapid expansion. It was not long before all Visa cards became known as Barclaycards and the business found itself in the unique position of owning the credit card generic. In consequence, approximately 50% of Barclaycard's growth came from non-Barclays customers.

The formula had longevity and, thanks to strong brand and product strategies, Barclaycard's high growth rate continued well into the 1990s, despite the introduction of annual account fees and the advent of the debit card.

'Access' meanwhile became a spent force. The coalition was eventually dissolved and the customer file divided between the participant banks during the 1980s.

By 1995, Barclaycard was over twice the size of the next largest bank credit card issuer in Europe and over 6m UK residents, around 13% of the UK adult population, held accounts. Cards in issue exceeded 8m.

2   The Growth of Competencies

As Barclaycard developed, so did its abilities. Over time, and aided by the availability of substantial scale economies, capabilities evolved into key business skills. Those that were unrivalled eventually became unique core competencies, creating sustainable competitive resilience.

A strategic review in the mid 1990s defined Barclaycard's competitive position in the following terms:

Core Competencies	Distinctive Capabilities	Assets
▪ Predictive skills and their exploitation ▪ Management of remote customer relationships	▪ Exploitation of communication channels ▪ Management of customer data ▪ Management of the Barclaycard brand ▪ Management of loyalty schemes ▪ Management of partnerships ▪ Management and delivery of security ▪ Ability and will to exploit and use systems ▪ Influence on Payment Schemes ▪ Managing risk at the margin ▪ High volume statistical modelling	▪ Customer data ▪ Large size and age of customer base ▪ Barclaycard brand awareness, stature and industry reputation ▪ Foothold in Europe ▪ Profiles (reward points) scheme ▪ Systems infrastructure ▪ Relationship with Barclays Bank ▪ Individual people with industry stature ▪ Automatic seat on Visa boards ▪ Teams with industry-leading knowledge ▪ Discrete business unit

The review concluded that Barclaycard's strategy, based on brand and added value, was still appropriate. More importantly for the purpose of this study, it also concluded that the core competencies of the business were portable into other territories.

3   Internationalization of the UK Credit Card Market

The entry of US 'monolines' to the UK in the mid 1990s precipitated a seismic shift in the competitive dynamics of the marketplace.

Until then, competition had been limited to some relatively harmless jostling between domestic players. The 'monolines', focused credit card specialists, brought with them deep actuarial skills that enabled them to undercut local prices and effectively 'cherry-pick' highly profitable high borrowers from UK issuers.

Barclaycard had been aware of the 'monoline' threat for some years and had taken it into account during strategic planning. The business knew that its strategy was sound and provided adequate defence, but it also knew that historically high margins were a thing of the past. For the first time, consumers had become acutely aware of price and the business needed to accept lower returns in order to compete.

Keen to maintain healthy levels of profit growth, Barclaycard started to look for new profit opportunities.

3.1   The Case for Market Development

Barclaycard recognised that opportunities for profit growth fell into the four broad areas defined by Anshoff and shown in the diagram below:

		Markets	
		Existing	**New**
Products — **Existing**		**Penetration** Leverage capabilities to drive harder into current market	**Market Development** Leverage capabilities to move into new territories
Products — **New**		**Product Development** Develop new capabilities in current market	**Diversification** Try something totally different

The business was already working hard in the UK and, in the light of increasing competition, knew that a more aggressive penetration strategy was unlikely to deliver sustained profit growth.

With projects involving on-line services, fixed and mobile telephone and procurement at an advanced stage, it also had a full and ambitious product development agenda.

Discounting diversification on grounds of both risk and appetite, Barclaycard decided to look for new markets. In addition to profit growth potential, the idea appealed because it promised to deliver file growth and cross-border scale, creating Group-wide cross-selling opportunities.

3.2 The Case for Europe

Barclaycard was determined only to enter markets where it could establish a sustainable competitive edge, so the choice of market was determined primarily by testing the extent to which core competencies could provide leverage.

A number of geographies were long-listed, analysed in detail and stress-tested. In each case, key performance criteria were metricated, transposed to the new environment and then benchmarked against both local and global competitors.

In addition, each area was assessed according to a list of weighted factors that were known to directly influence credit card profitability. The list included scale, propensity to use plastic, regulatory environment and an extensive range of other criteria.

Following an exhaustive analysis, the study concluded in favour of continental Europe for a number of reasons:

- The continuing trend towards market freedom was removing barriers to entry and creating opportunities within the financial services sector.
- At the same time, consumer attitudes were homogenising, leading to substantial mass-market potential.
- People were also starting to look more to value and quality, as issues of geography assumed secondary importance. This was challenging traditional supplier monopolies.
- Local card products were supply-driven and undifferentiated. Domestic banks had not developed the skills needed to extend lending beyond their own customer files and the market was under-supplied.

The study confirmed that Barclaycard's risk, marketing and remote customer management skills would provide a stronger competitive edge in continental Europe than in any other territory.

4 Market Entry

One of the advantages of having a clear generic strategy is that it gives both shape and direction to subordinate strategies.

Barclaycard had identified that competitive success in continental Europe would be determined by the extent to which it could leverage core competencies. Furthermore, analysis had shown that the route to achieving this lay in:

- Minimising operational and financial risk during implementation
- Competing through differentiation in the short term
- Developing the Barclaycard brand over the longer term

The challenge the business faced when deciding how to enter Europe was not, therefore, which entry strategy to use per se, but which would work best with the chosen approach.

A 'blueprint' for expansion was developed to help with this task. This was achieved by 'visioning' the ideal business and then modifying the output where necessary to accommodate strategic or wider commercial considerations. The result defined the ideal Barclaycard Europe as:

- UK Centred - tightly organised with strategy disciplined from Head Office
- Low cost - to support margins and competitive advantage
- Concentrating on revolving credit cards - trading directly on Barclaycard's expertise
- Differentiated - through positioning, added value and product extension
- Brand focused - featuring a common core proposition with local 'flavour'
- Mass-market - leveraging Barclaycard's risk and marketing skills
- Multi-domestic - with flexible imagery and offering to suit local needs
- Variable speed – with country entries tempered according to local conditions and accelerating as experience and capabilities increase

With over thirty years of investment to build a brand valued at over £1bn, it is hardly surprising that much of the internal discussion surrounding the 'blueprint' focused on the brand impact, both then and for the future.

A number of 'givens' rapidly helped to distil the debate to a single issue. These were:

- The more consistency between countries, the stronger the brand platform
- Although European consumers were generally homogenous, some local attitudes and habits were deeply rooted making absolute consistency impossible.

Barclaycard needed to know that it's chosen route, featuring multiple product variations, would not damage its long-term brand aspirations.

The only real option in such circumstances is to look at case studies. The grid below, borrowed from "The Reality of Global Brands" by Hankinson and Cowking, is probably the best demonstration of what can be achieved using permutations of product and brand.

		Brand	
		Standard	**Adapted**
Product	**Standard**	**Fully Global** Total consistency	**Brand Adaptive** Product remains the same, but brand proposition changes by market
	Adapted	**Product Adaptive** Consistent brand proposition, but product flexes to meet local needs	**Fully Adaptive** All facets flex

Research has shown that very few, if any, businesses can achieve absolute brand and product consistency. Even McDonald's ads chilli in Asia!

In addition, the traditional arguments for total consistency are hardly persuasive, pivoting around scale economies in advertising, an ability to attract global partners and 'opening other doors in new areas'. Whilst all are attractive academically, there is some doubt about achievability and the reality is that local flexing is likely to be a much more powerful and practical alternative, especially in a start-up situation. Kotler seems to agree.

Hankinson and Cowking cite Shell as a good example of 'product adaptivity'. The Shell example shows how products can be varied by territory under the umbrella of a common brand proposition.

On the strength of this and other data, Barclaycard decided that it could support a product adaptive approach providing central brand requirements were not substantially compromised in any one country.

5   Where and When to Flex?

Product adaptivity is a great idea in principle. Implementation is somewhat more complicated.

As the table below shows, the forces that were attracting Barclaycard to either end of the standardise-customise continuum for each country appeared equally compelling at first glance.

Case for Standardisation	Case for Customisation
▪ Brand consistency across all territories, creating opportunities for: ▪ Advertising economy ▪ Cross-border alliances ▪ Competition through differentiation ▪ Increasing brand equity ▪ Easier to manage operationally – 'one size fits all' ▪ Easier to implement business change ▪ Scale economy	▪ Speed to market ▪ Avoids challenging and potentially alienating local regulators ▪ Ensures best local product/ brand fit in each territory

When 'time horizon' was factored in to the analysis, however, it became clear that all of the impetus for customisation supported short-term tactical goals. Conversely, the case for standardisation was based on meeting longer-term strategic aims.

Benefiting once again from a clear generic strategy, Barclaycard was able to develop a series of principles to shape its activities. These were:

- Barclaycard branding is desirable, but not essential to all activities.
- Any use of the brand must be consistent with the UK
- The core features of the product must be the same; the offering must always include variable repayment revolving credit

This approach left each country free to build locally appropriate products without compromising or fettering Barclaycards longer-term strategy of creating a powerful and consistent pan-European brand.

As the paper goes on to show, products henceforth evolved very differently, but always around a consistent core, in different countries. The next three sections look at Germany, France and Spain respectively to demonstrate this.

5.1 Germany

Barclaycard recognised that Germany would be a keystone for its European business. With a population of over 80m, a strong economy and a high level of sophistication amongst financial service consumers, the business knew that the potential for revolving credit cards was enormous.

Only two things conspired to make life difficult:
- For years, the German banks' had pushed Eurocheque debit as their preferred payment card. Penetration had risen massively as a result, over 45m people held the card, and use had become habitual amongst consumers. Revolving credit cards had not developed. Only three banks offered the facility and none were German. Penetration was tiny.
- The domestic banks had priced Eurocheque favourably to retailers and introduced much higher rates for credit card transactions. Consequently, acceptance of revolving credit cards was very limited. Often, retailers who did accept the card would pressure customers to pay by Eurocheque instead, or add a transaction charge.

Germany was unique for Barclaycard because the parent company, Barclays Bank, had established a small credit card file as part of it's own European expansion drive during the early 1990s.

The card file was no longer integral to the bank's strategy and, recognising that it would benefit from expert management, Barclays transferred ownership to Barclaycard during the mid 1990s.

Although this gave Barclaycard Germany a running start, it also brought problems.

The product had been launched with a '2-for-1' joint Visa and Mastercard offer that was unrivalled in the German market at that time. The product specification remained largely unchanged for the following 6 years, however, and the USP disintegrated.

Additionally, traditional delivery channels were showing signs of wearout, probably helped by relatively high product pricing and over-use.

It rapidly became clear that a fundamental product overhaul and relaunch were needed. At the same time, the business also decided to explore other distribution options.

Research and common sense were used in equal measure to define the new consumer package that featured:

- Barclaycard UK brand imagery and guidelines
- Lower pricing
- A new Eurocheque card making Barclaycard a '3-for-1' product
- Improved, unbundled surround services (insurances, guarantees, etc)

Figure 1: German Relaunch Campaign

A massive programme of channel testing helped to determine the most effective means of distributing the product. Two new 'champion' channels were identified during the course of the study which also found that some of the older, more traditional channels had been reinvigorated by the changes.

Since the relaunch, Barclaycard Germany has enjoyed a compounded annual growth rate of between 40% and 50%.

The initiative was successful not only in absolute commercial terms, but also because it brought the German business within the brand parameters defined for Barclaycard Europe, despite introducing a totally new product concept.

5.2 France

France was attractive to Barclaycard because its population of around 60m offered scale potential and because it was a key market for other industries. Barclaycard would therefore need a presence in order to attract pan-European alliances.

All bank cards in France are regulated by the Cartes Bancaires (CB) cartel which, until recently, virtually prohibited revolving credit cards. For many years, debit cards were promoted as the banks' preferred payment card and revolving credit was left to retailers.

When Cartes Bancaires relaxed their rules during the mid 1990s, French banks found that they lacked the lending skills needed to offer revolving credit cards to non-customers. Faced with limited potential within their own customer bases, most decided that the prize was too small to justify investment. The analysis below shows the gap left for credit card specialists.

There are currently around 35m bank-issued debit cards and 25m retailer-issued credit cards in France.

Barclaycard saw the gap and recognised the potential for its product in France. The challenge, once again, was to find a way to flex to local conditions without compromising long-term strategy.

Four Cartes Bancaires rules in particular presented problems for Barclaycard:

- Cards had to conform to the prohibitive design that CB imposed on all issuers. This regulated virtually all of the card face, leaving little room for customisation.
- The name of the issuing bank had to appear on the face of the card. Brand names were not allowed.
- Co-branding, although permissible, could not be shown on the card face.
- The cards had to feature a microchip that was peculiar to the French market.

In short, Barclaycard France had to look like every other card, debit or credit.

Challenging the cartel was not an option. One of the largest international banks had withdrawn from the card market entirely following a failed attempt to disempower Cartes Bancaires. In any event, Barclaycard had a policy of co-operative working and did not wish to challenge the local infrastructure.

An approach based on compromise and compliance was selected. This involved:

- Tempering ambitions to replicate the UK card design and adopting the Cartes Bancaires version as fully as possible instead. Barclaycard then successfully pressed CB to 'stretch' their rules and allow the Barclaycard name and logo to appear on the card face.
- Restricting co-branding to areas other than the face of the card.
- Developing product features to differentiate in the absence of imagery. Barclaycard launched the first bank card loyalty programme (Millesime) in France.
- Using CB-accredited suppliers to produce cards with the standard French chip.

By adapting to the local environment, Barclaycard was able to gain entry to the French market (which other issuers had found so elusive) and also secure some concessions from the regulators to ensure sufficient differentiation from debit products.

5.3 Spain

Spain was the third country that, along with Germany and France, would create critical mass for Barclaycard in continental Europe.

A bank consortium also regulates the Spanish card market, but in this case there are no restrictive barriers to entry for non-domestic players and issuers have much greater freedom over card design. Entry and branding were not therefore a problem for Barclaycard.

With the highest per capita holding of bank-issued plastic cards in Europe, and a substantial number of storecards in circulation, Spain's 40m residents are more than familiar with credit cards. The population distinguishes itself however by being amongst the lowest users of revolving credit in Europe, primarily because of the cultural stigma associated with that type of borrowing.

Barclaycard therefore faced two challenges in Spain. Firstly, it needed to differentiate itself in a relatively well-supplied market. Secondly, it needed to legitimise the revolving credit element of the product.
The answer lay in positioning the product appropriately within the market and Barclaycard chose to work on two fronts in order to achieve it.

The first involved Barclays Bank. Over a number of years, Barclays had successfully established a private banking business in Spain. Targeting the high net worth segment, it had successfully combined strong brand building, service quality and high asset performance to create a superior wealth management operation, known locally as El Banco Azul (The Blue Bank).
Barclaycard knew that Spanish consumers would associate Barclaycard with Barclays and that the 'endorsement' would give immediate credibility to its product. It also knew that consumer awareness of Barclays as an elite brand, particularly around Madrid, was high and understood the importance of imagery in the Spain.

It became clear from research that the Barclays endorsement could contribute to a compelling consumer proposition.

Secondly, Barclaycard was aware that banker-customer relationships in Spain were weak. Banks would only provide facilities to established customers, who resented both the lack of choice and the parent-child nature of the relationship.

Due to its sophisticated risk management skills, Barclaycard did not need to have a customer relationship in order to make a positive lending decision and research showed convincingly that consumers would value an independent credit line highly.

Launch material made heavy use of both the brand and 'independence' message. In consequence, volumes exceeded targets, levels of credit-taking on the product were much higher than the market average and post-launch research showed that the positioning had achieved its objectives.

6 Summary and Conclusions

The fundamental choice facing every business that is looking to expand a brand beyond its domestic market is whether to standardise across all territories or adapt to each local market.

There is no 'hard and fast' rule to guide organisations in such circumstances and there is plenty of evidence to show that both adaptive and consistent strategies can work. The Barclaycard case study does however provide some helpful guidance.

Without doubt, strategic context is the leading consideration. If the business clearly understands its competencies and the basis on which it will sustain competitive advantage, then it has a start point from which to craft an approach that will be protect and even enhance its edge.

As the Barclaycard study shows, there is a strong strategic pull towards standardisation and a tactical pull towards local customisation. In normal circumstances, the strategic argument would be compelling, but Barclaycard actually generated the most short-term benefit from local tactical initiatives, so tactics should not be entirely discounted.

Barclaycard was able to do this only because it had developed an expansion approach that complemented its broader business strategy *and* then clearly defined a set of principles to regulate its activities. Once the framework was established, practitioners were free to organise their activities to optimise potential providing they played within the rules.

The Authors

Prof. Dr. Iskandar Abdullah is a faculty member at the Graduate School of Management, University Putra Malaysia, where he teaches marketing to MBA and Ph.D. students. Dr. Iskandar obtained his Ph.D. in marketing from the Michael Smurfit Graduate School of Business, University College Dublin, Ireland. He got his BBA from Western Michigan University and an MBA from Central Michigan University, USA, where he graduated with honors and initiated into a society known as Sigma Iota Epsilon (similar to Phi Kappa Beta in the liberal arts). Dr. Iskandar had also taught marketing courses for several years outside Malaysia including three years in Ireland and as visiting professor in Hong Kong and Singapore for the last two years. Besides being an academician, Dr. Iskandar has worked for several years in the advertising industry. He was previously an Account Director with J. Walter Thompson Advertising in Kuala Lumpur, Malaysia and assigned to handle international clients in the Asia Pacific Region. Later on he was appointed as Managing Director for Bloomingdale Advertising in Kuala Lumpur before re-joining the university in 1989.
E-mail: iskandar@putra.upm.edu.my

Anda Batraga has a Master's Degree in Commerce from the University of Latvia. She has been a full-time lecturer in the Institute of Marketing and Quality Management of the University of Latvia since 1992. She teaches Marketing, Marketing Communication and Advertising. Her Scientific Research deals with the development of Marketing Communication in Latvia. She is the author of several scientific publications.
E-mail: evf@lanet.lv

Ron Boddy has held a number of senior marketing appointments within the business and has been actively involved in all major change projects, including the move to dual (Visa and Mastercard) issuing and the introduction of annual fees. He was also responsible for introducing Barclaycard Gold, which is now one of the largest and most successful Gold card portfolios in the world. In 1996 he developed the case for expanding Barclaycard into continental Europe and oversaw the launch of businesses in France, Spain and Greece after spending a year as General Manager of Barclaycard Germany. He is a full Board member of Barclaycard Interna-

tional which now has businesses in Africa and the Caribbean as well as
Europe.
E-mail: Ron.Boddy@barclaycard.co.uk

Prof. Dr. Dae Ryun Chang is Professor of Business at Yonsei University
in Seoul, Korea. He received his Doctorate in Business from Harvard University, and his M.B.A. from Columbia University. He has held visiting
teaching positions at the Helsinki School of Economics and Business,
Australian National University, and Hong Kong University of Science and
Technology. He has published numerous journal articles in outlets such as
the Journal of Marketing, Management Science, and Decision Science. He
is a former editor of the Korean Marketing Review, the top marketing
journal in Korea. He is the author of four textbooks Integrated Advertising
Management, Advertising Management, International Marketing, and 2B
Marketing, all published in Korean. Dr. Chang's primary research interests
lie in integrated marketing communication, business to business marketing, marketing in newly industrializing countries, and marketing in the
telecommunications industry. Dr. Chang has been an advisor and lecturer
to many of the major corporations in Korea. He is currently on the board of
directors of Goodmorning Securities. Dr. Chang also serves on the executive steering committee of the Korean Association of Business Administration, the Korean Marketing Association, and the Korean Association of
Advertising Research.
E-mail: drchang@mail.yonsei.ac.kr

Ulrich Dimigen. Bank apprenticeship in Hamburg. Studies at the University of Fribourg (Switzerland) and the Brunel University of West London
(United Kingdom). Diploma in Business Administration at the University
of Fribourg. Stages and work for industrial companies in Germany and
South Africa. Since 2000 assistant at the Seminar for Marketing, University of Fribourg (Switzerland) and graduate student studying for a doctorate.
E-mail: ulrich.dimigen@unifr.ch

Prof. Dr. Cristina Etayo is a Doctor of Economics of the University of
Navarra, Spain. She finished a doctoral thesis on Economics and is presently giving classes in Business Management of Advertising and Public
Relations. Her researches are focused on Advertising and more concretely,
in the management styles of these types of businesses. Dr. Etayo has done

studies on how to manage businesses in the new information age and how to apply these models in cultural, organizational and operative circumstances within these companies. She is a member of the Investigation Group for Effective Communications (GRICE) of the University of Navarra and has collaborated in research projects for both local and community groups.

E-mail: cetayo@unav.es

George Frigkas studied Communication and Mass Media at the Panteion University, Athens and graduated in 1997. Since 1998 he conducted a Ph.D. research in the field of "Internet Advertising". Other academic fields studied: Political Science, the Balkans and European Union Issues. He worked in Advertising, Web Marketing, and Journalism. For the last 11 months he worked as editor in chief for the magazine "e.Market".

Martin Lee is the regional Creative Director in charge of *Dentsu Young & Rubicam* for the Asia Pacific region. He has worked on a large number of award-winning campaigns.

Prof. Dr. May O. Lwin is an Assistant Professor in the Marketing Department, Faculty of Business Administration at the National University of Singapore. Aside from advertising and promotions, her research interests include marketing regulations and ethics. She has published in journals such as Journal of Business Law, Journal of Current Issues in Research and Advertising and International Quarterly Journal of Marketing. She is also a co-author of Principles of Marketing: An Asian Casebook.

E-mail: may.lwin@anu.edu.au

Prof. Dr. Tony Meenaghan, Department of Marketing at the Graduate Business School in University College Dublin. His particular research interest is marketing communications and in particular commercial sponsorship. His work in these fields has been published in various journals such as *the European Journal of Marketing, the International Journal of Advertising, the Journal of Advertising Research, the Journal of Product and Brand Management, Psychology and Marketing* and *Sloan Management Review* amongst others. He is the author of *Commercial Sponsorship*, published by MCB University Press and is co-editor of *Perspectives on Marketing Management* and *Marketing Communications in Ireland,* pub-

lished by Oaktree Press. *Researching Commercial Sponsorship,* edited by
Professor Meenaghan was published by ESOMAR.
E-mail: Tony.Meenaghan@ucd.ie

Carlo Mondada: Studies at the University of Zurich and at the University
of Fribourg (Switzerland). Diploma in Business Administration at the University of Fribourg. Stages for industrial companies in Switzerland. Since
1999 assistant at the Seminar for Marketing at the University of Fribourg
(Switzerland) and graduate student studying for a doctorate.
E-mail: Carlo.Mondada@unifr.ch

Prof. Dr. Jürgen Rothlauf: Academic Background: Studies at the University of Erlangen/Nürnberg and University of Firenze. Current Position:
Associate Dean of Baltic Management Studies at the University of Applied
Sciences, Stralsund/Germany. Subjects: International Management and
Cross-Cultural Management. Professional Background: 1979-1980 Trai-
neeprogram at Kikkoman in Tokyo/Japan. 1980-1990 Trainer and Lectures
in the field of Further Education. 1991-1994 Senior Commercial Adviser
for GTZ in Riad/Saudi Arabia.
E-mail: juergen.rothlauf@fh-stralsund.de

Prof. Stella Lai Man So is marketing professor at the Chinese University
of Hong Kong. She teaches Marketing Management, Advertising and
Promotional Management. She received her MBA and her B.Sc. from As-
ton University at Birmingham in England. She was formerly Research
Manager in Reader's Digest and Asiaweek in Hong Kong. She was also a
Market Information Systems Manager of Union Carbide Eastern Inc. Be-
fore returning to Hong Kong, she was a lecturer at European University in
Antwerpen, Belgium. Ms Stella So has a wide range of consulting experi-
ence with many multinational companies and government offices, such as
the US Consulate, U.S. Meat Export Federation, Consulate General of the
Netherlands, Euromonitor Pubications LTD/PLC, Shell Petrol, Saatchi and
Saatchi Advertising, 4As Advertising Association, 2As Association, HK
Society of Publishers, Forbes Magazine, Capital Magazines, Asiaweek etc.
E-mail: stella@baf.msmail.cuhk.edu.hk

Prof. Dr. Paul O'Sullivan is Director of the Faculty of Business at the
Dublin Institute of Technology which is the largest Business School in

Ireland. He has been Senior Lecturer in Marketing Communications and Media Communications for over 15 years and has published widely in the academic literature and in industry periodicals. He is co-editor of Marketing Communications in Ireland (Oaktree Press 1997) and co-author of Marketing Practice in the Republic of Ireland and Northern Ireland 1991. He is a member of the editorial board of Irish Marketing Review and the Journal of Sports Marketing and Sponsorship. He was co-guest editor of the European Journal of Marketing (special issue on sponsorship) in 1999 and of the US based Journal of Psychology and Marketing in 2000. His research interests include Media, Advertising Creativity, Design and Marketing and Sports Sponsorship. He is a Director of one of Irelands leading Television Production Houses, a Board Member of a major Enterprise Trust, Former Chairman of the Small Enterprise Seed Fund and of the Joint Advertising Education Committee which services the needs of advertising in the Republic of Ireland.
E-mail: paul.osullivan@dit.ie

Dr. Tamás D. Szabó, Budapest University of Economic Sciences and Public Adminstration, associate professor in the department of marketing. Main research fields: media strategy, new media, Internet. Courses: advertising media planning, advertising strategy, marketing research, online marketing. Professional experiences: MATÁV (Hungarian Telecommunication Company): media manager, Optimum Media Direction Hungary (a member of the Omnicom Group): media manager, head of research department, COGNIT Consulting: managing director, Ad-Mark: marketing director.
E-mail: szabo@isc.bke.hu

Prof. Dr. Brad Thompson is an assistant professor of communications at the Pennsylvania State University. He has a Ph.D. in communications from the University of Colorado at Boulder. He earned a master's degree in journalism from the University of Missouri-Columbia. He was a journalist for 16 years. He worked at the Rocky Mountain News in Denver, Colorado, as a copy editor, assistant news editor, lifestyles editor and special projects editor. Before that he was a reporter, copy editor and wire editor at the Greenville News in South Carolina. In 2000-2001 he was awarded a Fulbright grant and taught at American University in Bulgaria. He teaches media law, news writing and reporting, news editing and other courses. With his wife, Beth Rogers Thompson, he co-authored an editing book for classroom use, Contemporary Editing Workbook. He continues to do ed-

iting on a freelance basis for corporate publications of Fortune's 500 companies. He also writes occasional op-ed articles for newspapers on media law and other issues.
E-mail: bthompson@nws.aubg.bg

Dr. Betty Tsakarestou. Lecturer, Panteion University of Social and Political Sciences, Athens, Greece. She has studied Political Sciences and Sociology at the Panteion University, Athens. She followed postgraduated studies in the field of Social Communication at the Université Catholique de Louvain-la-Neuve, Belgium. She has received her Ph.D. in Advertising and Communication at the Panteion University, Athens. Her thesis was on organizational cultures of advertising agencies and advertising message production in Greece. Since 1998 she is a lecturer at the Panteion University, Department of Communication and Mass Media, Athens. She lectures on Advertising, Public Relations and Business Ethics and Corporate Social Responsibility. She is head of the Laboratory of Advertising and Public Relations at the Panteion University. She has published articles on Advertising and Corporate Social Responsibility and she has contributed as a member of the organizing committees at several Greek and international conferences regarding the sponsorship, advertising, public relations and visual sociology. A book titled "Advertising in the Fordist and Post-Fordist era" is to be published in the autumn 2001 and currently she is researching on a new book on Corporate Social Responsibility and Cause-Related Marketing.
E-mail: btsaka@panteion.gr

Prof. Dr. Maurizio Vanetti. Since 1992 Professor for Marketing and Business Communication at the University of Fribourg (Switzerland). Teaching activities at the universities of Geneva and Lausanne. Partner at the virtual marketing campus network together with other Swiss universities. Author of the book 'La communication dans les PME' and of many articles of national and international level. Most recent specialization in the marketing for fairs and exhibitions, congresses and events. Practical consulting activities for enterprises and institutions.
E-mail: Maurizio.Vanetti@unifr.ch

H. Stadtler, C. Kilger (Eds.)

Supply Chain Management and Advanced Planning

Concepts, Models, Software and Case Studies

This book provides insights regarding the concepts underlying APS. Special emphasis is given to modelling supply chains and implementing APS in industry successfully. Understanding is enhanced through the use of case studies as well as an introduction to the solution algorithms used.

2000. XIV, 371 pp. 113 figs., 48 tabs. Hardcover
€ 41,95; £ 29,50; sFr 69,50
ISBN 3-540-67682-1

K. Mertins, P. Heisig, J. Vorbeck (Eds.)

Knowledge Management

Best Practices in Europe

One out of two companies have increased their productivity or saved costs with knowledge management. Best practices in knowledge management from leading companies are described for practitioners in different industries. The book shows how to integrate knowledge management activities into the daily business tasks and processes, how to motivate people and which capabilities and skills are required for knowledge management.

2001. XXII, 263 pp. 121 figs. Hardcover
€ 49,95; £ 35,-; sFr 83,-
ISBN 3-540-67484-5

Please order from
Springer · Customer Service
Haberstr. 7 · 69126 Heidelberg, Germany
Tel.: +49 (0) 6221 - 345 - 217/8
Fax: +49 (0) 6221 - 345 - 229
e-mail: orders@springer.de
or through your bookseller

All prices are net-prices subject to local VAT, e.g. in Germany 7% VAT for books.
Prices and other details are subject to change without notice. d&p · BA 42994/2 SF

Springer